The Complete Aquarist's Guide to
FRESHWATER
TROPICAL FISHES

Pterophyllum eimekei Angel Fish (to 5″)

The Complete Aquarist's Guide to
FRESHWATER
TROPICAL FISHES

Edited by John Gilbert

Consultant Editor: Raymond Legge

Peter Bird   Colin Roe

Donald Cook   Roy Skipper

George Cust   Michael Thomas

Albert Jessopp   Peter Utton

Harry Loder   David Walliker

WARD LOCK LIMITED
LONDON

Editor's Note

In designing this book, the sizes at which the photographs are reproduced have been dictated by the actual sizes of the fishes, as commonly seen in aquaria. With the larger fishes, some reduction in scale has been inevitable, but many of the smaller and medium-sized species are shown life size and none have been enlarged much beyond their normal length. A fish which normally grows to 6″ occupies more picture space than a fish which grows only to 2″.

A few words of caution are necessary regarding the interpretation of sizes mentioned in the captions. In most instances the figure indicates the maximum length to which the fish will grow in the wild. In cases where species kept in aquaria are noticeably smaller, this fact is mentioned in the relevant section of text. It should also be recognised that in giving such a figure no differentiation is made between the sizes attained by male and female; where there is an appreciable variation this too is mostly mentioned in the text.

Although the publishers would have liked to illustrate every fish mentioned, this has not been possible with some of the more uncommon species. The majority, however, are illustrated and placed as close as possible to the relevant text.

Text set in 'Monophoto' Baskerville by Keyspools Limited. Litho films from original colour transparencies and artwork and all printing by Smeets of Weert.

Reprinted 1973

ISBN 0 7063 1897 8

Printed in Holland

CONTENTS

Introduction

MANY CENTURIES AGO in distant China, a man took a fish from an outdoor pool and placed it in a bowl, the better to examine and appreciate its qualities; in so doing he became the first aquarist. The philosophical and aesthetic pleasure afforded by the colour, shape and movement of this fish must have been a rewarding experience, for the simple action of this anonymous enthusiast initiated a hobby which was to extend its bounds far beyond the Orient.

Appreciation of the grace and beauty of one of nature's creatures remains the chief motivation for the majority of fish keepers all over the world. For schools and universities, the aquarium is also an ideal medium for the study of biological principles. Others adopt the hobby with a view to financial gain, since there is a ready market for healthy stock bred in home aquaria.

Since the first known treatise on fishes, Chang Chi-en-te's 'The Book of the Vermilion Fish', written in China in 1506, many books on aquaria have appeared; but in a hobby which today covers such a vast field of interest it would be virtually impossible to find any single expert who could claim to speak with absolute authority on every aspect. For this reason the publishers have wisely engaged a number of writers who have gained wide recognition in their own particular sphere of aquatic interest. An occasional variation in style and phraseology is a small price to pay for such obvious gains. In any case, such a book is not intended to be read from cover to cover like a novel—although a beginner in the hobby may well do so to his advantage—indeed it is more of an aquarist's companion, a work of reference which any tropical fish keeper, whether his interest is aesthetic, scientific or commercial, will be fortunate to have constantly at hand.

In such a book, a veteran enthusiast must inevitably find himself re-reading familiar basic principles, advice on procedures and techniques which he knows off by heart; but although the facts do not alter with time, methods and equipment certainly do. Such a bewildering variety of gadgets and paraphernalia are now offered by the trade that many an aspiring aquarist must be convinced that tropical fishes cannot be successfully maintained without a great deal of expenditure and technical know-how. Nothing could be further from the truth, of course, for with simple materials, common sense and the observance of a few basic rules, a biologically sound and attractive environment can be established in an aquarium, so pleasing in appearance that it will be an asset to any home.

At a more advanced level, the aquarium offers a fertile field for the really diligent observer; indeed, many advances in biological discovery have arisen through the aquarist's observations. Any study in which there are still so many unsolved problems is bound to hold a profound interest for many, particularly regarding the question of breeding the rare or more demanding species.

A less tangible aspect of the hobby, not easily dealt with in aquarium literature, is the outlet it can provide for the creative urge which most of us have within us. The establishment of what, for want of a better term, is usually referred to as a 'balanced' aquarium, incorporating gravel, plants, rocks, tree roots or other features, provides fascinating variations and possibilities. It is difficult to describe the satisfaction to be derived from the search and collection of some of these materials in order to compose an aquascape, in which complete harmony in colour, form and texture is achieved. This, however, may be of little consequence if the aquarium is not itself fitted into an appropriate setting. It is not enough merely to place an aquarium incongruously upon some item of furniture; it should be part of the furnishing scheme, an integral part of the decor or a focal point of interest in a room.

Although the cradle of aquariology was in China, the first scientific paper on the theory and practice of the 'balanced' aquarium was published in England in 1850. By the end of the 19th century, however, Germany was firmly established in the forefront of aquarium culture and it was the tropical fishes which Germany exported to the U.S.A. in those early years that formed the foundation for the flourishing nation-wide interest the hobby enjoys in America today.

The International Commission on Zoological Nomenclature was instituted so that there should be universal acceptance and usage of correct scientific names but it is inevitable that authorities on both sides of the Atlantic will sometimes use a name that has been superseded or which may have been found synonymous with others in more general use. Classification work is continually in progress, but in so vast and complex a field there are bound to be discrepancies. Old familiar names are supplanted in the light of further research, colour variations within a single species may have given rise to a multiplicity of specific names, or conversely, what appeared to be only slight variations are found to indicate more radical differences necessitating new specific names. The same problem exists, to a much lesser degree, with the names of aquatic plants. The use of common or popular names alone is of course totally inadequate, for in many cases two or three, or even whole groups of closely related fishes of different species are referred to under a single common name. Consequently, throughout this book, the full scientific name and, whenever applicable, the common name of each species, is given.

The excellent quality of the illustrations will be an invaluable aid to recognition and identification, for there is no doubt that such pictures are much more readily absorbed than the most detailed of written descriptions.

Raymond Legge

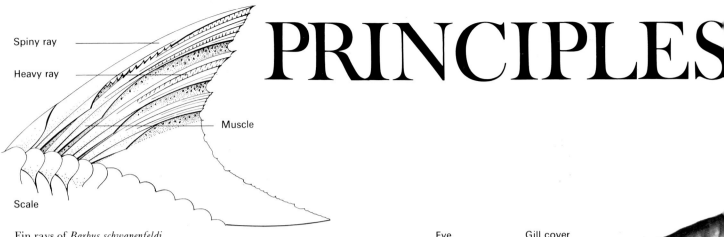

Spiny ray

Heavy ray

Muscle

Scale

Fin rays of *Barbus schwanenfeldi*

PRINCIPLES

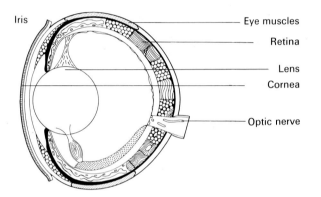

Iris

Eye muscles

Retina

Lens

Cornea

Optic nerve

Cross section of the eye

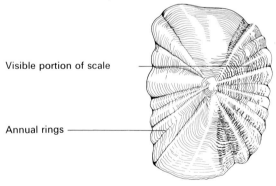

Visible portion of scale

Annual rings

Scale, magnified three times. Overlapping scales form in the dermis and are covered by another layer of skin, the epidermis.

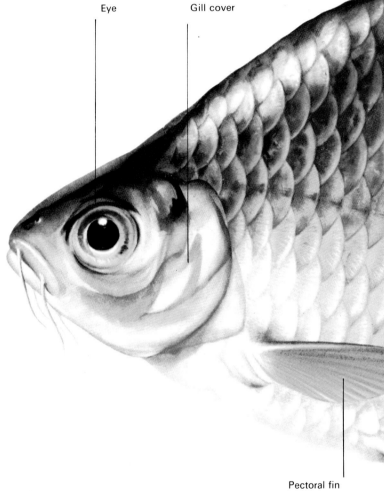

Eye

Gill cover

Pectoral fin

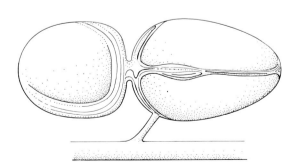

Swim bladder and pneumatic duct. The swim bladder functions mainly as a gas bladder, giving the fish the correct buoyancy for the depth at which it lives.

Any dictionary will tell you that a fish is a vertebrate animal adapted to live in water. It 'breathes' by extracting oxygen from the water through gills and is propelled and balanced by means of fins. 'Freshwater' and 'tropical' fishes are not essentially different from any other kind—these words merely designate the environment to which they have adapted. Keeping freshwater tropical fishes has grown up as a hobby because the freshwater and tropical environment has always been more easily approximated and maintained in the home aquarium than the 'coldwater' and/or 'marine' environment. Even today—with the availability of the most sophisticated aquarium equipment—the keeping of coldwater or marine fishes remains a relatively specialised and expensive pastime.

& MANAGEMENT

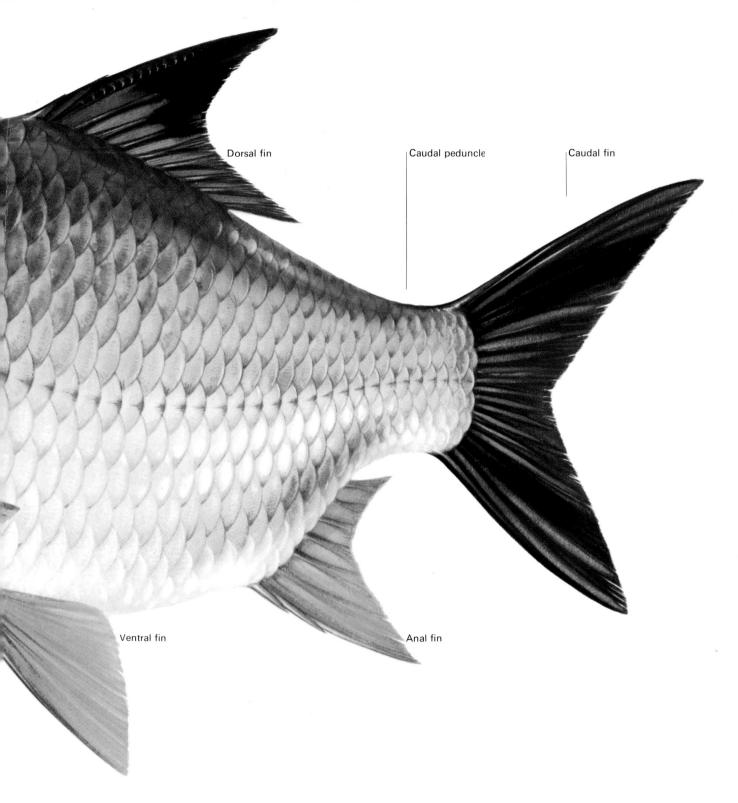

Dorsal fin

Caudal peduncle

Caudal fin

Ventral fin

Anal fin

THE KEEPING OF FISHES as pets has, during the last fifty years, developed into a popular and widespread hobby, but the beginnings of fish-keeping go back to antiquity. Early records show that Goldfish were kept as pets in China during the Sung Dynasty, a thousand years ago. In more recent times, Samuel Pepys made a diary reference, in 1665, to the keeping of fishes in the home.

In the Victorian era, the aquarium became a new and fashionable fad and was probably started in England by the work of Philip Gosse. He was responsible for the world's first public aquarium, the London Zoo 'fish house', opened in 1853. In 1854 he started to popularise home aquaria by writing the first of a series of books on the subject.

About this time a number of public aquaria were constructed throughout Europe, in Paris (1859), Hamburg (1864), and Naples (1873). The Crystal Palace Aquarium at Sydenham was opened in 1871, and was probably the first artificially lighted aquarium in the world.

The first tropical fish to be kept in home aquaria was apparently the Paradise Fish, *Macropodus opercularis*, which was introduced into Paris in 1868 by Carbonnier, and subsequently found its way to England and America. This was hardly surprising since the wide temperature tolerance of this species would have enabled it to be kept almost as a cold-water fish.

It was not, however, until the period between the two World Wars, that tropical fish aquaria became at all popular. Obviously, only a limited number of species were obtainable and because of importation difficulties, many of them were very expensive.

The aftermath of the 1939–1945 War saw a boom in the hobby. Better facilities for import, especially by air, enabled more and more species to become available at reasonable prices. The number of serious breeders increased. Local Aquatic Societies attracted a rapidly expanding membership. Aquarium shows and exhibitions, both on local and national level, gave a new impetus to the hobby.

In the 1950's the boom was followed by a slump. Many 'dabblers' in Great Britain found their interest waning and gave up, but on the continent of Europe and in the United States the hobby flourished and even gathered momentum. Fortunately, there were enough serious enthusiasts left in the United Kingdom to tide the hobby over a difficult period. Today the aquarium hobby has re-established itself with a vengeance and shows every sign of steady growth. Moreover, it is backed by a highly organised industry producing a wide range of products and equipment, all designed to ease the task of the aspiring aquarist.

CHOOSING AN AQUARIUM

The obvious first step is to buy or acquire an aquarium. There are many types available, but probably the most popular is the metal-framed rectangular tank, the glass of which is set in position by aquarium cement, a type of putty. For smaller tanks, a lightweight pressed steel frame is satisfactory, but for tanks larger than 18″ long and 10″ wide, angle-iron is the best material for the frame, being much stronger and less likely to become distorted and thus leak.

Ordinary aquarium frames are usually painted with high gloss paint or stove-enamelled to give a pleasant finish. Even better, though more expensive, are those in which the frame has been coated with nylon, epoxy resin or other non-toxic, rust-proof and durable material. In recent years a great variety of materials have been used in the manufacture of aquarium frames and the choice may now include anodised aluminium, plastics and stainless steel. At the same time, such advances have been made in adhesives that it is now perfectly feasible to cement plate glass sheets together, without any frame, to form an incredibly strong aquarium.

A moulded all-glass aquarium may be a temptation. The drawback is that it is difficult to get one in which the glass is really clear and free from visual distortion. Also, once an all-glass tank is cracked, it cannot be repaired and is quite useless.

A simple angle-iron tank is both strong and durable.

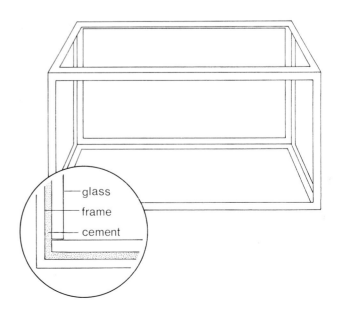

glass
frame
cement

Plastic tanks are available in a variety of sizes and shapes. Most of them are small and have the disadvantage that the plastic tends, in due course, to scratch and become opaque.

A number of sophisticated designs are on the market, worth considering by those who wish to have something out of the ordinary.

The bow-fronted aquarium is a variation of the angle-iron rectangular tank, in which the front glass is bowed, rather like a television screen. It has a magnifying effect and is most decorative. Bow-fronted tanks are also available in plastic, and there are a number of variations, with built-in heating and lighting equipment.

One design of aquarium has an additional sheet of glass, running the length of the tank and forming a compartment at the back, which is part of a filtering system to keep the water clear.

There is doubtless a great deal to be done, both from the functional and decorative point of view, in the field of aquarium design, and research on the subject is to be encouraged. But until a perfect aquarium is designed, the serious beginner would be well advised to purchase the angle-iron framed tank, in as large a size as can be accommodated, preferably not smaller than 24″ long, 12″ wide and 12″ deep. Obviously, a limited number of fishes can be kept in any one tank. If you buy a small one, you will sooner or later wish to replace it with a larger one. It is also easier to keep a larger tank in good condition.

Tanks are available in many sizes from 6″ × 6″ × 6″ upwards from aquarium suppliers. The most common sizes are:

LENGTH	WIDTH	DEPTH
12″	6″	6″
14″	8″	8″
18″	10″	10″
24″	12″	12″
36″	12″	12″

Some of the larger tanks are also made 15″ deep in order to give a larger 'picture' effect. These tanks can be very decorative, but will not hold any more fishes than the shallower varieties. The governing factor is the absorption by the water surface of oxygen from the air. This is determined by the surface area and not the depth. Where deeper tanks do play a useful part, both decoratively and functionally, is in the housing of larger fishes with deep bodies, of which the Angel Fish is a good example.

Having bought your tank, place it on a level surface and test it by filling it with water. A word of warning here. Water is very heavy and a 24″ × 12″ × 12″ tank filled with water weighs over 120 lbs. A simple way to calculate water capacity is to multiply the height, length and width of the tank and divide by 231. Thus a tank measuring 24″ × 12″ × 12″ would hold nearly 15 gallons (3456 divided by 231). A cubic foot of water is equal to $6\frac{1}{4}$ gallons, and one gallon of water weighs 10 lbs. It is, therefore, essential to have a strong stand. This can be a table or similar piece of furniture, or you may prefer to buy an angle-iron stand made specially for the purpose. Never attempt to lift a tank

Two tanks showing the importance of surface area in relation to water depth. The top tank, with its shallower depth, allows greater oxygen absorption.

A bow-fronted angle-iron tank creates a magnifying effect.

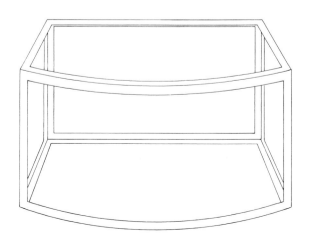

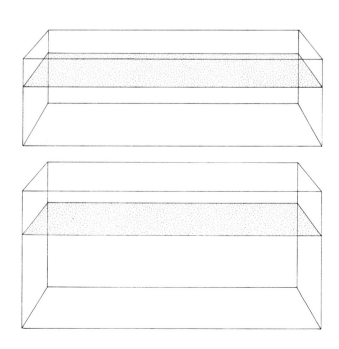

which is full of water as the frame may distort and cause it to leak.

Sometimes a newly purchased tank will leak a little, but it should soon dry up. If the leak persists or if you are in any doubt at all, take it back to the dealer. In any event, the water will have to be emptied before the setting-up stage.

Tank covers in metal or plastic, fitting over the top of the aquarium and made to hold lamp bulbs, can be bought in matching colours. They keep dust out, condensation and fishes in. Some aquarists prefer a sheet of glass which can be fitted on clips, in which case provision must be made for lamps.

However, such covers will not necessarily provide complete protection against the risk of poisoning and death of fishes by household sprays, pesticides or even tobacco fumes. Paraffin-based sprays are particularly dangerous. Be careful to keep all such noxious substances away from the tank.

SITING THE AQUARIUM

There is no doubt that a tastefully furnished aquarium, appropriately sited and incorporated into the decor, can be a great asset to any room. No effort should be spared to make it an integral part of the furnishing scheme, and indeed, it can become a focal point in the room. It is not difficult to flank an aquarium with pleasingly bound volumes on a bookself, fit it into a neat cabinet that will conceal accessory equipment, or build it into a wall recess.

LIGHTING

It is far safer to stand the tank away from any window and supplement with artificial light. In any case, some artificial light is essential in order to see the aquarium to the best advantage at all times and to promote plant growth. The amount and type of light required is a matter of experience. As a general guide, 40 watts per square foot of surface area may be used, and this may be increased or decreased according to the natural light available. Fluorescent lighting is quite successful, and is more economical as a lower wattage may be used. Some forms of this lighting are not suitable for plant growth, but the 'warm white' type is often used.

TEMPERATURE

Most tropical fishes thrive at a temperature of between 73° and 77°F. This is the temperature one might expect on a warm summer day, neither lukewarm nor hot. But natural temperatures are unpredictable and in order to achieve an even,

Three of several types of tank covers. Covers may be purchased already fitted with lights.

satisfactory temperature throughout the year it is essential, in the so-called temperate climate zones, to employ a heater and thermostat.

The usual type of heater, which is quite inexpensive, consists of an electric element sealed in a glass tube. An insulated wire carries the electric current into the tube, immersed in the water.

The thermostat is an automatic switch which cuts off the current when the pre-determined temperature is reached. There are two main types. One, like the heater, is enclosed in a glass tube, and is immersed in the water. The other type is an external thermostat, and is clipped to the outside of the tank, close to the glass.

There are various types of thermometers made especially for aquarium use. The long tubular types may be mercury or alcohol filled. Mercury is generally considered to be more accurate and also reacts more quickly than the alcohol type. Some are designed to float in the water, while others have a rubber sucker attached, so that they can be positioned on the tank glass. Neither is very expensive. Another type is dial-shaped, with a needle which points to the temperature. This thermometer is attached to the glass by a suction disc, and is more expensive than the other types.

All the temperatures mentioned in this book are given in degrees Fahrenheit. Old customs are hard to shed and experience shows that during this transitional period of switching from Fahrenheit to Centigrade reckoning most people tend automatically to think in terms of the former measurement. For easy reference, therefore, the approximate Fahrenheit–Centigrade equivalents are given in the following diagram.

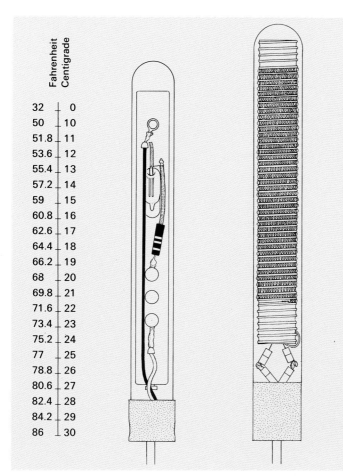

Fahrenheit	Centigrade
32	0
50	10
51.8	11
53.6	12
55.4	13
57.2	14
59	15
60.8	16
62.6	17
64.4	18
66.2	19
68	20
69.8	21
71.6	22
73.4	23
75.2	24
77	25
78.8	26
80.6	27
82.4	28
84.2	29
86	30

Aquaria may be lighted either by incandescent tungsten lamps or by fluorescent tubes.
The advantage of incandescent illumination is that it is cheap and simple to install, that it encourages plant growth and that it highlights the natural colours of the fishes. On the other hand, tungsten bulbs are short-lived and heavy on electricity consumption, they produce intense heat which may damage surface plants and they do not provide an absolutely even distribution of light.

Most aquarists therefore favour fluorescent lighting which, although requiring expert guidance on installation, is cheaper to operate, does not heat the water surface to excess, is obtainable in a variety of lengths, colours and wattages and illuminates the tank or tanks evenly.

A thermostat and a heater. Both are enclosed in a glass tube. The heater must always be covered by water before it is switched on

BASIC PRINCIPLES OF AQUARIUM LIFE

Before proceeding to the actual setting up of a tank it is worth mentioning, very briefly, the general principles which govern aquarium keeping.

The aquarium may be regarded as a world in miniature, a small-scale reproduction of life in a pond or river. Fishes absorb oxygen from the water by means of gills, the oxygen being converted into carbon dioxide, which is passed out in the water expelled from the gills. Oxygen is constantly being absorbed from the air by the water surface and diffuses through it. (This is why the surface area of an aquarium is so important.) The process of absorption and diffusion, however, is very slow. When a fish is unable to get sufficient oxygen or when the carbon dioxide content of the water is high, it will gasp at the surface. This usually indicates that there are too many fishes in the tank.

In the presence of light, plants absorb carbon dioxide and evolve oxygen. This process is called photosynthesis, whereby the plant is able to build up its tissues by utilising the carbon from the carbon dioxide in conjunction with materials absorbed from its root system.

It will be seen that the process of photosynthesis complements the breathing process of the fish, and it has been said that fishes are dependent on plants to produce the oxygen they require. This is not entirely true since fishes can and do survive in tanks devoid of plants, the absorption by water of oxygen from the air being independent of the presence of plants. Nevertheless, plants do play a part in ensuring the saturation of water with oxygen and also help to remove the toxic carbon dioxide.

Plants also feed on the waste matter produced by the fishes, and therefore help to prevent the formation of toxic substances. In nature, this waste matter is the beginning of a food cycle in which larger organisms feed in turn upon smaller organisms, with the larger organisms eventually forming an important source of food for the fishes. Unfortunately, in the limited space of the aquarium, natural foods such as daphnia are consumed before they have the opportunity to breed, and it is therefore necessary to introduce food. This process too can be a source of contamination in the comparatively cramped area of the aquarium, so that care must be taken never to over-feed.

SETTING UP THE TANK

Having checked the tank for leaking and placed the stand in the required position, all is now ready for setting up the aquarium.

The floor of the tank should be covered with a suitable compost to a depth of about 2″. Aquarium compost or gravel can be bought quite cheaply and consists of a coarse sand or gravel, the particles of which are about $\frac{1}{8}$″ in diameter. This is definitely the best grade to use. A coarser gravel does not promote good plant growth and allows food particles to lodge between the pebbles. A fine sand packs too densely and does not allow the plant roots to penetrate easily.

Some aquarists use a layer of peat or soil under the gravel in order to provide a nutritious planting material. The beginner is advised not to do this as it may contaminate the water. Also, unless great care is taken, this under-layer or substrate may rise to the top, resulting in an unsightly and troublesome mess. This is definitely something for the experienced aquarist only.

The aquarium compost as obtained from the shop is usually dirty and needs to be washed thoroughly before use. This is best done by placing the compost in a bowl, a little at a time, and allowing the water tap to run on it. You can stir it with the hands to speed up the process, tipping off the dirty water now and then, taking care not to lose the gravel or block the sink waste with it. Continue until the water in the bowl remains clear when stirred up, then repeat the process with another batch of gravel.

Now place the compost in the tank. It is best to slope the level from back to front so that it is about 1″ deep in the front and 3″ at the back. The level does not have to be completely uniform and will depend on the setting you have in mind. For example, the corners of the tank might be filled liberally and the compost sloped off to almost nothing in the centre of the front of the tank.

Rocks usually form an important part of the decorative scheme and certainly add greatly to the picturesque qualities of the aquarium. But a few words of warning are needed here. Some rocks, being highly alkaline, dissolve slowly to create unsatisfactory conditions. In general, it is best to avoid soft sedimentary rocks, limestones and artificial features in untreated cement, but there are plenty of others to choose from, as most of the igneous rocks, sandstones and slates are perfectly safe. They can be tested with a drop of hydrochloric acid, and if the acid foams it indicates the presence of injurious calcareous material.

Pleasing set-pieces are obtainable from most aquatic dealers, but a great deal of enjoyment and satisfaction can be obtained from the acquisition of colourful and attractive rocks from the more rugged localities of coastal, mountain, river or lake terrain.

Rocks should be firmly bedded into the compost so that food particles will not lodge beneath them and contaminate the water.

Tree roots, gnarled branches and driftwood are also popular decorative features, but any such material should be thoroughly cleaned of all foreign matter before use.

Now that you have prepared your basic design with compost and rocks, pour a few inches of water into the tank. It is best to use a watering can, with rose attachment, to avoid undue disturbance. The water should be of approximately the desired temperature.

It is a good idea at this stage to fit the heater and thermostat (if of the submersible type) in order to avoid later disturbance of plants. Follow the maker's instructions to the letter and invest in a special holder, fixed to the glass by means of a rubber or plastic sucker, to keep the heater in position. Fix the heater to the side rather than the back of the tank—such a position is less obtrusive —setting it horizontally, or at a slight angle, about 1″ from the bottom. Do not bury the heater in the compost. With care you can arrange your natural rock setting to conceal both heater and thermostat. Make quite certain, however, that you can place the thermostat as far away as possible from the heater. If it is too close, you will not obtain an even heat distribution. Do not at this stage connect thermostat and heater to the electricity supply.

PLANTING

The choice of plants to create a decorative aquarium is very much a matter of individual taste, and the aquarist must often use his own judgement in assessing how to use them. Some knowledge of the growth habits of plants, however, is valuable, as some will grow more rapidly than others and must be given more space in the initial planting.

Once you have selected your plants, you must decide how to arrange them. It is usual to place the tallest plants at the back and the smaller ones near the front. Plant more densely at the back of the tank and continue round the sides to the front

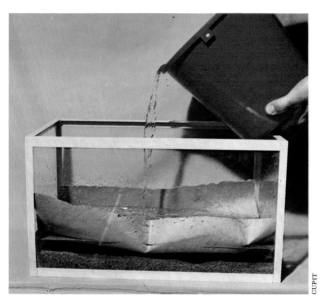

Filling a tank after protecting plants and gravel.

corners. It is more effective to use groups or clusters of the same species of plant, rather than single specimens. (See page 31 *et seq.*)

When planting is completed, fill the tank with water, taking great care not to disturb the gravel and uproot the plants. A simple way to avoid this is to cut two or three pieces of brown paper to the size of the tank area and place them over the plants, rock and gravel. Then, using a watering can, with rose attached, pour the water slowly over the paper. When the tank is filled, remove the paper. An alternative method, not so effective, is to place a saucer or plate in the unplanted area of the tank and pour the water onto this from a jug or other vessel.

After filling the tank, check that the thermostat and heater are correctly positioned and fixed according to the manufacturer's instructions. They may then be connected by plugging into the electricity supply. Thermostats are normally set to the correct temperature range, i.e. 73°–77°F., but it is advisable to check by means of a thermometer.

WATER

Water is the most essential part of the aquarist's 'equipment' but only too often it is taken for granted. In fact, the nature of water varies considerably. In some places it is 'hard', in others 'soft'. Pure water is a simple chemical compound, known to the chemist as H_2O. But although H_2O is a fixed, invariable substance, it will dissolve gases, salts and organic matter, and it is this dissolved matter that changes its nature. It is testimony to the hardiness of many fishes that they are able to thrive in water quite different in sub-

stance from that in which they are found in nature.

Water is obtained from many sources, but all of it comes originally from the sea by way of evaporation and rainfall. Rain may run off the surface on which it falls, forming lakes, streams, rivers, ponds and so forth, or it may percolate into the soil, giving rise to various underground sources. Rain water, initially pure, is polluted on its journey by gases and other impurities, particularly in industrial areas. For this reason, whilst rain water is suitable for the aquarium, care should be taken that it is not contaminated, especially if collected from a roof. It is always advisable to allow it to stand for several days, before introducing it into an aquarium.

Water in lakes or rivers will vary according to the nature of the rock formation. Limestone will cause the water to be hard and alkaline, but where the rocks are impervious to water action it will remain soft. If peat is present, the water will be soft and acid, possibly discoloured.

In the equatorial regions where tropical fishes are found, streams and ponds are often overhung by dense vegetation which falls into the water and decomposes. This causes acid conditions, similar to that produced by peat.

All water for domestic use is required to be pure and wholesome. This means that it must be non-injurious, free from disease organisms and toxic substances and from excessive amounts of dissolved substances. In other words, it must be fit to drink. Nevertheless, within these limits it will still vary according to the source from which the supply is obtained.

The beginner need not worry too much about this, as most tropical fishes quickly adapt themselves to the water in which they are kept. But problems often arise in trying to breed certain types of fishes when the chemical content of the water becomes more important. For example, soft water with a certain pH may be recommended, and it is as well to understand exactly what this means.

Hardness: Most natural waters contain dissolved salts which are consequently found in tap water. These consist mainly of chlorides, sulphates and bicarbonates. The calcium and magnesium forms of these salts are responsible for 'hardness', while an excess of chlorides gives the water a brackish taste. Carbonates only occur in small amounts, as calcium carbonate (chalk) is almost insoluble. It will, however, dissolve in water containing carbon dioxide, becoming converted to bicarbonate. Magnesium carbonate, being more soluble than calcium carbonate, also forms a more soluble bicarbonate. Boiling the water will break down the

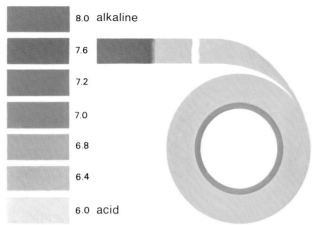

8.0 alkaline

7.6

7.2

7.0

6.8

6.4

6.0 acid

A representation of the 'indicator' dyes used to measure the acid or alkaline content of water in a tank.

bicarbonates and the less soluble carbonates will be thrown down. The phenomenon is seen as 'scale' in boilers and 'fur' in kettles.

Hardness which can be removed by boiling is sometimes referred to as 'temporary' hardness. 'Permanent' or non-carbonate hardness is due to the chlorides and sulphates of calcium and magnesium and cannot be removed by boiling.

Water hardness is measured as if it were all due to calcium carbonate, and is variously expressed in different parts of the world. In France, for example, one degree of hardness is equal to one part of calcium *carbonate* dissolved in 100,000 parts of water, while in Germany, each degree of hardness indicates one part of calcium *oxide* in 100,000 parts of water. The English or 'Clark's' degree of hardness is given in terms of grains of calcium carbonate per gallon of water. The United States adopts a similar system except that the gallon (231 cu. in.) is smaller than the imperial gallon (277¼ cu. in.) and their degree of hardness correspondingly less. A convenient formula is 1 French degree = 0.56 German degree = 0.70 English (Clark's) degree = 0.585 U.S. degree. Because of the confusion which can arise from this multiplicity of figures, it is more accurate and scientific to quote hardness in terms of parts per million. One Clark's degree is approximately equal to 14 parts per million.

Water with a hardness of less than 100 parts per million is usually regarded as 'soft', 100 and 200 is 'slightly hard', and over 200, 'hard' or 'very hard'.

The hardness of aquarium water may be adjusted by diluting with distilled or rain water.

Metals: Because some metals are slowly dissolved by water, especially soft water, care must be taken in introducing them into the aquarium. Copper, zinc and lead are all toxic to fishes. Lead will dissolve only in soft water, a protective deposit

forming on the metal in hard water. If the water supply comes through a copper boiler or pipes it is advisable to flush the water thoroughly before drawing supplies for the aquarium.

pH Value: pH is a measure of acidity or alkalinity in a fluid. It need not unduly concern the average hobbyist, intent only upon the establishment of an interesting and decorative aquarium, but as it has a very considerable influence on the breeding and rearing of fishes, its importance should be borne in mind. Neutral water is said to have a pH of 7, while water with a pH of less than 7 is acid, and greater than 7 alkaline. In nature, acid water is usually due to the presence of peat or decaying vegetation. Carbon dioxide (CO_2) also acts as an acid and pH will therefore vary with the CO_2 content. Alkalinity is frequently due to calcium bicarbonate, which is also responsible for hardness. Therefore, in nature, hard waters are usually also alkaline.

The pH is measured by the use of 'indicators'—dyes which change colour at different values. Indicators are available as solutions or papers and there are various methods of using them. These simple methods are acceptable for general purposes, but for greater accuracy instruments called 'comparators' are used. A simple form of comparator set is available from most aquarium dealers.

Acidity may be produced in the aquarium by the use of peat. Long fallen oak or beech leaves have also been recommended. Phosphoric and tannic acids are among suitable chemicals, but care must be exercised by the inexperienced. It is rarely necessary to reduce pH below 6. A low pH and a high carbon dioxide content also cause a more rapid corrosion of iron, lead, copper and zinc.

The influence of water conditions on the breeding, growth and development of fishes and plants has long been known. But our knowledge of the water requirements of individual fishes and plant species, and of the effect in water of factors other than hardness and pH, is far from complete.

SELECTION OF FISHES

When the tank has been filled with water, the proud owner will be tempted to step back and admire it. Restraint is now recommended. Do not be in too much of a hurry to buy fishes to put into it. It is a good idea to leave it for a few days, or even a week or two, to settle down. Some of the plants may rise to the surface, having become detached

A pair of Green Swordtails, *Xiphophorus helleri*, typical Live-bearers. The upper fish is the female.

from their anchorage. These will need to be re-planted with the aid of planting sticks. Water which starts to turn green is receiving too much light and this should be reduced either by using smaller bulbs or, if due to natural light, by shading the back and sides of the tank.

Most people will wish to collect a community of different species of fishes, all living together in harmony. When buying a fish which is not familiar, it is advisable to ascertain its habits and to see whether it is suitable for a community tank.

Tropical fishes may broadly be divided into two groups, the Live-bearers and the Egg-layers. The Live-bearers give birth to live young and are rather easier to breed. With some species, however, this can become an embarrassment, especially when space is at a premium. Live-bearers do not normally look after their young and will, in fact, eat them.

Sexing of Live-bearers is fairly easy as the anal fin in the adult male forms a rod-like gonopodium. The anal fin is situated on the underside of the fish, immediately in front of the tail or caudal fin. In the female, it is the normal fan shape, as in most fishes.

Egg-layers include the majority of our tropical fishes. In general, the sexes are similar in ap-pearance and are almost equally colourful.

When buying, it is useful to know what to look for in a healthy fish. It will, of course, have an appearance which is normal to its species, but in general the scales will be bright and glistening, and the fins spread out and not carried folded to the body. In particular, the dorsal fin will be held erect. Lack of colour is not necessarily an indication of ill-health. Most fishes tend to lose colour when frightened or if the water is too cold, but this is only a temporary condition. A fish which swims in an erratic manner, however, or rubs itself against objects in the tank, may be diseased or have parasites. (See page 231 *et seq.*)

Make sure you buy fishes only from a reputable dealer who is known to sell good, healthy specimens and who will offer reliable advice on care and breeding.

The swimming habits of fishes vary according to species. Some tend to swim near the bottom, while others frequent the surface. Many swim in the middle area. All one can say is that a fish should swim in a manner normal to its species. The beginner would be well advised to study the sections in this book dealing with individual species in order

A planting stick is a convenient aid when adding new plants to an aquarium setting.

Floating a jar in the tank, enabling the water temperature in the container to adjust to that of the aquarium, helps to acclimatise newly purchased stock.

to be able to identify and learn something of their varied characteristics. As he gains experience he will easily be able to form a mental picture of a healthy specimen of any given species.

In a well kept aquarium, sickness or disease is rare. Fishes have a great resistance to disease as long as they are not weakened by bad treatment, feeding or over-crowding. Aquarists who have a number of tanks should use one for quarantine so that new fishes can be segregated for about two weeks. By this time, any latent disease will have developed and may be treated without risk of infecting the established tanks. The beginner, who is likely to have only one tank, must simply guard against buying unhealthy stock.

The fishes will probably be supplied in a plastic bag or glass jar. In either case it is necessary to prevent undue chilling. In very cold weather, the container should be wrapped in a piece of blanket, felt, or some other insulating material. The handyman can make a simple carrying box, with a handle and built-in insulation, to take one or two jars.

When you get the fishes home, do not tip them straight into the tank. In spite of precautions, the temperature of the water in the container will probably be different from that in the tank. Float the jar or plastic bag gently in the tank. After about fifteen minutes to allow the temperatures to equalise, the fishes should be carefully released. It is good policy to feed any fishes already occupying the tank, before introducing the newcomers. A well fed fish is less likely to resent intruders!

Some of the new fishes may be pale and hide away in corners. This is only a temporary state of affairs. Leave them alone and they will soon recover both their colour and energy.

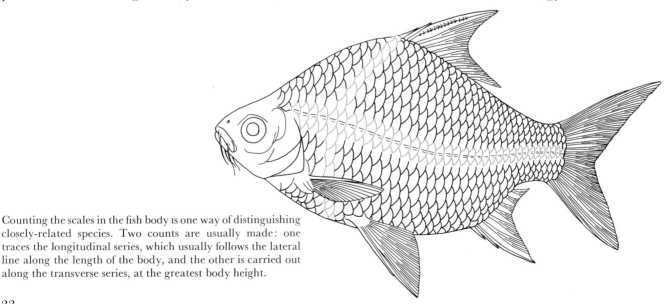

Counting the scales in the fish body is one way of distinguishing closely-related species. Two counts are usually made: one traces the longitudinal series, which usually follows the lateral line along the length of the body, and the other is carried out along the transverse series, at the greatest body height.

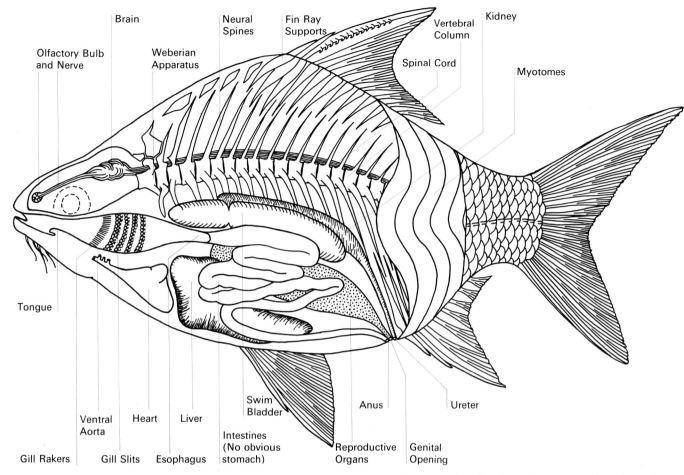

Olfactory Bulb and Nerve · Brain · Weberian Apparatus · Neural Spines · Fin Ray Supports · Vertebral Column · Kidney · Spinal Cord · Myotomes

Tongue

Gill Rakers · Ventral Aorta · Heart · Gill Slits · Liver · Esophagus · Intestines (No obvious stomach) · Swim Bladder · Reproductive Organs · Anus · Genital Opening · Ureter

The serious aquarist will wish to know something about the internal anatomy of fishes in order to understand the breathing, breeding and other processes of fish life.

Basic caudal fin shapes will help in identifying groups and species of fishes. There are many variations and developments of these shapes.

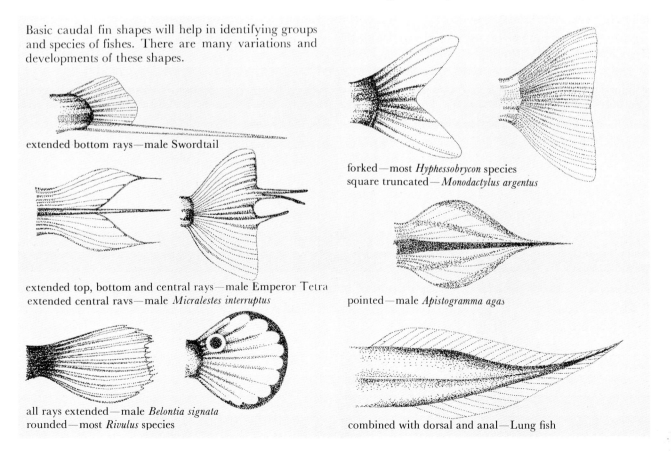

extended bottom rays—male Swordtail

forked—most *Hyphessobrycon* species
square truncated—*Monodactylus argentus*

extended top, bottom and central rays—male Emperor Tetra
extended central rays—male *Micralestes interruptus*

pointed—male *Apistogramma agas*

all rays extended—male *Belontia signata*
rounded—most *Rivulus* species

combined with dorsal and anal—Lung fish

AQUARIUM MAINTENANCE

The aquarium, once established, should need little attention, provided care is taken not to over-feed the fish and the light is correctly controlled. For normal maintenance there are a number of inexpensive pieces of equipment on the market.

Scraper: Algae, an elementary form of plant growth, will usually make an early entry into the aquarium. There are many different types, including a brown variety, which sometimes appears on the tank glass and which is an indication of insufficient light. The green algae usually indicates an over-abundance of light and these conditions can be corrected. In either case, they should be removed from the glass, otherwise viewing will be impaired.

For cleaning the inside of the tank glass, use a scraper, either of plastic or metal, which is made to hold a razor blade.

There is a type of algae which often appears as green threads or wool. This can usually be removed by putting in a stick which has a rough surface and twisting it in the clumps of algae. The threads are wound around the stick and pulled out.

Syphon: Algae scraped from the surface of the glass will settle to the bottom of the tank, and a black deposit, consisting partly of fish excreta, will also appear. This is known as 'mulm' and should be removed periodically by a syphon tube.

The syphon tube is essentially a length of rubber or plastic tubing of about $\frac{1}{4}'' - \frac{3}{8}''$ internal diameter and long enough to extend from the inside bottom surface of the tank, over the top and down to the floor. The syphoning process can be started by placing one end below the water surface and

sucking at the other end. As the water level rises, remove the tube from your mouth, pinch it closed and place it in a clean receptacle standing on the floor. The water will then flow into the receptacle and the end of the tube in the tank can be lowered near the bottom and used like a vacuum cleaner to remove the mulm. This will be deposited in the container. When all the mulm has been removed, the syphon tube can be stopped simply by lifting it from the tank. After a few minutes the mulm will settle and the clear water can be decanted and returned to the tank. Any gravel should also be washed and replaced.

Shops offer modifications of this simple apparatus, thus reducing the risk of taking a mouthful of dirty water. For those who find it difficult to master the technique described, an alternative is to hold one end of the tube to a tap, turn on the water until it flows from the end of the tube, close both ends with the fingers and carry the tube to the tank with the ends raised high, removing the fingers when one end is below the water surface.

Feeding rings: These are not essential, but some aquarists like to use them as they prevent dry food from spreading over the surface and, if uneaten, sinking to the bottom over a wide area. Basically, they consist of a glass or plastic tube bent into a circular or triangular shape, and are usually attached to the side of the tank by a rubber sucker.

Aerators: Aeration, in its simplest form, consists of blowing a stream of air bubbles into the water. Some have doubted the value of this, arguing that water takes up oxygen from the atmosphere at a constant proportion (dependent on temperature

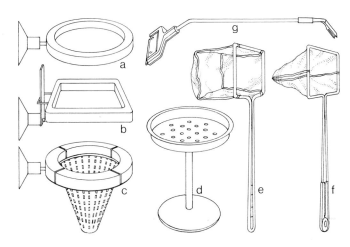

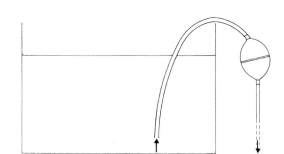

a Simple feeding ring. **b** Floating feeding ring. **c** Worm feeder. **d** Feeder for base of tank. **e, f** Different size fish nets. **g** Scraper for removing algae.

Diagram showing syphon correctly positioned on a tank.

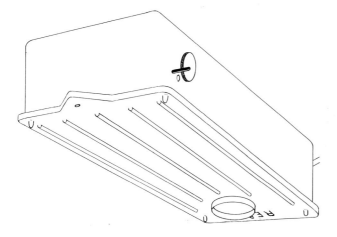

A simple electric motor for pumping air. This is one of several types which can be purchased.

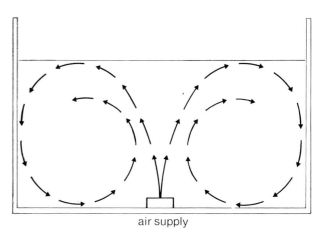

air supply

Circulation of air bubbles in water by aeration process.

and atmospheric pressure), and that no more oxygen can be absorbed by pumping air into the water. This is not altogether true, since the absorption of oxygen at the water surface and its diffusion throughout the water is a slow process, and the oxygen level near the surface is higher than at the bottom of the tank. The aeration process causes a constant disturbance of the water surface, covering it with ripples. Thus the surface area is increased and the absorption of oxygen facilitated. Furthermore, the diffusion of oxygen is accelerated by the mixing process. It is also probable that the flow of bubbles through the water helps to remove carbon dioxide and other noxious gases which may be present.

Certainly, one can keep more fishes in an aerated tank, probably twice as many, as in an unaerated one. The main disadvantage is that fishes that have been accustomed to aeration will suffer if moved to an unaerated tank or if the aerator is switched off. This can be dangerous, especially in well stocked tanks.

An electric pump for working an aerator is not expensive to buy, though more elaborate and substantial models which will operate several aerators are also obtainable. The pump is attached by a length of rubber or plastic tubing to a diffuser stone. This consists of a piece of porous stone, usually in the shape of a cube or cylinder, into which a piece of rigid tubing is fixed. When the tubing from the pump is attached to this, air is forced through the porous stone and emits an underwater stream of fine bubbles.

Filters: The same pump can be used to operate a filter. Incorporated in aquarium filters is what is known as an air-lift. The principle is as follows. A stream of air bubbles is forced into the bottom of a tube held vertically in the water and reaching from near the bottom to above the surface. As the bubbles

rise up the tube they carry some of the water with them. At the top of the tube a mixture of water and air is expelled. By this simple device the air pump is converted into a water pump. If the water is now allowed to fall on to a filter bed, which will remove any particles, clean water will run back into the tank.

This is the basic process involved in the aquarium filter, but of course there are many different types. The filter bed frequently consists of nylon wool, but but may also contain granules of activated charcoal (carbon) which will also absorb noxious gases from the water. Sand and gravel can also be used as filtering media. Whatever the material used, it will have to be changed from time to time as it becomes saturated with the matter filtered out.

Commercial filters are usually made of plastic, and the simpler models are made to fit into an inside corner of the tank so that the water runs directly back into the aquarium. More complex models are fitted to the outside, with tubes carrying the water to and from the tank. A simple but effective form of filter can be made from a flower pot filled with sand. A simple air-lift is pushed into the sand and

An air-lift works both as an air and water pump, performing the dual role of aeration and filtration.

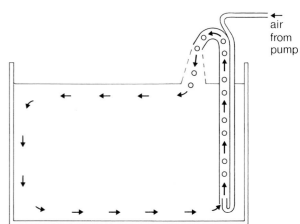

air from pump

connected to a pump. As the water is expelled from the top of the air-lift, more water passes through the sand to replace it. Thus the sand in the pot acts as a filtering medium. This form of underwater filtration is the basis of some systems which have been produced in which the filter bed is below the water surface.

Carrying this idea a stage further is the sub-gravel filter, in which the aquarium gravel itself is the filtering medium. This is made of plastic and consists of a raised hollow base, containing many slots, which is placed on the glass bottom of the tank and covered with gravel. From the base a wide and a narrow plastic tube lead upwards. The narrow tube is attached to an air pump. The wider tube allows the air bubbles to escape from below the base, without unduly disturbing the tank.

Most snails suitable for freshwater aquaria are found in the tropics, but several species from Europe are frequently seen. Normally they feed on the remains of animal food and algae so it is not necessary to provide special food other than pieces of lettuce for the known plant-eaters.

Among the freshwater snails found in Europe are **a**: *Melanoides tuberculata* Malayan Burrowing Snail which grows up to 1″ in length and is suitable for the temperate aquarium.
b: *Planorbis corneus* Great Ramshorn Snail. Although this is a cold-water species and grows to 1¼″ in diameter, it is often used in temperate aquariums.
c: *Lymnaea ovata peregra* Wandering Snail should be avoided as it produces a substance which may convulse fishes.
d: *Ampularius ampularia* is not suitable for the average aquarium as it eats the higher aquatic plants but it is kept as a producer of infusoria.

The advantage of a filter is that the water is kept clean and clear. It also provides some of the advantages of aeration. It is not, however, essential, and in a well balanced aquarium the various biological processes described previously will ensure a healthy environment for your fishes.

Snails: There are a number of varieties of aquatic snails, which are often recommended as scavengers, to help keep the tank clean. They are of doubtful value, however, since at tropical temperatures they tend to be prolific, and their excreta counterbalances the cleaning. Furthermore, some species will not hesitate, if hungry, to eat aquatic plants.

In addition to the equipment already described the following are basic essentials.

Nets: A fish net should not be too small. It is easier to catch a fish with a large net. However, it is a good idea to have about three nets, say 3″×2″, 4″×3″, and 5″×4″. The smallest net should be of a fine mesh and can be used for feeding daphnia and other live foods.

Jars: A few 2 lb. jam jars are necessary for transferring fishes or, if need be, isolating them.

FOODS AND FEEDING

Dried Foods

There are now a number of dried foods generally available for tropical fishes, some better than others. Ideally, they should contain all the essential items of a fish's diet, protein, fats, carbohydrates, together with vegetable matter, mineral salts and vitamins. For small fishes they must be finely ground. Some are in the form of flakes and these can be crumbled between the fingers.

Such dried foods can be used as a basic diet, but should be supplemented from time to time with other foods. They should be fed sparingly, for if they are left uneaten they will pollute the water. A good rule is to feed only as much as will be eaten in five minutes. This can soon be discovered by experience and the amount may then be repeated three or four times a day. Beginners are often advised to feed only once a day. This is to reduce the risk of over-feeding, since more fishes die as a result of polluted water through over-feeding than from starvation. Nevertheless, provided the amount

Right: *Daphnia* or 'water fleas' (to ⅛"). Far right: *Cyclops* (to ⅛"). Lower right: Gnat larvae. Lower far right: Glass worms or 'phantom larvae' (to ⅝")

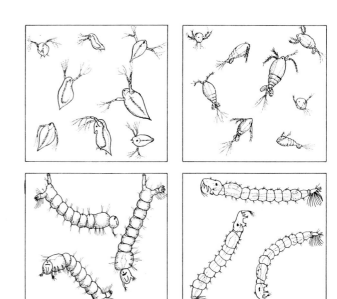

given is rigidly controlled, no harm will come from frequent feeding.

Many household foods are excellent for fishes. Cooked meat or fish, finely chopped with a knife or razor blade, or a small piece of cheese or boiled yolk of egg, finely crumbled, are all suitable. Fresh or frozen prawns or shrimps, similarly treated, can also be given. But the portions must be extremely small, as these foods will quickly pollute a tank. Yolk of eggs and liver, for example, if not eaten in a few minutes, will cloud the water very quickly.

Live Foods

Most species will thrive on live foods and the following are some of the main types available.

Daphnia: Daphnia or 'water fleas' are small crustaceans, not really fleas proper. They are found in ponds, during spring and summer, and are often sold in pet shops. Their food value is not very great but they are relished by all fishes, who doubtless benefit from the exercise of chasing and catching them. Daphnia do not survive for very long in a small volume of water and should be fed to the fishes quite soon after purchase. Alternatively, they can be put into a large bowl or bucket of water, when they will last a little longer.

Daphnia may also be collected from ponds, using a large net, which may be trawled through the water in figure-of-eight patterns. When collected in this way, they must be carried home in a container of water, tipped into a large enamelled basin or bowl and scrutinised carefully in case other creatures, such as dragon-fly larvae, which are harmful to fishes, have also been scooped up.

Cyclops: Cyclops are slightly smaller than daphnia and have a different habit of movement. They are accepted by most fishes but may attack small fry. The female has two egg sacs carried at the end of the body, which makes it identifiable.

Gnat larvae: These are found in summer in ponds, water butts and even small containers, which have become filled with rain water. They rise to the surface of the water, quickly dive to the bottom if disturbed, only to rise again a little later. This is the time to scoop them out with a net. Do not feed

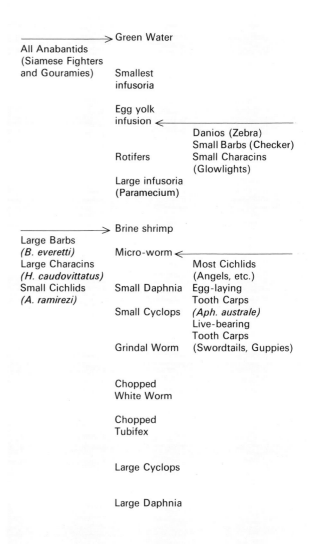

This chart shows the suggested first food for fry of differing species. With some species it is best to provide two sizes, *e.g.* for most Characins provide infusoria and brine shrimp. The next size food should be provided as soon as the fry are large enough.

too many and do not keep them for too long or they may change into gnats, not pleasant to have around the house. If the eggs, which are laid raft-like on the surface of the water, can be found, they may be floated in the tank and the larvae will be eaten as they emerge.

Glass Worms: These are similar to mosquito larvae, transparent, and known as 'ghost larvae'.

Blood Worms: The larvae of flies or midges, these are usually found in the mud at the bottom of a pond or water butt. They are bright red in colour, about $\frac{1}{2}''$ long, and are very nutritious.

Tubifex Worms: Tubifex are long thin worms, sometimes found in mud at the bottom of rivers and ponds. They are difficult to collect and it is simpler to buy them from aquatic stores. Tubifex live in very dirty conditions and must be thoroughly cleaned before they are fed to fishes. Ideally, they should be kept in running water, as in a bowl beneath a dripping tap. It is better not to use tubifex at all, than to use it inadequately cleansed.

Grindal Worms: These are a smaller variety of white worm, cultured in the same way, but preferring a more tropical temperature, of $70°-75°$F.

Earthworms: These provide an excellent and nutritious food for all but the largest aquarium fishes, such as the Cichlids, but they must be chopped up before feeding—one reason why they are not used more frequently.

Enchytrae or White Worms: These can be bred and form an excellent occasional diet for fishes, though they should not be fed too frequently as they are rather fattening. They live in the earth and may be bought as a culture, embedded in a lump of soil.

They are usually bred in a wooden box about $12'' \times 8'' \times 6''$ deep, or in an old aquarium. A sheet of glass is cut to a size slightly smaller than the top of the box, which is filled with about $4''$ of soil or leaf mould. Place the culture on top of the soil, which should be damp, but not wet. Dampen a piece of bread and push into the soil just below the surface. Then place the glass on top of the soil. The box should have a lid or another piece of glass fitting over it.

The worms, which look like pieces of white thread about $\frac{1}{2}''$ long, breed readily. On removing the sheet of glass, some of them will be found around the bread and may be removed with a pair

of tweezers. Try to remove the worms without soil, but if this is not possible, tip them into a small container of water and then remove with the tweezers. Remember to keep the soil neither too dry nor too wet, and do not use too much bread or it will go mouldy. Replace it only when it has been eaten by the worms.

Micro-worms: A minute worm which is used for feeding small fry. Micro-worm, like *Enchytrae*, is bought as a culture but is grown in a different way. A small saucerful of ground oatmeal is mixed with a little water and the culture placed on this. The saucer is covered with glass and shaded with a piece of cardboard. Kept at a temperature of $70°-75°$F., the worms multiply and climb the sides of the saucer, where they can be removed with a brush.

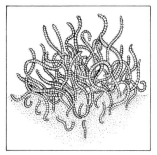 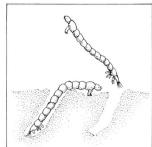

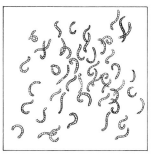 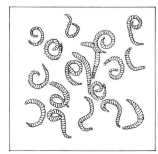

Upper left: Tubifex worms (to $1''$). Upper right: Blood worms (midge larvae—to $\frac{1}{2}''$). Lower left: Grindal worms (*E. buchholtzi*—to $\frac{1}{2}''$). Lower right: White worms (to $1''$)

The culture becomes foul in about ten days, so it is advisable to start with a fresh culture every five days or so and to use three saucers in rotation. Special plastic breeding receptacles for micro-worms are commercially available.

First Foods for Fry

The tiny new-born fry must have food small enough for them to eat. In the case of live-bearers, the young are born fully developed and are therefore able to forage for food without difficulty. Consequently, they are easier to feed than egg-layers, which are usually very minute, and born with a yolk-sac on which they feed for the first few days.

The young of live-bearers may be fed on finely powdered dried food which is often sold under the name of 'fry grain'. They may also be given any of the adult foods which can be produced in a small enough form. Micro-worms and very small daphnia are also suitable.

Infusoria: The fry of egg-layers are usually first fed on 'infusoria'. This is a general name given to microscopic organisms which breed in water containing infusion of plant leaves and other materials. Infusoria cultures may be prepared by adding crushed lettuce leaves, banana skins, pieces of potato, or hay, to a bowl of water and allowing it to stand. The water turns cloudy and then, after several days, clears. Lettuce leaves can also be used

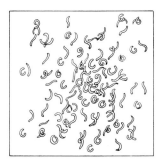

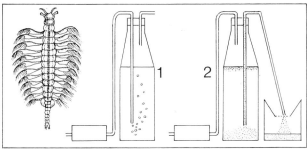

Upper left: Micro-worms (to $\frac{1}{16}$"). Upper right: Infusoria. Above: Hatching method for Brine shrimps

by drying in an oven and crumbling. They may be stored in this form all the year round. A cupful of dried lettuce leaves, added to 5 gallons of water, produces a fairly rich culture in about four days.

Infusoria cultures can be ladled out by the jarful and tipped directly into the dry tank. For the more ingenious, a 'drip' system can be devised. It consists basically of a bottle with a stopper, through which passes a tube. This tube is attached to a length of plastic tubing which leads into the fry tank, the bottle containing the infusoria culture being suspended above it. Rate of flow is controlled by an adjustable clamp. This arrangement will provide the fry with a constant supply of food.

For those who prefer less troublesome methods, there is a proprietary liquid food, sold in a tube, which is used by adding a few drops to the tank. In addition to providing instant food value, this preparation initiates growth of infusoria in the tank.

Ampullaria or **Apple Snails:** These are large water snails, which can be fed on lettuce leaves. The excreta of these snails is rich in infusoria-supporting substances, so that the water becomes full of them and can be used as a culture.

Yolk of egg: A small piece of hard-boiled egg yolk, placed in a piece of linen, may be dipped into the tank, lifted out and gently squeezed. A few drops only of the cloudy liquid should be allowed to fall into the tank. This is an excellent alternative to infusoria but care must be taken not to over-feed with this, as it can quickly foul the water.

Brine Shrimps: These are marine shrimps which can be cultivated quite simply from eggs, also available in a dried form. One simple method, illustrated here, requires a bottle, a stopper, several lengths of plastic tubing and a sieve. Fill the bottle two-thirds full of tap water and add a heaped teaspoonful of common salt. Drop in a quantity of brine shrimp eggs. Keep the water at a temperature of about 75°F. and aerate it vigorously. The long tube is inserted through the stopper so that it reaches to the base of the bottle. The other end is attached to an air tube connected to the pump. The short inlet tube may in turn be attached to additional appliances (diagram 1).

The larvae will hatch within twenty-four to forty-eight hours (the shells floating to the surface) and the air supply should then be cut off. The air tube is removed from the pump and placed in position over a container to which is fixed a rectangular sieve. Air is blown through a tube connected to the short outlet tube so that the minute shrimps near the base of the bottle are siphoned out and sieved into the container (diagram 2).

Micro-worms make a good second or third food, while fine dried food and sifted daphnia can also be used at this stage.

Most aquarists evolve their own variations and techniques in the culture of live foods. Individual preferences and methods change with the development of enthusiasm and experience.

To sum up, a fish fed entirely on dried food will not do as well as one fed on a mixed diet containing fresh and live foods. Correct feeding is essential to health and growth.

A variety of decorative tropical aquatic plants

AQUATIC PLANTS

IDEALLY, an aquarium is a miniature world with animal, vegetable and mineral provided in quantities required for the balance of life, both animal and vegetable. None of us is sufficiently skilled scientifically to work out correct combinations, but fortunately exact amounts are not necessary for a comparatively successful balance between animal and vegetable in an aquarium, given the desirable mineral additive.

This mineral additive is divided into two sections; that required by the plants, and that required by the fishes to provide an approximate water condition to that of their natural habitat. It is generally appreciated that fishes excrete certain substances required by plants, and plants, having absorbed these substances, make some repayment to the fishes, mainly in the form of oxygen for respiration. Plants are able to take in inorganic matter and are also able to absorb certain organic by-products.

Both plants and fishes, however, are happier under certain ecological conditions. For sub-aquatic plants and fishes this means certain chemicals and physical requirements, such as a special range in density of the water, i.e. the amount of dissolved minerals present in the water, and the pH (hydrogen potential) which, loosely speaking, is the acidity or alkalinity of the water. Light is also important.

Plants in an aquarium serve two purposes, the first being their contribution biologically to the balance of the aquarium, and the second their aesthetic and decorative contribution. The type of plant is dictated by the nature of the fish population and the expected amount of excretion from it. For instance, small, rapidly respiring fishes, with relatively small appetites which consequently produce little excrement, can be kept with plants requiring neutral or alkaline conditions. The more voracious of the carnivorous fishes which produce strong acidic excrement will, however, require some heavily-rooted plants, able to absorb the deposits and to tolerate relatively acid conditions. Take care, however, that the tank is not too heavily populated with fishes of this type, for the superabundance of food matter encourages excessive multiplication of undesirable algae.

There is no doubt that a beautifully planted aquarium will in itself be decorative, a miniature tropical garden far easier to maintain than some of the floral decorations which are kept in many homes. So if you aim for a pleasing underwater effect, even before you introduce any fishes, the prospects of eventual success are considerably enhanced.

Naturally, in starting an aquarium, you will have some idea of what you want to achieve. Your aim may be fairly modest—to create a small underwater world giving some extra beauty and interest to life. Alternatively, you may be attracted to some special type of sub-aquatic plant life and wish to cultivate it successfully in the home. Or you may wish to keep for special interest a particular species of fish, whose requirements differ from those of most species. Such fishes, for example, may require either strong or dim light, alkaline or acid water, still or turbulent conditions; so you may have to provide a home giving acid conditions, dim light and still water, or alkaline conditions, strong light and fast-moving or aerated water. With fishes that are vegetarian, furthermore, you will need to provide adequate vegetation to prevent them devouring your carefully prepared sub-aquatic plant life and destroying the beauty of the aquarium.

AQUASCAPING

The lowest level of the aquarium bed should always be at the front, so that all waste matter automatically falls in this direction, is visible and thus easily removed. Ideally, the depth of gravel at the front should be $1'' \times 1\frac{1}{2}''$ rising to $3'' \times 4''$ at the back, depending on the width of the aquarium, giving a rise in level of approximately $1''$ in $3''-5''$. If the rise is greater, it tends anyway to level out in time so that one sees a line of gravel above the base of the front glass, and thus less waste matter tends to lie around the whole of the aquarium base.

Rockwork may be very pleasantly incorporated, particularly in larger aquaria. Natural water-worn limestone and rocks from the seashore are both pleasing and safe. Soft sandstones, limestones and sedimentary rocks may cause trouble and should be avoided. Artificial rocks, arches, caves and monstrous backgrounds should be treated with caution, and are not recommended. Rockwork should not be placed too near the front glass, otherwise a crowded appearance results and cleaning becomes difficult; it should blend in with the gravel and rise up from it, not giving the impression of something stuck in merely to fill in space. Bulky pieces of rock should only be used in large aquaria as they considerably reduce the planting area. Thin sections of rock should be chosen for small and narrow aquaria as plants placed behind wide rocks give the appearance of being a great distance away.

After placing the gravel and arranging the rockwork in the aquarium, you should consider the type of plants which will suit the arrangement of the tank. It is not enough to make a haphazard selection of attractive plants and stick them in at random. The rate of growth of the plants must be considered so that the foreground may be composed of plants which will neither grow too quickly nor too large, and the background of much larger plants with faster rates of growth, since it is not so necessary to keep them continuously pruned to a constant height.

In arranging the aquarium, the whole pattern will sometimes be planned in relation to some special plant, such as a fine Amazon Sword Plant, or a large, beautiful species of unusual form or colour, such as *Barclaya longifolia*. This was particularly the case some fifteen years ago when few plants were generally known. Many plants in plentiful supply today were then rare and prized possessions and such specimens were, because of their value, given importance in the setting out of an aquarium. Today, however, we have some 200 species of aquarium plants, most of which are regularly available from a good water plant nursery; so it is relatively simple to choose plants of a colour, form and size to suit even the most sophisticated aquascapes. There are short plants for the foreground, tall plants for the rearground, small bushy plants for rock crevices, large important-looking plants for special features, and a wide variety of dark green, light green, brown and red plants to give colour contrast.

Having decided upon the general shape of your aquascape, it is relatively simple to choose the plants with which to furnish it, having regard, of course, to their special requirements. If you are on hard water supply, for instance, it would be foolish to choose plants known to be more suited to soft water. Two important families of plants, Araceae (including *Cryptocoryne* and *Anubias*) and Alismataceae (including *Echinodorus* and *Sagittaria*), broadly speaking like soft and hard waters respectively. There are exceptions in each case, but most fall into these two categories. Both groups give a wide range of form of plant so that one can choose feature, group and thicket-forming plants from each.

Planting should proceed from front to rear, heavy thickets being best situated at sides and rear to give adequate swimming space and clear viewing of the fishes. Clear spaces need not be left bare, but may be filled with short plants. An interesting experiment is to furnish an aquarium after the manner of a specific geographical area, such as part of the Amazon, populating it with plants and fishes from the same part of the world. The advantage of this is that the occupants will enjoy the same ecological conditions. This is comparatively simple if you live in a soft water area. Very hard water in your district

makes the selection of your stock a little more difficult, and you may have to add equal parts of distilled water or boiled rain water to the tap water when filling the aquarium.

Most forms of aquarium gravel and rocks tend in time to harden the water, so that it may occasionally be necessary to give partial water changes if the hardness rises above 12° (Clark's). Inexpensive hardness-testing kits are readily available. Fresh tap water, which may be overcharged with air and perhaps contain chlorine, harms plants, so that it is best to allow the aquarium water to stand twenty-four hours before planting. Always keep a supply of a few gallons of standing water for use when topping-up or partially changing. Continuous topping-up to replace evaporated water causes a considerable increase in dissolved minerals, so that partial water changes may be necessary to counteract this. Certain plants, however, such as some of the *Cryptocorynes*, react very badly to sudden water change, so this should always be done gently and over a period of an hour or two, according to the amount of water being changed.

In arranging the rockwork, adequate sub-gravel space should be left to allow roots to spread, while in planting, roots should not be bunched up tightly but spread out. Great care should be taken not to damage roots in handling and planting. Immediately after planting, the period of light should be shortened to about four or six hours per day in order to hasten root development. It is also important that the plants should be established to some depth before the introduction of fishes, and a period of fourteen days seems reasonable.

AVAILABILITY OF PLANTS

As in all branches of horticulture, there are periods of plenty and periods of shortage in plants, certainly in good cultivated specimens as against those shipped in from the tropics. Plants collected in the wild too often appear to have been collected without any knowledge or care, usually arriving without roots, apparently having been torn from the beds rather than dug out and the roots washed clean. This is a great pity, as one would gladly pay a higher price for a plant in good condition than one which may take more than six months to grow to saleable size and condition. Probably more than ninety per-cent of imported plants die off long before they reach an aquarium.

From October to March, only slight growth is made by the fast-growing green plants which need abundant light, whereas slow-growing rain forest plants, such as *Cryptocorynes*, make reasonable growth during the winter and are in fair supply the whole year round. So the difficult time of year to find abundance and variety of aquarium plants is from the end of the winter until early summer (in Europe, from January to May).

When planting an aquarium, you must make up your mind whether you are prepared to give the continual small attentions required by fast-growing plants, or whether you wish simply to plant and leave the tank unattended for many months. The advantage of fast-growing plants is that they do not tend to collect the parasitic algae which often abound on the slow growers. The leaves of the slow-growing plants last for perhaps two years—time enough for many forms of algae to establish themselves—whereas the leaves of the others may be pruned away in three months or less. Fast-growing plants also absorb far more food, which, in a tank of slow-growing plants, is more readily available for algae. On the other hand, algae can be kept under control biologically by adjusting the light and introducing sufficient algae-eating fishes.

Many of our aquarium plants are in nature accustomed to spending part of the year growing emerse (the dry season), when they normally flower and produce seeds, and part of the year submerse (the rainy season), when they multiply by vegetative means (i.e. runners and plantlets). Usually the emerse and submerse forms of leaves are completely different. Amongst the most striking examples of this are such plants as *Synnema triflorum*, *Armoracia aquatica*, *Bacopa myriophylloides* and *Ludwigia arcuata*. Emerse-grown plants reduce to a minimum the danger of introducing algae, but some plants lose the emerse leaves on transfer to submerse conditions, and one has to wait until new leaves develop. If, when setting up the aquarium, a fair amount of mature water is mixed in with the new water, much less harm is likely to be caused to the plants, particularly if the natural water comes from the tank or tanks in which the plants have been grown previously.

The following catalogue describes those plants best suited to the tropical aquarium:

Acorus gramineus: A species of spiky, rush-like plants from East Asia. In nature they are marsh plants but, generally speaking, they last well under water. There are several forms: a dwarf one, which grows to a maximum of 2″–3″, an intermediate one, growing from 4″–12″, and a robust variety, growing up to 18″ tall. There is also a variegated horticultural form, which grows normally to about 9″.

Acorus gramineus

Alternanthera sessilis, with red stem and foliage, is an unusual decorative plant

Alternanthera sessilis: A red, moisture-loving plant with long lanceolate leaves, up to 3″ long and ½″ wide, carried on branched woody stems. The colour varies, according to light and cultivation, from a rich wine-red to a dark reddish-green. The stems are usually bright red. It lasts for some months under water provided the water is not too hard, in which event it sheds its leaves rapidly. It is normally grown as an emerse plant, with cuttings or rooted cuttings transferred to the aquarium. It should be regarded as a temporary decoration rather than a permanent feature in the aquarium.

Genus *Anubias*: A genus of tropical bog plants from the African continent, which are extremely robust and do well in soft and slightly acid water. Most of them have tough, wax-like foliage and are very

Anubias lanceolata, a bog plant, grows to 12″ in the aquarium

Aponogeton crispus. The leaves, carried on single spikes, are up to 2 feet long

Anubias barteri, with arrow-shaped leaves. *Anubias* species grow best half submerged

Aponogeton undulatus. The wavy leaves grow up to 9″ in length

slow in growing. A dwarf species, *Anubias nana*, usually does not grow over 6″. *A. lanceolata* may grow to 24″ but usually keeps to within 12″ in the aquarium. This plant was once named the Water Aspidistra. Most of this family have lanceolate leaves, with the exception of *A. barteri*, the leaves of which are arrow-shaped.

Genus *Aponogeton* is comprised of tropical and subtropical submerged aquatics from Africa, Asia and Australasia. In the African species, the florets are all carried on twin spikes, and in the Asian and Australasian, on single spikes. The most useful plants in the aquarium are *Aponogeton crispus* and *A. undulatus* from Ceylon, *A. ulvaceus* from Madagascar and the extraordinary *A. fenestralis*, the Lace-leafed Plant, also from Madagascar.

Genus *Bacopa*: The genus *Bacopa* is a family of sub-tropical, moisture-loving plants which do relatively well under water. *Bacopa caroliniana* and *B. monniera* are suited to both tropical and cold water aquaria, the other members of the family only being suitable for tropical tanks.

Genus *Blyxa*: The genus *Blyxa* is Asian and Australasian in distribution, the most useful member of the family being *Blyxa japonica*, which is essentially tropical, and beautiful when grown in soft water.

Genus *Cabomba*: The genus *Cabomba* is found in the American continent southwards from the southern states of North America. They are very beautiful aquarium plants with divided, fan-like leaves opposite one another on ascending stems. A highly

35

Aponogeton fenestralis, the Lace-leafed Plant, so named after the 15″ long veined leaves

Aponogeton ulvaceus has transparent leaves up to 20″ long

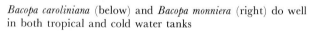

Bacopa caroliniana (below) and *Bacopa monniera* (right) do well in both tropical and cold water tanks

36

Blyxa japonica grows well in soft water

Cabomba caroliniana from America. The stems, with their fan-like leaves, grow to $4\frac{1}{2}$ feet

Ceratophyllum demersum, Hornwort, a decorative branching plant

decorative family, the commonly available species being *Cabomba caroliniana*.

Ceratophyllum demersum **Hornwort:** Though somewhat brittle, this is a very handsome plant when grown at lower temperatures and in good light.

Genus *Ceratopteris* **Floating Fern, Indian** or **Sumatra Fern:** This genus has two members. *Ceratopteris cornuta* is the Floating Fern, a useful plant for shading an aquarium from strong light. It produces quantities of plantlets on the leaf edges, and the thick roots, which hang well down into the water, are extremely useful as refuge for small fishes. *C. thalictroides* is known as the Indian or Sumatra Fern, an extremely beautiful plant of a bright pale-green colour, reproducing also by formation of plantlets on the leaves.

Genus *Cryptocoryne :* This large genus consists mainly of bog plants, which enjoy the rainy seasons submerged. Distribution is entirely in tropical and sub-tropical South-east Asia. Emerse and submerse foliage varies enormously and the large range of shape and colour found amongst members of this genus make it one of the most valuable decorative plants. Many *Cryptocorynes* are not in commercial supply and those described here are chiefly those which are generally available and also desirable for use in the tropical freshwater aquarium.

37

Ceratopteris thalictroides, the Indian or Sumatra fern, is an underwater species. The illustration above shows the plant rooted in gravel: on the right it is shown floating on the surface where the different leaf development is apparent.

Cryptocoryne beckettii, a beautiful and prolific species

38

Cryptocoryne affinis: Known in the trade as *C. haerteliana*, this is one of the most prolific members of the genus, having long lanceolate leaves with a bluish-green upper surface and reddish-purple underside. The mid-rib and main side nerves are conspicuously pale white. The species grows up to 12″ in height but normal aquarium height is 6″–8″.

Cryptocoryne beckettii: Widely but incorrectly known in the trade as *C. cordata*, which is an entirely different plant. It has two forms, wide-leafed and narrow-leafed. Growing to 9″ in both varieties, it is a robust plant with olive-green to dark-brown leaves, the undersides being rich reddish-purple.

Cryptocoryne blassii: This is one of the more recent introductions. It is a plant growing up to 18″ in height, having rich reddish-brown foliage with brilliant burgundy-coloured undersides. An extremely handsome plant when well established.

Cryptocoryne ciliata: A relatively large species with light to mid-green foliage, attaining an aquarium height of up to 20″, although frequently taller in nature. The species has wide distribution from India through to New Guinea, displaying various types of foliage, from broad cordate to narrow lanceolate in shape. Whilst most members of the *Cryptocoryne* family prefer soft and slightly acid water, this plant will stand relatively alkaline and even slightly brackish water.

Cryptocoryne ciliata does well in slightly alkaline or brackish water

39

Cryptocoryne griffithii displays many attractive colour variations

Cryptocoryne nevillii, dwarf form

Cryptocoryne wendtii, an exceptionally strong grower

Cryptocoryne griffithii: Found in Malacca, this plant has broad ovate leaves with bluntish-pointed tips. It grows to about 10″ in height and varies in colour from pale green to dark green and even brown, with reddish-purple undersides. There are often very conspicuous reddish-brown flecks on the upper surface, and a brown form carrying these most attractive markings has been distributed under the fancy name of *C. maculata*.

Cryptocoryne nevillii: This is a useful plant, particularly in its dwarf form, which grows normally 1″–2″ high. A very useful plant for foreground thickets, the leaves being a good bright colour, varying from light to mid-green.

Cryptocoryne thwaitesii: This is one of the most distinctive members of the genus, a relatively small plant not exceeding 6″ in height, with leaves varying from ovate, with pointed tip and cordate base, to narrow lanceolate, with slowly tapering base. The edge of the leaf is coarsely serrated and the surface rough, leathery and extremely tough in texture. The colour ranges from warm olive-green to reddish-brown, and the mature plant shows extremely pretty mottling on the upper surface.

Cryptocoryne wendtii: From South-east Asia. It is probable that this plant is as widely distributed as *C. ciliata*. Variation within the species appears to be very considerable, probably because different races are found in different localities. For this reason, it is conveniently divided into four distinct forms, only one of which shows its clear origin.

Nevertheless, more than one form of this plant is widely found in Ceylon. It is a strong grower, requiring no special conditions. Colour forms of the plant include the typical one, olive-green with purplish underside, growing to about 9″ in height; a rich reddish-brown form with heavy dark brown marmorations and rich purple underside, growing normally to no more than 5″; a narrow pale green form, growing up to 10″; and a small reddish-brown form, not normally growing above 3″–4″.

Cryptocoryne willisii: This is one of the well-known members of the family, described at one time also as *C. undulata*. It has long, narrow, lanceolate leaves with an attractive crinkled foliage, and varies considerably in colour from pale green to rich reddish-brown, often with a bright reddish-purple underside. It grows to about 12″.

Cryptocoryne willisii, with narrow crinkled leaves

Didiplis diandra, Water Hedge.

Echinodorus brevipedicellatus, Junior Sword Plant

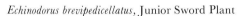

Didiplis diandra **Water Hedge:** Although usually in short supply, this is a plant worthy of mention. Native to North America, it makes a thick bushy mass, hence its common name.

Genus *Echinodorus:* The genus *Echinodorus* is comprised mainly of bog and submerged aquatics, most of which come from the American continent. It is closely related to the genus *Sagittaria,* which is also mainly an American genus. Most members of the genus are heavy feeders so that a small amount of food should be provided for them, particularly in the new aquarium. Many of them have the added advantage of thriving in relatively poor light.

Echinodorus berteroi **Cellophane Plant:** In the young plant, the leaves are light green and translucent, strap-like in form, with very short stems;

but each successive leaf appears to broaden slightly and the stem to lengthen until eventually it produces heart-shaped leaves on long thin stems, first floating at the surface and later erect and emerse. This plant is very useful in medium and large aquaria. Should it become too large and robust, it should be cut right back, when it will start its interesting cycle of development all over again.

Echinodorus brevipedicellatus **Junior Sword Plant:** This species is very useful for the smaller aquarium, normally growing to a maximum of 8″. It resembles a small, broad-leafed Amazon Sword Plant.

Echinodorus grisebachii **Chain Sword Plant:** A small perennial bog plant enjoying completely and, if need be, permanently submerged conditions. Multiplication of this plant is by runners and, once established, it grows very rapidly. If the plant is not permitted to produce runners, or if they are severed as soon as they form, it can grow up to 8″ in height, with leaves 1½″ broad. Under normal conditions, however, with runners remaining, it grows to 3″–4″, with leaves up to ¾″ in breadth. It can make dense thickets and is a useful foreground plant for the medium to large aquarium.

Echinodorus paniculatus **Amazon Sword Plant:** This well-known plant is slightly variable in form. These forms are probably merely different races found in different localities, the leaves varying from slender (1″–1½″) to broad (4″–5″). There appears to be no variation within the race, that is to say a narrow-leafed race remains narrow-leafed,

41

Echinodorus grisebachii, Chain Sword Plant

Echinodorus paniculatus, the popular Amazon Sword Plant, requires a large tank for good growth

Echinodorus tunicatus has attractive heart-shaped leaves growing flat from the stems

Below: *Echinodorus tenellus*, Pigmy Chain Sword Plant, readily available and suitable for small tanks

producing stock with identical narrow leaves. A particularly handsome specimen may grow to 15″ or even 18″ in height, with 30 to 40 leaves. Further investigation may lead to fresh conclusions.

Echinodorus tenellus **Pigmy Chain Sword Plant, Narrow-leafed Chain Sword Plant:** A very widely distributed plant with many races within the species, varying so greatly that it is hard to accept that all are con-specific. The smallest variety grows only to 2″–3″, frequently remaining no taller than 1″, and the largest reaches 12″ in height. The two usual varieties, commonly known as Pigmy Chain Sword and Narrow-leafed Chain Sword, are both in fair commercial supply and are quite useful and attractive plants.

Echinodorus tunicatus: Pale green, heart-shaped leaves up to 8″ long and 5″ wide (although usually half this size in aquaria) with very strong, prominent mid-rib and six longitudinal nerves. The leaves are normally carried at right angles to the stems, making it quite a distinctive member of this genus.

Genus *Eleocharis:* This genus has two members which are particularly useful in aquaria.

Eleocharis acicularis **Hairgrass:** This is a bog plant with creeping root-stock, bearing long stems terminating in a brown spikelet and having no leaves. The submerged plant may attain a length of more than 6″ and its slender beauty makes it a very

Eleocharis acicularis, Hairgrass, a delicately beautiful submerse plant

Elodea ernstiae, another large plant, suited, like *E. densa*, both to tropical and cold water aquaria

Elodea densa, a large submerged plant, growing to 12 feet.

decorative plant. It is well suited to both cold and warm aquaria. Submerged, spikelets do not form.

Eleocharis vivipara **Umbrella Hairgrass:** This plant has hair-like stems growing 10″–12″ high and ending in terminal buds which produce plantlets. These in turn produce stems with terminal buds, bearing smaller plantlets almost *ad infinitum*. A very graceful plant and most decorative in aquaria.

Genus *Elodea*: This genus consists of entirely submerged aquatics, many of which are of great value in an aquarium. All are relatively rapid-growing plants and therefore excellent oxygenators. Consequently they need a large amount of attention to keep them tidy in an indoor aquarium.

Elodea densa: Pale to dark green translucent, lineal leaves with rounded tips, arranged in whorls on ascending branched stems. Considerably larger than other members of the family, it is suited to tropical or cold aquaria.

Elodea ernstiae: Formerly known as *E. callitrichoides*, this plant is useful for both cold and warm aquaria. Small lanceolate leaves, green to olive and sometimes reddish-brown, are carried in whorls.

Hydrilla verticillata: A submerged water plant not unlike the genus *Elodeas* in form, the leaves are $\frac{1}{2}$″–1″ long and are carried in whorls, spaced from $\frac{3}{4}$″–1″ apart. Suited to temperate or warm aquaria.

PENGILLEY

Hydrilla verticillata, with its whorls of leaves, strongly resembles the *Elodea* species

Right: *Hygrophila guianensis*, Willow-leafed Hygrophila

Right, below: *Hygrophila polysperma*, submerse form, easy to grow and propagate

PENGILLEY

CUPIT

Genus *Hygrophila*: This genus has two members used frequently in aquaria.

Hygrophila guianensis **Willow-leafed Hygrophila:** Pointed lanceolate leaves up to 5″ in length and ½″ in width. Colour pale green.

Hygrophila polysperma: More common in aquaria, this plant has pale green lanceolate leaves carried on thin, rather woody stems. It enjoys good light and if kept well pruned can form most handsome thickets. The leaves are about 2″ long.

Genus *Lagenandra*: The genus *Lagenandra*, closely related to the genus *Cryptocoryne*, is quite useful in the tropical aquarium.

Lagenandra lancifolia: This has thick, fleshy, mid- to dark-green leaves, tough of texture and broad lanceolate in shape. The species grows to a height of 9″ and is suitable for most tank sizes.

Lagenandra ovata: This is the giant of the genus, growing to over 36″ in height, but in the larger aquarium it will normally not exceed 18″. It has pale green, pointed lanceolate leaves, extremely tough of texture and thus able to withstand the

44

CUPIT

Lagenandra lancifolia, smallest of the three commonly imported genera

Right: *Lagenandra thwaitesii*, the most beautiful and popular member of the genus

PENGILLEY

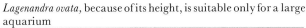

Lagenandra ovata, because of its height, is suitable only for a large aquarium

PENGILLEY

onslaughts of the larger fishes. It also has the advantage of being able to stand relatively hard or even slightly brackish water.

Lagenandra thwaitesii: A most distinctive and beautiful plant. The dark green lanceolate leaves, with broad, greyish-silver edges, are carried on reddish stems of about the same length. The height may be up to 18″ in nature but 9″ is normally the maximum aquarium size.

Genus *Lemna* **Duckweed:** A genus of small floating aquatics which provide shade and are at the same time of considerable food value. Goldfish and many tropical varieties devour them greedily.

Lemna gibba: A thick Duckweed, with bright green rounded fronds up to $\frac{1}{2}$″ in diameter.

Lemna polyrhiza: The largest of the Duckweeds bearing large round fronds attaining a size of $\frac{1}{2}$″ in diameter, with dark green upper surface and purple lower surface.

Lemna trisulca **Ivy-leafed Duckweed:** This is a most attractive species, with light green translucent fronds, elliptical in shape and about $\frac{1}{2}$″ long. It

45

Limnophila sessiliflora, Ambulia, a popular plant with whorls of pinnate leaves

floats just below the surface, whereas the other members have the upper surface of the fronds above the water. It is worth mentioning here *Wolffia arrhiza*, formerly known as *Lemna arrhiza*, which has small fronds less than a millimetre in diameter and is the smallest known flowering plant.

Limnophila sessiliflora **Ambulia:** This is a very beautiful and easily grown aquarium plant. Pale green whorls, up to 3″ in diameter, make very decorative tall thickets if pruned regularly and given fairly good light.

Genus *Ludwigia:* The genus *Ludwigia* is a group of bog plants which do well under water. The three

members of this genus normally available are:

Ludwigia arcuata: When grown as a bog plant this has narrow lanceolate leaves about ¾″ in length and ⅞″ in width. Submerged, the leaves completely change their form to sharply pointed lineal and attain a length of up to 1½″. An attractive and dainty plant, it is pale green under tropical conditions, reddish-brown at lower temperatures.

Ludwigia natans: This is the strongest growing member of the genus. The broad lanceolate leaves are pale to mid-green in colour, becoming reddish in strong light, and have bright red undersides when cultivated in lower temperatures and in good light. Suitable for both cold and warm aquaria.

Ludwigia arcuata, showing submerged pointed leaves

Ludwigia natans, a strong grower, withstanding a wide range of water temperatures

Ludwigia palustris displays emerse and submerse leaf forms

Marsilea hirsuta, the Four-leafed Clover, thrives underwater in almost any temperature

Micranthemum micranthemoides, an elegant creeping plant, grows only at high tropical temperatures

Right: *Myriophyllum brasiliense*, a feathery, semi-submerged bog plant

Nuphar luteum. Seedlings only are recommended for this rapid grower

Ludwigia palustris: Not quite such a strong growing plant as the former and does not last quite so well submerged as the other two members of the genus.

Marsilea hirsuta **Four-leafed Clover:** Does quite well for almost indefinite periods submerged, with a wide range of temperature from 40°F. up to high tropical. A curious and decorative plant.

Micranthemum micranthemoides: A dainty pale green plant with ¼″-long elliptical leaves, carried on ascending stems, it creeps along the bottom of the aquarium to make very pretty thickets. It should be grown in strong light and only at the warmer temperatures. Clipping the tops keeps it under control and induces numerous side shoots.

Genus *Myriophyllum:* This genus has a number of members used in aquaria but they are not really useful indoor plants.

The two best are listed below.

Myriophyllum brasiliense: This is a creeping bog plant with coarse aerial leaves and submerged, feather-like foliage carried in whorls of four, sometimes six, on ascending stems. The colour varies from yellowish to mid-green.

Myriophyllum elationoides: Quite suitable for the lower as well as tropical temperatures, with very fine and dainty foliage, carried in whorls of three or four, rarely five.

Nomaphila stricta, similar to genus *Hygrophila*, with emerse and submerse forms

Nuphar sagittifolium, the handsome, long-leafed Cape Fear Spatterdock

Nomaphila stricta: A very close relative of the genus *Hygrophila*, with large, pale-green leaves with pointed tips, varying in shape from broad to narrow lanceolate and carried on woody stems. A good plant but a ready prey to snails.

Genus *Nuphar:* This genus has four useful members.

Nuphar japonicum: This is a very beautiful plant, quite variable in form and colour, having broad arrow-like leaves, attractively waved at the edges. *Nuphar japonicum var. rubrotinctum* is a distinctive variety with attractive reddish-brown foliage.

Nuphar luteum: This has large, pale green leaves, up to 9″ across. Seedlings only should be used of this plant, as rhizome cuttings tend to outgrow even large aquaria very quickly. Even seedlings become too high after a year or two.

Nuphar pumilum: Similar but much smaller than the above, with pale green translucent foliage. A most attractive plant for both cold and tropical aquaria.

Nuphar sagittifolium **Cape Fear Spatterdock:** A beautiful and decorative plant with long, wavy, arrow-shaped leaves, bright pale green in colour,

Nymphaea x daubenyana, a small Water-lily with heart-shaped floating leaves

Rotala indica, showing typical lanceolate submerse leaves

Rotala rotundifolia, similar to but larger than *R. indica*

Sagittaria latifolia shows marked variations between aerial and submerged leaves

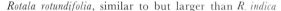

and carried on slender stems. It should be planted with a little soil round it to prevent the rhizome rotting away at the end where it has been cut from the parent plant.

Nymphaea x daubenyana: A small hybrid Water-lily, suitable for the tropical aquarium. The floating leaves are heart-shaped or oval, pale to bright green above, pale green to reddish beneath. The flowers are pale blue with pointed petals, growing on long stalks. Young flowering plants are formed from the base of the leaf and are easily propagated in pots plunged to the rim in water.

Genus *Rotala:* This genus has two useful members for aquaria.

Rotala indica: This is a pretty little plant, the rounded emerse leaves and elongated lanceolate submerse leaves becoming reddish-purple at the lower temperatures in good light. It has a creeping habit, which makes it useful in the foreground of aquaria.

Rotala rotundifolia: This is a larger plant than *R. indica*, otherwise the description is similar, with the same basic colour at lower temperatures.

51

Genus *Sagittaria*: This genus has quite a large number of species used in aquaria, but the two most useful and usual plants for the aquarist are mentioned below.

Sagittaria latifolia **Giant Sagittaria:** Submerged leaves are broad and lineal of shape, with rounded tips up to 18″ in length and a little over 1″ in breadth. Aerial leaves are lanceolate, carried on long stems. Suited to warm or cold aquaria.

Sagittaria subulata: This has long, slender, lineal leaves, broadly pointed at the tips. Grass-green in colour at the higher temperatures, it may become reddish-brown in strong light at the lower temperatures. Oval, floating leaves carried on long, slender stems often develop in the flowering season. The plant grows to 15″ or more in height.

Synnema triflorum **Water Wistaria:** A most variable plant, the shape of the leaves varying from oval, with tiny serrations on the edges, to divided leaves with large serrations. Submerged, the leaves are pale green and of fine, rather fragile texture. Aerial leaves are dark green and thick, with a tendency to hairiness. Only suited to tropical aquaria.

Synnema triflorum, Water Wistaria, grows emerse or submerse

Right, above: *Vallisneria spiralis*, a very popular aquatic plant

Right: *Vallisneria spiralis forma tortifolia*, the Corkscrew Vallisneria

Left: *Sagittaria subulata* has long, ribbon-like leaves and grows to 15″ or more in height

Genus *Vallisneria*: This genus has a number of members, of which *Vallisneria spiralis* and its varieties are the most useful.

Vallisneria spiralis: This has narrow lineal leaves from pale green to reddish-brown in colour. It may grow up to 3′ long, although 18″ or less is more usual in the aquarium.

Vallisneria spiralis forma tortifolia **Corkscrew** or **Twisted Vallisneria**: This is rather thicker and broader than the former plant with leaves attractively twisted like a corkscrew.

A group of *Cheirodon axelrodi*, Cardinal Tetras. (See page 62)

RELATED FAMILIES

CHARACIDAE form one of the largest families of fishes; at present more than 1,300 species are known. This number increases every year as new species are discovered in inaccessible parts of the tropical world.

Although some are widespread, the African species of Characins are few in number and only seen in aquaria on odd occasions. Most species come from South and Central America with a few from as far north as the southern states of the U.S.A. By far the largest variety are to be found in the vast basin of the Amazon river and this is the natural habitat of the majority of Characins seen in small aquaria. From this area come the genera *Hemigrammus* and *Hyphessobrycon,* an extensive group of popular aquarium fishes which are commonly known as 'Tetras' from their sub-family name Tetragonopterinae.

There is no typical Characin shape. Some of the *Hemigrammus* and *Hyphessobrycon* species are long and slender compared with the genus *Metynnis* which is short, deep bodied and best described as disc-shaped.

One feature which is common to all species is the presence of teeth. In some species of Piranha these are so large that the fish has difficulty in closing the mouth, but with the usual aquarium species a much closer inspection is required to see them.

In most species a small adipose fin, set between the dorsal and caudal fins, is present. This feature is also to be found in the genus *Corydoras*—one of the family of Catfishes.

For most people, the object of setting up an aquarium in the home is to enjoy its beauty, and unless the conditions are correct the fishes will not look their best. Obviously, the conditions under which the fishes live in nature are the most suitable, and these should be reproduced if possible.

For the most part, the small Characins which are kept in aquaria are shoaling fishes living in the shallows of large bodies of water, small streams and pools, with a profuse growth of water plants near at hand to provide refuge from the attacks of larger fishes. These waters are well shaded by plants and trees so that only an occasional beam of sunlight filters on to the water. The water is very soft and is continually freshened by the tropical rainfall.

These then are the conditions which must be aimed for in the artificial surroundings of the aquarium if the fishes are to thrive and look well.

Ideally, the aquarium should be set up using soft water and, if possible, lime-free gravel. With many of the readily available gravels the water will very soon absorb some of the calcium and become hard. Thickets of plants should be provided to give the fishes a sense of security and a refuge if they are frightened. The tank should have a darkened background and only low-powered bulbs used to provide subdued lighting. If floating plants such as Duckweed or *Salvinia* are used the strength of the lighting may be increased. The water temperature can be anywhere between 75°–80°F. but remember that the light bulbs will increase the surface water temperature, especially if long periods of lighting are required.

Water changes continually in nature so if possible some of the water in the aquarium should be replaced at frequent intervals. If adequate supplies of soft water are not always available, mild aeration or, even better, filtration can be used.

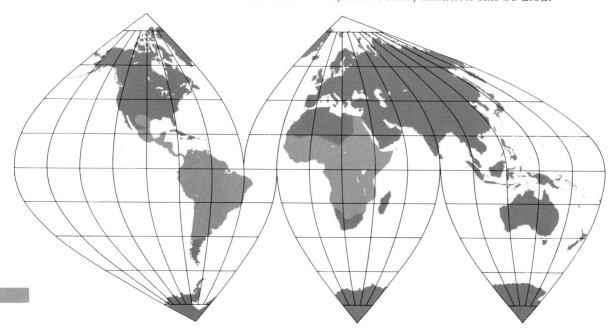

Distribution of Characins in Tropical Africa, and Central and South America

FOODS AND FEEDING

Although in nature the majority of the Characins are carnivorous, their diet in the home aquarium is fortunately not so demanding and they will usually take most foods that are offered. As their natural foods consist of small aquatic insects, larvae and fish fry, together with anything edible on the water surface, you should always try to provide a proportion of live foods if the fishes are to thrive.

During the summer months adequate supplies of both daphnia and tubifex can be obtained to satisfy their needs, and an occasional trip to the nearest pond will usually produce such delicacies as mosquito larvae, blood worms, glass worms or fairy shrimp. Such foods provide a welcome change from the routine of the more easily obtained daphnia and tubifex. Of course, a daily feed of any of the well-known dry foods will be taken quite readily.

Providing a variety of foods during the winter months presents a few difficulties which can, with a little effort, be overcome. With all the ponds very cold, if not frozen over, daphnia and most of the insect larvae have disappeared, although it is possible to find blood worms and glass worms in small numbers. Even tubifex worms which, during the warmer months, are a bright reddish-brown in colour, look grey and decidedly unpalatable, even to a fish. During this time foods from the household refrigerator can be used to excellent effect. Scraped beef, beef heart or liver, either raw or cooked, are accepted with relish by most fishes but care must be exercised as any over-feeding will quickly cause trouble. Any pieces that remain uneaten should be removed after a few hours.

Other foods that can be tried are raw fish—most Characins will, if hungry, soon eat their not-long-dead relatives—shrimp, prawn, crab, lobster and shellfish. In fact, if it is edible by human standards it is worth trying on the fishes.

Another food which can be cultured and which the fishes enjoy is the white worm and its smaller cousin, the grindal worm. These worms have a high fat content and should not be fed too heavily.

If the aquarist is not too squeamish, one of the best foods that is available all the year round is the garden earthworm. Small specimens can be washed and chopped up with a sharp razor blade to a size suitable for the fishes.

The feeding of most Characins, as can be seen, does not present too many problems, but there are one or two genera which require special attention.

First, the Piranhas. Any aquarist who decides to keep these fishes must be prepared to make a special effort as their basic diet in nature is raw meat—not scraped, but in chunks! They also take live fishes. (Ownership of Piranhas is banned in some American states because of the possible introduction of these fishes into streams and their ability to inflict dangerous wounds on men and beasts. Persons interested in acquiring these fishes should check with their state division of Fish and Wildlife for any restrictions that may apply.)

Second, the *Metynnis*. Although very similar in appearance to the Piranhas, these fishes are basically herbivorous and should not be kept in well planted tanks. They like the soft-leaved plants such as *Sagittaria* and *Vallisneria*, which they quickly reduce to short stumps. They will not touch the hardier plants such as *Echinodorus* and *Cryptocoryne* provided adequate vegetable food is offered. Lettuce leaves thrown on the surface of the water will quickly be torn to pieces and devoured. They should also be given a proportion of their diet in live foods, such as daphnia and tubifex.

There are also a few other species of Characin that like to nibble at plants to supplement their diet. One of these is *Hemigrammus caudovittatus*—the Buenos Aires Tetra. It too appears to eat only the softer plants, so the addition of small pieces of lettuce now and then may save the cultivated plants from damage.

To summarise, you should always aim at providing as varied a diet as possible for your fishes, remembering special requirements of certain species.

BREEDING

With the vast number of species in the family, it is not surprising to find different methods of spawning. Even when the majority follow the same pattern some species are very easy and some are extremely difficult. With more experience and technical knowledge, species which were considered difficult ten or fifteen years ago are now being spawned by relative newcomers to the hobby.

However, the following notes apply to a considerable number of the popular Characins and the method described may be used for many others with very little variation.

Before thinking of spawning any fish there is one important condition to be satisfied. One must have a pair! This may seem obvious to many readers but frequently, especially with Characins, aquarists have tried to induce either two females or two males to spawn. With old, mature fishes the different sex characteristics are usually more easily discernible, but young specimens often look very much alike. One fairly reliable method is to view the fishes from above; the females show in their outline the slight bulge caused by the roe, whereas the males have a straight line contour. This distinction is seen much earlier from above than from the side. In many species mature specimens show easily recognisable differences, the male displaying extended finnage and more intense colours, as well as being considerably smaller than the female.

If you decide to breed a particular species, you would be well advised to purchase (from two or three different sources to increase the chances of acquiring unrelated pairs) at least half a dozen young, healthy fishes and raise them yourself to sexual maturity. Careful study during this period will show which are the males and which are the females and which two fishes 'pair off'. Although Characins rarely show the same discrimination when pairing as the family Cichlidae, it is sensible to try to breed from a pair which attract each other. When the sexes are obvious, separate them. If you leave them all in one tank, there is the risk that they will spawn there just when a controlled spawning is contemplated.

If the varied diet recommended for Characins has been adhered to, there is no need for any special conditioning for breeding. Obviously, during the winter months, when live foods are difficult to obtain, the fishes may not spawn as readily or prolifically, but during the summer, provided conditions are right, they should spawn regularly.

When you have a pair of fishes which are mature and in condition to spawn, you are ready to consider the setting up of the breeding tank.

Most Characins lay eggs which are termed semi-adhesive. Some will stick to whatever they touch and others will fall to the bottom of the tank. Once laid, the fishes take no further interest in them other than to regard them as food. Therefore, the spawning tank must provide sufficient cover for the scattered eggs, especially if they spawn in your absence and you are unable to remove the fishes once spawning has been completed. The base of the tank may be covered with a layer of small pebbles, glass marbles or well boiled peat. This will take care of the eggs which fall to the bottom. A dense clump of plants may be provided to take care of the adhesive eggs, but as plants are not easily cleaned many aquarists prefer some form of artificial medium such as nylon mops, coconut fibre or the commercially produced 'Aqua-Fern'.

The tank itself need not be large; a standard 18″ × 10″ × 10″ will suffice for all but the smallest species.

Many Characins spawn so readily that no special measures are necessary to induce them to do so, but others are much more demanding. For these it will be found advisable to obscure the back and end glasses, and even the bottom, with dark paper or paint, to exclude unwanted light. Again, almost sterile conditions may be found necessary and the tank should be thoroughly cleansed before filling to a depth of about 8″ with mature rain water that has been standing for some time on peat, and which will be a pale brown colour. Raise the temperature to 80°F. and place the spawning medium in the tank, having first sterilised it in boiling water. Cover the front and top with a sheet of brown paper and leave the whole set-up for at least twenty-four hours to allow things to settle. Remember to place the heater as far as possible from the spawning medium to prevent eggs being damaged when the heat switches on.

The selected pair of fishes should be placed in the tank in the evening so that they have a little time to get used to their new surroundings before dark, and the paper should again cover the tank.

With luck, when the paper is carefully lifted in the morning, a few white eggs will be seen. The spawning act can be turbulent and quite a few eggs do not get fertilised—these are the opaque white ones. The fertile eggs are small and nearly transparent, making them extremely difficult to see. Watch the fishes, and if they appear to have finished spawning, return them to their original tanks. Cover the spawning tank and leave until the evening. When it is dark, lift the newspaper again and shine a light in from the top. By this time the fry will have hatched and may be seen diving for cover away from the light. Replace the cover and leave for a further twenty-four hours.

With some species spawning does not take place the morning following their transfer to the breeding tank, so if nothing has happened the pair should be left for up to four days before separating the fishes and trying again later.

When the young fishes become free-swimming they will require feeding very small foods, and an infusoria culture or hatching of brine shrimp should have been prepared well in advance. Many a good spawning has been lost because of an inadequate food supply at this crucial stage.

As the young fry grow, larger foods such as micro-worm and fine cyclops and daphnia may be introduced, remembering that the fishes are able to take larger sized foods than is generally appreciated. The original spawning tank will quickly prove inadequate with the rapid growth of the fry and they should be transferred to larger quarters after about two weeks. When this is done count the number in the spawning. Estimates are usually fifty per-cent lower than actual fact at this stage and of course subsequent crowding will seriously stunt the growth of the fishes.

AFRICAN SPECIES

Alestes longipinnis : Most of the genus *Alestes* are large fishes generally unsuited to the average home aquarium, but *A. longipinnis* can be accommodated in larger tanks. The species grows to about 5″ but is not particularly colourful. Apart from a red eye and a short black stripe running forward from the tail for a short distance into the body, the overall colour is silver. The dorsal fin of the male is long and pointed, the female's shorter and rounded.

Arnoldichthys spilopterus : A beautiful little fish, easily recognised by the very large iridescent scales on the upper half of the body. This is an ideal aquarium species which likes to swim in open water. It does not grow larger than 3″ and is not often available

Although, as mentioned earlier, the majority of Characins spawn in the manner described, some species do not follow this pattern and they will be dealt with under their separate descriptions.

Of course, with over 1,000 members in the family, it is not possible to describe them all. The following species are the most popular and therefore those which the aquarist is most likely to see.

as it has apparently not yet been bred in captivity. Both sexes have a large black spot in the dorsal fin.

Micralestes interruptus **Congo Tetra:** This fish is undoubtedly the most beautiful Characin so far introduced to the hobby from Africa. Like the previous species, it has large scales which reflect all the colours of the rainbow, but to a much brighter degree. Both sexes produce uneven extensions to the middle rays of the caudal fin although they are shorter in the female than in the male. The male also develops a flowing dorsal fin with sexual maturity. An ideal community fish for the medium to large aquarium. It is a prolific spawner, the non-adhesive eggs sinking to the bottom.

Micralestes interruptus Congo Tetra (to 4½″)

PENGILLEY

A shoal of *Arnoldichthys spilopterus* (to 3″)

Alestes longipinnis Long-finned Characin

60

SOUTH AMERICAN SPECIES

Abramites microcephalus **Marbled Headstander:** Reaching about 5″ in length, this is the largest of the aquarium 'headstanders'. The body has alternating dark and light brown bars and the fins, with the exception of the tail, show similar hues of brown. The adipose fin has a bright yellow spot.

Anoptichthys jordani **Blind Cave Fish:** The Blind Cave Fish is an interesting example of evolution. Thousands of years ago, specimens of *Astyanax fasciatus mexicanus* became trapped in underground streams at San Luis Potosi in Mexico. As they lived in total darkness, they had no use for their eyes and thus gradually lost them. Although these fishes cannot see their food, they are quite capable of fending for themselves in the community aquarium, their sense of smell being very highly developed. The sense of touch must also be very strong as they rarely bump into anything solid, including the glass of the tank. It is a curiosity rather than a colourful fish, the body being pale pink with colourless fins.

Aphyocharax rubripinnis **Bloodfin:** The Bloodfin is one species which appears to have suffered from continuous commercial breeding as the red colour in the fins which gives the fish its common name no longer has the intensity it had a few years ago. A relatively cheap fish, because it is easily spawned, it should be purchased in numbers as it looks much happier in a shoal of its own species.

Charax gibbosus **Hump-backed Headstander:** Not a particularly attractive fish and the habit of swimming around with its head down, which gives it the common name of Hump-backed Headstander, is really its only claim to fame. Although it looks a little vicious, it is in fact quite a peaceful species, growing to 3″ or 4″ in the aquarium.

Anoptichthys jordani Blind Cave Fish (to 3¼″)

Abramites microcephalus Marbled Headstander (to 5″)

Right: *Aphyocharax rubripinnis* Bloodfin (to 2″)

61

Cheirodon axelrodi **Cardinal Tetra:** Probably the most brilliant fish kept in freshwater aquaria to date, the Cardinal Tetra, with its bright blue-green and red colouring, is a comparative newcomer to the hobby. Named after a well-known American aquarist, the first specimens were sent from South America to the U.S.A. in 1956. They proved very difficult to spawn but fortunately, with more experience, they are being produced in reasonable numbers by commercial breeders in Europe and the U.S.A. and very few wild specimens are now imported. An ideal aquarium fish but a little shy, unless in the company of its own species.

Cheirodon axelrodi Cardinal Tetra (to 1½")

Copeina arnoldi (to 3")

Charax gibbosus Hump-backed Headstander (to 4")

62

Copeina arnoldi: This timid little fish is not really an ideal community species as it spends most of its time swimming among the plants in the aquarium. Both sexes have an extended top lobe to the caudal fin, the male's being much longer than the female's. These fish have a method of spawning totally different from any other Characins, and they also display interest in their eggs when laid, which is very unlike the Characin family as a whole.

The spawning pair of fishes select a site for their eggs above the surface of the water; in nature an overhanging leaf, the stem of a reed or any object situated above the surface, in the aquarium often the cover glass. The fishes leap from the water side by side and after several dummy runs deposit a few eggs at a time until spawning is completed. Spawnings average about 100 eggs. The male then takes up position under the spawn and, using his long tail, periodically splashes water upwards to prevent dehydration of the eggs. The fry hatch in thirty-six to forty-eight hours, when the brood care instinct vanishes; so the parents should be removed unless adequate cover for the fry is provided. These fishes will spawn in a part-filled aquarium which has either large plant leaves or a strip of slate projecting above the water surface to act as a spawning ground.

Corynopoma riisei **Swordtail Characin:** The Swordtail Characin is another species which is not particularly colourful, but because of its finnage makes an interesting member of the community aquarium. The main body colour is silver with a pinkish flush, and the fins are clear. The male's finnage is again longer than the female's, and the lower lobe of the male's caudal extends as in the live-bearer species *Xiphophorus helleri*—hence its common name. The most unusual features of this fish are the gill cover extensions, which in the male extend for more than half the body length, with a spoon-shaped ending.

The spawning procedure of this species is of particular interest in that the male transfers sperm in a capsule to the female's vent—the method is not really understood—and there they are stored. When the female releases her eggs, which may be some time later, they are immediately fertilised. It appears that the sperm can stay alive for a long period as the female may have several subsequent spawnings without the presence of the male.

Exodon paradoxus: A fish which is not too popular because of its size—up to 4″ in the aquarium—and also its quarrelsome nature. Quite a colourful species when young but rather drab when mature.

Gymnocorymbus ternetzi **Black Widow:** When young, Black Widows look very attractive, with the rear half of the body and the large anal fin black, but unfortunately, as the fish matures, the black fades to grey. One of the most popular Characins, easily spawned and therefore cheap to buy.

Hasemania marginata **Silver Tip** or **Copper Tetra:** There is often confusion in distinguishing this Tetra from its close relative, *Hemigrammus nanus;* indeed there is little more than the absence of an adipose fin and a slightly less intense black marking at the base of the tail in *H. marginata* to distinguish them. Both are spritely little fishes, the males, when mature, having a beautiful copper body colour and both sexes brilliant white tips to dorsal, anal and caudal fins. They require some time to acclimatise to new surroundings before looking their best.

Hemigrammus caudovittatus **Buenos Aires Tetra:** This is a species quite commonly found in aquaria but is more suited to larger tanks, as it grows to 4″. Unfortunately, it is one of the species of Characin that, if not well fed, will nibble the softer plants and also the thin fins of such fishes as Angels and Gouramis. Being sub-tropical, it prefers temperatures a little lower than those required by other Characins. In other respects, care and breeding are as for all *Hemigrammus* species.

Gymnocorymbus ternetzi Black Widow (to 2¼″)

NIEUWENHUIZEN

Exodon paradoxus (to 4″). A quarrelsome fish, this specimen has lost a tip from its caudal fin

Hemigrammus erythrozonus **Glowlight Tetra:** This species is one of the most beautiful of Characins if the correct conditions are provided for it. The red line which runs from the nose to the base of the caudal fin becomes brilliant and the tips of the fins white if the fish is kept in a tank with plenty of plants and subdued lighting. The Glowlight Tetra, being quite easy to breed and therefore relatively cheap, is indispensable for the Characin community aquarium. It grows only to about 1¾″.

Hemigrammus ocellifer **Beacon** or **Head-and-Tail-light Fish:** The alternative common names of this fish derive from the bright golden spots in the top of the eye and the base of the tail. Males of this species and some other Tetras have an unusual characteristic in that the leading rays of the anal fin develop a hook which catches in nets when the fish is caught. Care should be exercised when detaching the fish, as the fin and even the body could be torn. Another very common and cheap Tetra, and an ideal community fish.

Hemigrammus pulcher: A fish quite similar to *H. ocellifer,* but noticeably deeper bodied, having a short black bar or wedge in the rear part of the body. It is not seen so frequently in aquaria as *H. ocellifer,* as it is not too easy to spawn.

Hemigrammus caudovittatus Buenos Aires Tetra (to 3″)

Right: *Hemigrammus erythrozonus* Glowlight Tetra (to 1¾″)

Hasemania marginata Silver Tip/Copper Tetra (to 1½″)

KAHL

Hemigrammus ocellifer Beacon/Head-and-Tail-light Fish (to 1¾″)

Right: *Hemigrammus pulcher* (to 2¼″)

KAHL

Hemigrammus rhodostomus: Because this fish is difficult to breed and not brilliantly coloured, it is not often seen. When viewed in a well planted and softly lighted tank, the red nose and black striped tail intensify in colour, making the species quite attractive. The male is slimmer than the female.

Hyphessobrycon flammeus **Flame Tetra:** Another fish which has deteriorated badly through continuous in-breeding, the Flame Tetra is rarely seen nowadays with the bright red colour that it should have. A fish which most beginners to the hobby try to breed, as it is not difficult to induce to spawn.

Hyphessobrycon griemi: A fish similar to the previous species, but more delicately coloured. It is only rarely seen, as in dealers' tanks it loses most of its colour under the bright lights.

Hyphessobrycon herbertaxelrodi **Black Neon:** Another recent introduction to the hobby, the Black Neon is a fish that takes quite some time to reach maturity. When it does, the females are a little larger than the males. Under subdued lighting, the pale bar which runs from behind the eye to the base of the caudal becomes green, and the black line below intensifies. It is not too difficult to spawn, especially if two or three pairs are used together, and makes an ideal community fish.

Hyphessobrycon heterorhabdus: Similar to *H. herbertaxelrodi* but not often available as it is not easily bred. Females again are larger than males and the green stripe is replaced by two thin lines of red and gold. The fins are colourless or pale yellow.

Hyphessobrycon innesi **Neon Tetra:** Without doubt the most popular and well known of the Characins, the Neon Tetra, which once commanded very high prices, can now be purchased quite cheaply. Its brilliant electric blue-green and red colouring is eclipsed only by that of the Cardinal Tetra, its slightly more opulent relative. Although not very easy to spawn, continental breeders have mastered the problem and produce them by the hundred.

Hyphessobrycon pulchripinnis **Lemon Tetra:** The Lemon Tetra is not one of the most colourful Characins but is a peaceful, active little fish. When acclimatised it can look quite attractive, with the yellow stripe in the dorsal and anal fins a bright lemon colour.

Hemigrammus rhodostomus (to 1½″)

PENGILLEY

KAHL.

Hyphessobrycon flammeus Flame Tetra (to 1¾″)

NIEUWENHUIZEN

Hyphessobrycon griemi (to 1¼″)

CUPIT

Left: *Hyphessobrycon herbertaxelrodi* Black Neon (to 2″)

Hyphessobrycon heterorhabdus (to 2″)

NIEUWENHUIZEN

Hyphessobrycon innesi Neon Tetra (to 1½")

Hyphessobrycon pulchripinnis Lemon Tetra (to 2")

KAHL

NIEUWENHUIZEN

Hyphessobrycon rosaceus **Rosy Tetra** and *H. ornatus:* Though there is confusion in the nomenclature of these closely related Blood Characins, they may be distinguished by the sickle-shaped dorsal fin in the male *H. ornatus*. The females are virtually impossible to tell apart and it is highly probable that hybridisation occurs. Both are elegant and ideal community fishes, the body and fins being strongly flushed with red in mature specimens while the dorsal is blotched with black, the leading edge and tip enamel white.

Hyphessobrycon rubrostigma **Bleeding Heart Tetra:** This fish, so called because of the large red spot in the centre of the body, is similar to *H. ornatus* in general appearance, but quite a bit larger when mature. They can grow to 3½" and therefore do best in larger tanks. Being none too easy to breed, they are rather expensive. They dislike changes of water and many young specimens are lost very early after purchase. Soft, slightly acid water is essential for growth and health.

Hyphessobrycon callistus and *H. serpae:* Two more Blood Characins so closely related that it is inevitable that confusion will arise, the more so since there are three less common species, *H. bentosi*, *H. copelandi* and *H. minor*, belonging to this group of very similar fishes. All have pleasantly glowing red bodies, but in varying degrees of intensity. *H. callistus* is distinguished by an elongated black shoulder-blotch, an almost totally back dorsal fin and a black-edged anal fin. In the *H. serpae* the

shoulder blotch is barely visible and the fins are much less heavily marked in black, for unless the aquarium is well planted and the lighting soft, most of the colour fades from adult specimens. However, if a spawning is successful, the young make extremely attractive members of a Characin aquarium collection.

Megalamphodus megalopterus **Black Phantom Tetra:** Although of a different genus, the Black Phantom Tetra is very much like *Hyphessobrycon rosaceus* in body shape, but quite a bit smaller. Not often available, as it is difficult to spawn, this species has a dark tint to the body and nearly black dorsal, caudal, anal and ventral fins. The dorsal of the male grows long and flowing with maturity. There is another species, *M. sweglesi*, which has red fins instead of black.

Metynnis schreitmuelleri: There are quite a number of species in this genus but this is the only one normally available, and then only occasionally. It is not suitable as a community fish because of its size and its habit of devouring plants. In a large tank with thick, strong plants and fed with a large proportion of vegetable matter, a few of these fishes make a very pleasant display.

Moenkhausia sanctae-filomenae **Red Eye Tetra:** The Red Eye Tetra can also become a little large for normal community aquaria and does not have a great deal of colour, apart from a black bar in the base of the caudal and a red patch on the eye.

KAHL

Hyphessobrycon rosaceus Rosy Tetra (to 1½″)

HANSEN

Hyphessobrycon ornatus (to 1½″)

PENGILLEY

Left: *Hyphessobrycon rubrostigma* Bleeding Heart Tetra (to 3½″)
Hyphessobrycon serpae (to 1¾″)

PENGILLEY

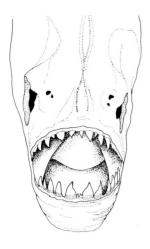

Teeth arrangement of a typical Piranha

Metynnis schreitmuelleri (to 6″)

Above: *Megalamphodus megalopterus* Black Phantom Tetra (to 2″)

NIEUWENHUIZEN

Moenkhausia sanctae-filomenae Red Eye Tetra (to 2¾″)

NIEUWENHUIZEN

Nematobrycon palmeri Emperor Tetra (to 3″)

Pristella riddlei X-Ray Tetra (to 1¾″)

KAHL

Nematobrycon palmeri **Emperor Tetra:** The Emperor Tetra was introduced to the hobby in the early 1960's and since then has become a firm favourite. Although not difficult to spawn, it is not very prolific, and since the fry grow slowly the adults are usually expensive. Mature males are easily distinguished by extended dorsal and three-pronged caudal fins. A very beautiful and useful community fish.

Pristella riddlei **X-Ray Tetra:** A firm favourite for years, the X-Ray Tetra is an ideal community fish. Always on the move, it is not as timid as most other Characins. It is easily bred, always available and cheap to buy.

Rooseveltiella nattereri: **Piranha:** This fish is the most common of the Piranhas, about which many stories, some true, some exaggerated, have been written. It is, in any event, not a community fish. They have been bred in aquaria and it would appear that fish farms in the tropics are producing them in numbers as recently batches of quite small specimens have been available. They are usually kept singly in large tanks and fed on small fishes.

Similar in appearance and behaviour are the various *Serrasalmus* species.

Thayeria obliqua: **Penguin Fish:** Another very common Characin, the Penguin Fish has the habit of swimming with a tail-down attitude. This does not prevent the fish from being one of the fastest Characins in the aquarium and one of the most difficult to catch. Apart from a black bar extending from the gills to the tail root and then into the slightly extended lower lobe of the tail, there is little colour. It is a prolific spawner, usually at least 400–500 in a spawning, and can therefore be relied on as being readily available.

Below: *Thayeria obliqua* Penguin Fish (to 2½″)

NIEUWENHUIZEN

Rooseveltiella nattereri Piranha (to 11″)

RELATED FAMILIES

Of the African family Citharinidae there are a few species that appear occasionally in dealers' tanks. *Nannaethiops unitaeniatus* and *Neolebias ansorgei* are small, timid fishes quite suitable for the community aquarium, the latter being the more colourful, with the iridescent hues of the African Characins.

Occasionally some of the genus *Distichodus* are imported, but as they are fairly large fishes when mature, only young specimens are suitable for the smaller aquaria. *Distichodus sexfasciatus* is one of the smaller species, but even he will grow to 10″ long.

The Anostomidae are a South American family of fairly large fishes, suitable for large aquaria.

Anostomus anostomus: This fish has a very elongated body, up to 6″ or 7″, with three dark brown or black stripes running along the entire length. The dorsal and caudal fins show red near the base, fading towards the outer edges. Fairly peaceful among fishes of similar size, it likes to swim with a slight head-down attitude.

Chilodus punctatus **Spotted Headstander:** This is a species suitable for most aquaria as mature specimens reach about 3½″. It is an interesting fish with an attractive checkered body pattern of dark and light brown, and a black and red patch on the dorsal. It has a very pronounced head-down swimming tendency.

Occasionally, one of the species of the South American *Leporinus*, such as *L. fasciatus*, *L. frederici* or *L. arcus* is available, but since they grow to at least 12″ they are obviously unsuited to all but the largest aquaria. The same applies to *Prochilodus insignis*, another South American species.

The Gasteropelecidae are another exclusively South American family comprising the species known as Hatchet Fishes. All have very deep bodies and with rapid beating movements of the large pectoral fins are able to propel themselves out of the water and glide for short distances. All are fascinating aquarium fishes, quite easily kept in a fairly long and well covered tank.

Neolebias ansorgei (to 1¼″)

Serrasalmus brandti Piranha (to 12″)

Distichodus sexfasciatus (to 10″)

PENGILLEY

Prochilodus insignis (to 12″)

Below: *Chilodus punctatus* Spotted Headstander (to 3½″)

NIEUWENHUIZEN

Nannaethiops unitaeniatus (to 2½″)

PENGILLEY

PENGILLEY

74

Anostomus anostomus (to 7″)

Far left: *Leporinus fasciatus* (to 12″)

Carnegiella strigata Marbled Hatchet Fish (to 2″)

Nannostomus beckfordi Golden Pencil Fish (to 2½″)

Nannostomus unifasciatus (to 2½″)

Gasteropelecus levis Silver Hatchet Fish (to 2½″)

Carnegiella strigata **Marbled Hatchet Fish:** Probably the most commonly seen species, with a pattern of irregular light and dark brown bars diagonally across the body. Its maximum length is about 2″.

Gasteropelecus levis **Silver Hatchet Fish:** This species is also frequently available, slightly larger than *Carnegiella strigata*, with a plain silver body.

Gasteropelecus sternicla **Common Hatchet Fish:** The silver body has a black stripe extending from gill cover to tail.

The Hemiodontidae family, also from South America, is known chiefly for the Pencil Fishes from the genera *Nannostomus* and *Poecilobrycon*, all of which are very attractive and popular aquarium

KAHL

Gasteropelecus sternicla Common Hatchet Fish (to 2½″)

fishes. Experts cannot agree as to whether the two genera should be separated but to simplify matters they may all be classified under *Nannostomus*. They all have long, slender bodies, with relatively small mouths, and the majority have horizontally striped body patterns. These patterns fade at night and are replaced by irregular dark blotches. Their movements tend to be spasmodic but when resting the pectoral fins are always fluttering.

Nannostomus beckfordi beckfordi, Nannostomus beckfordi anomalus, Nannostomus beckfordi aripirangensis
Golden Pencil Fish: Three species which are so difficult to distinguish from one another that all share the same common name. As they are so closely related it is possible that hybridisation has occurred, making identification of their offspring

Nannostomus marginatus (to 1½")

impossible. All are best described as torpedo-shaped, with two horizontal black and gold bars on their flanks. Females have little other colour but the males have red in the dorsal, anal and caudal fins, intensifying at spawning time.

Nannostomus eques: One of the more interesting species, which normally swims at a rather oblique angle as if permanently looking for food on the surface. The body has the typical alternating dark and light bars of the genus, the central dark one running from the snout through the eye and the length of the body down into the enlarged lower lobe of the caudal fin. The light bar above often continues into the tail, giving the effect of a central dividing line. The anal has black and red blotches, tipped, like the ventrals, porcelain-white.

Nannostomus harrisoni: This fish is similar to *N. beckfordi*, though somewhat larger. It is not particularly colourful.

Nannostomus marginatus: This fish is shorter and more stocky than the other species and one of the most colourful, showing three dark bars, with a golden strip above the much wider central bar. There is a thin red line between the black and gold, and the dorsal, anal and ventral fins have bright blotches. Always in good colour in the aquarium.

Nannostomus trifasciatus: Undoubtedly the most beautiful of the Pencil Fishes, this is similar in colour to *N. marginatus*, with the addition of red in the caudal fin, but is altogether larger and more graceful. Unfortunately, it is not one of the easiest to spawn and hence is not often available.

Nannostomus unifasciatus: The body colour of this species is yellow-brown with a broad dark brown longitudinal band extending from the mouth to the caudal peduncle. A very distinctive feature is the red caudal fin and the fish has a habit of swimming at an angle, with a pronounced head-up attitude.

78

Nannostomus harrisoni (to 2¼″)

Nannostomus trifasciatus (to 2¼″)

Nannostomus eques (to 2″)

Aphyosemion sjoestedti (to 5″) and *Roloffia occidentalis* (to 3½″)

THE classification of Egg-laying Tooth Carps is more confused than that of other fishes. Taxonomists are working to improve this state of affairs; at present both the old and new scientific names, as well as popular names, are in general use.

The large family of Cyprinodontidae contain both live-bearing and egg-laying species. Those who keep fishes as a hobby would prefer them to be classified separately but the taxonomist, studying the subject more scientifically, sees enough similarities to justify their classification as one family.

The Egg-laying Tooth Carps, better known as Killifishes, are small fishes, usually with large dorsal and anal fins. The caudal fin in the males of many genera is also large and lyre-shaped. The pectoral fins are often of a good size and the fishes are expert jumpers. The mouth is usually large and situated well forward.

Killifishes are found in every continent except Australasia. Although the majority live within the tropics, even Europe has some species of interest to aquarists. *Aphanius iberus* is found in Spain and Algeria and *Valencia hispanica* is another Spanish Killifish. These fishes are rarely kept, however, except by specialists.

The African genera are distributed as follows:

Aphyosemion: found on the west coast of Africa. This very large genus, with some beautiful fishes, has recently been split geographically into two separate genera. The genus *Aphyosemion* consists of those species east of the Dahomey Gap (between Ghana and Nigeria), while the new genus *Roloffia* contains all species west of the Dahomey Gap.

Aplocheilichthys: from Lagos south as far as Angola.

Epiplatys: this genus, with over a dozen species known to aquarists, is also West African, ranging from Sierra Leone down to the Congo. One fish, *Pseudepiplatys annulatus*, was originally classified as *Epiplatys* but has now been put into a new genus.

Nothobranchius: East African coast, from Kenya down to Mozambique.

Pachypanchax: Madagascar and neighbouring parts of East Africa.

In Asia and the Near East there are a number of *Aphanius* species; in the Far East the two main genera are *Aplocheilus*, wide-ranging, with species in India through Ceylon to Malaya; and *Oryzias*, also widespread, with *O. melastigma* in India and Ceylon, *O. celebensis* in the Celebes, *O. javanicus* in Indonesia and *O. latipes* in Japan.

North America has the genus *Fundulus*, ranging from Canada to Florida, while the genera *Cyprinodon*, *Chriopeops* and *Jordanella* are found in Florida.

From Central America comes the Cuban Killie, *Cubanichthys cubensis*, and a number of species of the genus *Rivulus*, which has members ranging from Panama southwards to Santos, Brazil.

South America has some very colourful and interesting Killifishes in addition to the southern members of the genus *Rivulus*. *Cynolebias* contains the Dwarf Argentine Pearl Fish, *Cynolebias nigripinnis*, one of the most beautiful of all aquarium fishes. The genera *Pterolebias*, *Cynopoecilus* and *Rachovia* all have interesting species which are kept by some hobbyists; *Austrofundulus dolichopterus* is a member of a Venezuelan genus, new to aquarists in Europe.

Killifishes live in small pools and streams, often in areas with considerable overhead vegetation and overgrowth of plants, to shade them from bright lights, which they dislike. The tropical Killifishes live in areas of heavy rainfall where the water is often very soft and, because of decaying plants, on the acid side. The water may reach temperatures of up to 80°F in the dry season, but natural shade often keeps it down nearer the 70°F mark. In these areas of heavy rainfall, decaying pond vegetation and slow-flowing streams, mosquito larvae and aquatic crustaceans are abundant. The very large, frontally-positioned mouth of many of these fishes indicates that they are skilled catchers of moving food, and in fact they should be given plenty of live foods.

Some species live in geographical areas where the dry and rainy seasons are particularly well differentiated—savannah regions, for example, where a main rainy season of a few months is followed by a long dry season with scarcely any rain to relieve the hot days. Ponds tend to dry up and as the water evaporates many fishes die of asphyxia. For this reason some Killifishes are known as annual fishes, living only from the beginning of the wet season to the critical moment during the dry season when the ponds disappear. Yet despite the difficult habitat, these fishes have developed methods of perpetuating their species. They bury their eggs in the mud at the bottom of the pond. When it dries out, the parents die, but the buried eggs are protected from desiccation for several months. Within hours of the arrival of rain, the eggs hatch and the cycle begins again. These are called egg buriers or substrate spawners.

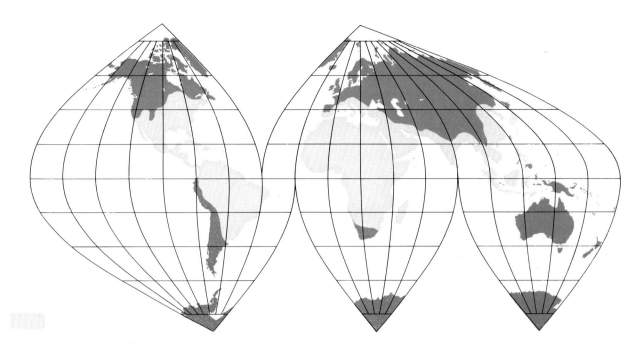

Distribution of Egg-laying Tooth Carps in Africa, southern Europe and Asia, and parts of America

Killies living under less extreme conditions do not need to bury their eggs, but lay them on the roots of top plants. These are called the egg hangers or top spawners. There are also a number of species which lay their eggs on the bottom mud, and which form an intermediate group.

BREEDING

The Egg-laying Tooth Carps are the easiest of all fishes to breed, given the special conditions they require. It must be remembered, however, that these are not fishes for the community aquarium.

The vast majority of this family must have soft, acid water. A few will accept slightly alkaline water but even these do better in acid conditions. The easiest way to get soft water is from the tap, but this is only possible where the public water supply comes from upland surface reservoirs set on high, peaty moorlands. In those areas where the water comes from deep wells and is very hard, you must either collect rain water or buy demineralised water. If the atmosphere is clean, rain water may be collected from the glass or plastic roofs of greenhouses or porches, and conducted by plastic guttering and drainpipes into plastic dustbins. Water collected from galvanised iron, asbestos, cement or concrete surfaces, however, is not satisfactory, as it picks up alkalines and salts producing hardness. Alternatively, a mixture of one part hard tap water with nine parts demineralised water is usually very satisfactory.

This soft water, no matter how obtained, is now acidified by adding previously boiled peat. For this purpose, buy ordinary peat—i.e. without any added chemicals or fertilisers. Boil this in a saucepan in soft water for five minutes. Let it cool and then strain off the water and squeeze the peat as dry as possible. This removes excess acid and prevents any risk of the water becoming too acidic and killing the fishes or damaging the eggs.

Killifishes may be kept in small tanks, some of the smaller species even in plastic food containers $12'' \times 6'' \times 4''$. Fill the tank with water and add enough of the boiled and squeezed peat to give about $1''$ in depth. The peat will float at first but in a few days will form a layer about $1''$ thick on the bottom. This is the ideal substrate for Egg-laying Tooth Carps. Do not use gravels, as most of them contain calcium salts which will make the water hard. The pH should be between 6 and 7.

Keep the tank at a temperature of $70°–75°$F, and avoid giving them too much light. Bright lighting causes them to panic. Never use a light directly over the tank. Natural light or a central light fitting in the room are usually adequate.

Killifishes must have live food for successful breeding—daphnia, mosquito larvae, white worm or tubifex. Snails must not be allowed into the tanks or they will eat the eggs. One way to prevent snail spawn gaining access is to exclude plants, which in any event do not grow well in these tanks, due to insufficient light. Nor is the peat substrate a good planting medium. A glass tank cover is essential on all tanks as the fishes are excellent jumpers and leap out of uncovered tanks.

So much for the basic set-up required for successful breeding. Procedure from now on depends upon what method of breeding is naturally used by the fishes. The majority deposit a few eggs at a time on the roots of floating plants. In the aquarium these egg hangers may be given a mop of nylon wool on which to hang their eggs. Wind a dozen turns of green nylon wool around a piece of cardboard 6″ long and then cut one end. These pieces are then fixed to a cork, and this provides a floating mop.

The fishes should then be conditioned in the breeding tank. One male with three females is a good combination. Pairing a single male and female may result in his killing her by an over-vigorous courtship, whereas more than one male will lead to fighting rather than breeding. The eggs, one, two or three at a time, are then laid on the nylon mop, to which they adhere. They vary in size from $\frac{1}{16}$″ to $\frac{1}{8}$″ in diameter, depending upon the species. After a week of spawning there may be up to 200 eggs on the mop, according to the species and condition of the fishes. Remove the mop, put it in a jam jar full of water from the tank, and provide a new mop for the parents. Put a lid on the jam jar and label it (use a china marking pencil) with the name of the species and date removed from the parents. Alternatively, you can pick the eggs carefully off the nylon mop with your fingers and put them directly into the jam jar. If they are sticky and adhere to the fingers, use a child's paint brush to transfer them to the jar.

The eggs do not have a shell but are covered with a thick membrane, through which the eyes of the developing fishes may be seen during the latter part of the incubation process. But even with good parents, up to thirty per-cent of the eggs may not be fertilised and will not develop. These will either become fungused or disintegrate over a few days. It is immaterial whether these are removed or left in position. The majority of the eggs will hatch within fourteen to twenty-one days of laying and the fry are large enough to feed immediately on newly hatched brine shrimp. Apart from *Aphyosemion bivittatum*, they grow extremely rapidly. Because the parents have been allowed to spawn for a week together before removing the eggs, some eggs are seven days older than their brothers and sisters, and the rapidly growing older fishes may eat their newly hatched younger brethren. You may therefore have to separate the larger specimens from the smaller ones. Give the fry small daphnia, chopped white worm or chopped tubifex as soon as they are big enough to take them. Many species are sexually mature when three or four months old.

For the breeding of the egg burier group, set up a Killifish tank in the usual way. Use enough peat to ensure a 1″ layer of peat on the tank bottom. Put in your fish—one male and three females. These fishes are often sexually mature at eight weeks and dead within one year so the breeding period is short and sharp, the males chasing the females and fighting one another relentlessly. Thus the correct ratio of male to female is especially important. Give the fishes as much live food as they will eat. The male courts the females vigorously, chasing each in turn as they catch his eye. He swims alongside the willing one, overlaps his dorsal fin over her back and together they plunge into the peat, leaving a few specks floating in the water above the spot where they have disappeared. After a few seconds the male reappears, followed shortly afterwards by the female, who will have laid an egg in the peat. This is repeated a few times daily. At the end of ten days, remove all the peat, using a fine mesh nylon net, and provide a further supply. If well fed, the adults will continue spawning. Drain the water from the netted peat containing the eggs and transfer it to a plastic box. Do not put the lid on at this stage. Mark clearly on the box the name of species, date of spawning and date removed from the water. Leave the box open for a few days until the peat dries out to a 'just moist' state. Then put the lid on the box and keep it at between 68°–72°F. If a box is unavailable, put the peat in a plastic bag, tie and knot the neck, label and incubate.

Leave the box or bag to stand for three or four months, depending upon the species, then add water from the Tooth Carp tank to the peat and stir. Within a few hours the fry will hatch. They will be very shy at first and dive into the peat, particularly if you expose them to a bright light. They will immediately eat newly hatched brine shrimp and growth is extremely rapid with good feeding of increasingly large live food. The fishes are mature within six to eight weeks. Eggs which do not hatch when water is added should be 'dried out' again, incubated for another two weeks, then given more water. In every batch of eggs there are a few which have a longer than normal incubation period. In the wild, this is a safeguard to protect the species from extinction if the rains are late.

There are a few species e.g. *Aphyosemion sjoestedti*, who prefer to lay their eggs on the surface of the peat. The eggs of this intermediate group do not need to be dried out but have an incubation period of about five to seven weeks.

Individual species that vary from the main patterns are mentioned in the following catalogue section. This does not attempt to deal with all known species, but describes some representative and interesting Killifishes kept by aquarists.

Aphanius iberus Spanish Killie (to 2″)

Aphanius mento (to 2″)

Aphyosemion australe Chocolate Lyretail (to 2½″)

Aphyosemion bivittatum (to 2¼″)

Aphanius iberus **Spanish Killie:** One of the Killi-fishes that lives outside the tropics, found in Spain, Morocco and Algeria. In Spain it is found in the south, living in shallow ditches quite close to the sea. These ditches, used to irrigate the rice fields and orange groves, may occasionally be flooded by the sea at exceptional tides. Water temperatures vary considerably, according to season. Moreover, the water is reported to be often alkaline and hard, so this is evidently a most unusual species. The male is blue-green with fifteen or sixteen narrow transverse bars on the body. All the fins are dark blue, the caudal having transverse bands and a pale blue margin. The female is a less colourful olive-green. The fishes are easy to sex and grow to 2″ in length. They are egg hangers and the incubation period is eight to fourteen days.

Aphanius mento: Comes from Iran, Syria and Turkey and is found in freshwater pools and in lakes. It is also unusual among the Killifishes in that it prefers hard, alkaline water. The males grow to 2″ in length and are olive-brown with silvery blue spots. These increase in number and become almost black when the fish is in breeding trim. They are best spawned in the ratio of three females to one male, as the males fight. They are egg hangers and good fishes will provide 100–200 eggs per week. The fry hatch in ten days at 72°F.

The genus *Aphyosemion* contains at least twenty species known to aquarists. They are confined to West Africa and all of them are beautiful fishes. There is much active work going on to improve the classification of this genus.

Aphyosemion australe **Chocolate Lyretail:** This fish lives in small, temporary streams in the rain forest areas, where the water is acid and soft, with the temperature rarely exceeding 75°F. The male is a bright reddish-brown with numerous red spots. The caudal fin is lyre-shaped, with pointed upper and lower prolongations, the edges of which are lined reddish-violet. The female is brown with red spots and has a rounded caudal fin. The Lyretail grows up to 2½″ in length and is a typical egg hanger, the eggs taking two to three weeks to hatch. From personal experience, they do not seem to survive longer than eighteen months from hatching, though recent specimens appear to be tougher than the original introductions. There is a golden colour variety (Golden Lyretail).

Aphyosemion bivattatum: There are a number of strains of this egg hanger, which were once given specific names—*bivittatum hollyi*, *bivittatum multicolor*, etc. The general colour of either sex is reddish-brown, with two dark longitudinal bands. All the fins are brighter, extended to points in the male, rounded in the female. They grow to $2\frac{1}{4}''$ in length, and are easy to breed, with an incubation period of fourteen to twenty days. The parents do not appear to molest their young. The only problem with this species is its very slow rate of growth—half as fast as the rest of the genus.

Aphysemion bualanum: Both sexes are distinguished by long drawn-out dorsal and anal fins. The male is brownish, blue-green under some lighting, with irregular red dots and red-black lines. Dorsal, anal and ventral fins are blue-green, with red dots and lines. The female is basically blue-green.

Aphyosemion calliurum: This species exists in two colour variations, yellow and blue. The males grow to 3″ and the females are somewhat smaller. It is a very typical member of the genus and an egg hanger, tending to swim in the lower half of the aquarium. Experiments by the British Aquarist Study Society show that the optimum temperature for incubating the eggs is 71°F.

Aphyosemion christyi: Formerly known as *Aphyosemion cognatum*, this is one of the smaller species, growing to 2″. It comes from the lower Congo, where it lives in ponds, pools and ditches. Colouration is pale brown with red spots, and the characteristic lyre tail in the male. The female has hyaline fins that contrast with the coloured fins of her mate. It breeds in the usual way for egg hangers. Experiments by the British Aquarist Study Society have shown that eggs incubated at 78°F. have a mean incubation period of fourteen days, while those at 67°F. take twenty-three days.

Aphyosemion cinnamoneum: The male is a bright cinnamon yellow-brown, with gold-bordered blue tail, ventral and anal fins. The female is basically grey-brown, with greenish fins. Eggs incubated at 72°F. hatch within twenty to twenty-two days. Use soft water with fibrous peat for breeding.

Aphyosemion filamentosum: This beautiful fish is so-named from the filament-type extended rays of the caudal and anal fins. Colouration of the male ranges from green-blue to violet, with numerous red spots and blotches. The female is less colourful.

Aphyosemion gardneri: This very widely distributed species grows to $2\frac{1}{2}''$. There are two colour varieties

Aphyosemion calliurum (to 3″)

Aphyosemion bualanum (to $2\frac{1}{2}''$)

Aphyosemion cinnamomeum (to $2\frac{1}{4}''$)
Aphyosemion christyi (to 2″)

Aphyosemion filamentosum (to 1¾″)

Aphyosemion gardneri (to 2½″)

Aphyosemion melanopteron (to 1¾″)

Aphyosemion spurrelli (to 3″)

—yellow and blue. The female is very similar to all *Aphyosemion* females, pale tan in colour. It is most important, incidentally, if you have more than one species of *Aphyosemion,* not to get the females mixed up. It is possible to cross-breed certain species, but the offspring are usually sterile. A pair of *Aphyosemion gardneri,* if kept separated for about ten days to condition them, can produce over 50 eggs a day for a few days.

Aphyosemion melanopteron: Adult males of this relatively new species are orange to brownish-orange, with diffuse red spots; the females are grey to light brown. The dorsal fin and the dorsal and ventral margins of the caudal fin are almost entirely black in the male; the fins of the female are colourless, but the lower jaw is black. Eggs are deposited along floating spawning mops and hatch within fifteen to twenty days. Growth of fry is rapid.

Aphyosemion sjoestedti **Blue Gularis:** Although the scientific name of this fish has recently changed, its common name remains the same—much to the relief of the ordinary hobbyist. It lives in the Niger delta and males can grow to 5″ in length. The upper part of the male's body is reddish-brown, the sides are green and blue, the abdomen bluish. His characteristic feature is the tri-lobed caudal fin, the upper section blue-green with red stripes, the middle yellow, and the lower part blue with red stripes. The female is dark olive-green with red spots.

This fish ranks as one of the intermediate group of spawners. It does not hang its eggs on the roots of top plants nor does it bury them in peat. A recommended method of breeding is to add to the peat a handful of boiled, squeezed peat fibre which is sold as a filter medium. This sinks to the bottom and the fishes lay their eggs on it. The fibres, with eggs attached, may be removed about once a week and placed either in half-filled jam jars or half-filled plastic food boxes. If you have the time and inclination to count eggs, you can remove them from the fibre and simply put them straight into the water in the jar. These are then left at about 72°F. for five weeks when the eggs start hatching. The young can be fed immediately on brine shrimp.

Aphyosemion spurrelli: Often confused with *A. gardneri,* the males are bluish-violet, brown on the back, light brown on the belly, with numerous red to maroon markings over the entire body. Fins are yellowish, tinged with red and blue. Females are brownish, with clear to yellowish fins. This species spawns on bottom mops, peat or sand.

87

Aplocheilichthys macrophthalmus (to 1¼″)

Aplocheilichthys spilauchena (to 2¾″)

Aplocheilus lineatus (to 4″)

Aplocheilus dayi Ceylon Panchax (to 3″)

Aplocheilichthys macrophthalmus: This species from south-west Nigeria displays colour variations. In some males the caudal fin shows a V-shaped orange-red marking, in others a marbled pattern of blue, brown or orange-red spots. Ventrals, anal, dorsal and caudal fin have narrow or broad orange-red margins.

Aplocheilichthys spilauchena: Distributed from Senegal to the Congo, this species does well in brackish water. Its basic colour is yellow-green, with a blue tinge in certain lighting. The fish has a white spot on the nape and the male has red and white spots on dorsal and anal fins, missing in the female.

There are three species of genus *Aplocheilus* which are common to aquarists.

Aplocheilus panchax (to 3¼″)

Aplocheilus dayi **Ceylon Panchax:** This fish is widely distributed in Ceylon, in streams and ditches. In the wild the male grows up to 3″ in length. The male is well coloured, gold and metallic green on the back, with a light blue abdomen. The caudal fin is rounded, yellowish-green with red spots, the outer margins being red-banded.

Austrofundulus dolichopterus (to $1\frac{3}{4}''$)

It prefers the usual soft acid water with temperatures ranging from $72°$–$78°$F. Experience shows that for spawning they prefer peat fibre, floating in the middle and lower third of the tank, to nylon wool mops. The incubation period is about fourteen days. Imported fishes are more sensitive to changes in water conditions than those which have been bred in an aquarium.

Aplocheilus lineatus: This is the largest member of the genus, growing to $4''$. It is widely distributed in southern India and Ceylon. The male's colour ranges from olive-brown to yellow. The front end is covered with brilliant red spots, with dark transverse bands farther back. The eye is bright green. Females are darker, less colourful, with a 'Panchax' spot on the dorsal fin.

Aplocheilus panchax: Widely distributed throughout India, Burma and Malaysia, the colouration of this species is very variable, the male being grey-yellow, with a bluish sheen by reflected light, the bluish dorsal and yellow caudal fins being edged with black. The female is less colourful. There are few breeding problems with this undemanding fish.

Austrofundulus dolichopterus: This is a recently introduced Killifish from Venezuela, approximately $1\frac{3}{4}''$ long, its ground colour being pale brown and the sides of the body having a spotted appearance. The nape and top of head are dark brown.

Austrofundulus transilis: Also from Venezuela, the body colour of the male ranges from silvery blue to tan, deep blue in breeding hue. There are dark, brownish-red spots all over the body and the dorsal, anal and caudal fins are blue-green, with variable spots or bands. The caudal fin is lyre-shaped, edged with black.

Among the most popular of the South American *Cynolebias* genus are the following:

Cynolebias bellotti **Argentine Pearl Fish:** This species is found in eastern parts of South America, at latitudes of $30°$–$40°$S. The colour of the male is dark to grey-blue, with white spots over the head, body and most of the fins. The female is slate-blue, with white belly and dark spots. In nature it is most active during the cool winter months (May–October), disappearing during the summer

Austrofundulus transilis (to $5\frac{1}{2}''$)

Cynolebias bellotti Argentine Pearlfish (to $2\frac{3}{4}''$)

drought. The species survives because the parents bury their eggs in the mud and silt of the ponds in which they live. The eggs are dependent on the dry period for their development. It has been observed that in areas containing this and other Killifishes, mosquitoes are rare, due to the fishes' voracious eating habits. This has prompted authorities to experiment with them in malaria control, for example in the rice-growing areas of southern California. In aquarium conditions the eggs must remain in the 'dried out' state, in barely moist peat, for four months.

Cynolebias nigripinnis **Dwarf Argentine Pearl Fish:** The male of this species, which grows no longer than $1\frac{1}{2}''$ from the tip of its nose to the end of its tail is a wonderful little fish, and no photograph can ever do it justice. Very briefly, the male's colouration is dark royal blue with white pearl-like spots, while the female is olive-brown with darker blotches. It comes from the same regions as *Cynolebias bellotti* and needs the usual aquarium conditions for egg buriers. The male fish will fight more fiercely than Siamese Fighting Fishes if there are females around, so you must provide one male to three females. They are sexually mature at eight weeks, and eight months is about their maximum

KNAACK

PENGILLEY

Cynolebias whitei White's Pearlfish (to 4″)

Cynolebias nigripinnis Dwarf Argentine Pearlfish (to 1½″)

life expectation. So try to buy young specimens.

The female requires plenty of live food to keep her in breeding condition. Breed this fish in the normal way for egg buriers and keep the eggs 'dry' for sixteen weeks. The young will hatch within a few hours of adding water, and will grow very rapidly if well fed. Some hatchings produce 'belly sliders'—fry that never seem to be able to swim off the bottom. This may be due to damage caused to the developing embryo by acidity, as a result of not boiling and squeezing out the excess acid in the peat prior to use.

Cynolebias whitei **White's Pearl Fish:** This is an annual fish from ponds and pools in Rio de Janeiro State. The male can grow to 4″ in the wild, the female to 2″. The basic colouring of the male is chocolate-brown with golden spots, and bands of gold on the anal and caudal fins.

Spawning is by egg burying—the fishes diving deeply into the peat to deposit their eggs. The incubation period of eggs in the 'dried-out' state is sixteen weeks. The fry feed immediately on newly hatched brine shrimp and are sexually mature at about 1½″ (males) and ¾″ (females).

There are at least thirteen species of West African *Epiplatys*, which are occasionally seen in aquaria, of which the following four are typical.

Epiplatys chevalieri : A native of the Congo, the male is olive-green to brownish-red, with yellowish flanks and creamy-white underside. There are several rows of longitudinal red spots, sometimes close enough to form an unbroken band. The female also has red-brown spots but is altogether less striking. Like others of the genus, it is a predatory fish but not known to have bred in captivity.

Epiplatys dageti **Red-chinned Panchax:** Known for many years as *Epiplatys chaperi*, this fish comes from Monrovia in Liberia. The male is 2½″ long when adult and in good condition is a very pretty fish, with a black back, grey to blue-green sides and a yellow belly. Chin and throat are brilliant reddish-orange. The caudal fin is lyre-shaped with prolongation of the lower rays. The female is altogether duller. They will eat dry food but prefer and do better on live food. Pike-like in form, they tend to swim just under the surface. The best temperature for spawning is 75°F. and the eggs take ten days to hatch. Fry from parents spawning for the first time are said to be predominantly male, those from older parents predominantly female.

Epiplatys chevalieri (to 2¾")

Epiplatys dageti Red-chinned Panchax (to 2½")

Epiplatys longiventralis : Care and breeding of this species is similar to *E. dageti.* There are several dark transverse bands on the flanks, the characteristic longitudinal rows of brownish-red spots, and red spots all over the dorsal and anal fins.

Epiplatys sexfasciatus **Six-barred Panchax:** This fish is found from Liberia southwards to the Congo. The back is dark grey, the sides olive-brown, the belly yellow-white. There are six wide transverse bands on the lower part of the body only. The males grow fairly large (4") but their peaceful temperament makes them very suitable for beginners. A word of warning, however—they are very good jumpers, so the aquarium must have a tight, full-fitting lid or the occupants will leap out. They are best kept at 75°–78°F. Although less predatory than most Killifishes, they will eat fishes of other species smaller than themselves. They spawn readily on nylon wool mops, and the parents eat neither eggs nor fry even if the mop is left in the tank for longer than the normal incubation period of fourteen days.

The genus *Fundulus* contains many species, which are not much kept by aquarists. They generally

Epiplatys longiventralis (to 2¼")

Epiplatys sexfasciatus (to 4″)

breed best at temperatures of 72°–74°F. The eggs, which in nature are laid on plants, do best on nylon wool in tanks and take about ten to fourteen days to hatch.

Fundulus catenatus **Chained Top Minnow:** This fish comes from the eastern states of the U.S.A., extending from Virginia to Texas, and grows to 8″ in the wild. The basic colour of the male is olive-green with numerous red spots on the flanks, the fins being dull yellow with red spots. The female is yellow-brown with rows of indistinct brown spots. Give the fish typical Killifish conditions with temperatures ranging from 68°–72°F. They will spawn best on clumps of peat fibre, and the young take about ten days to hatch.

Fundulus chrysotus **Golden Ear:** From South Carolina to Florida and found in brackish waters and fresh water. The male, which grows to 3″, is olive-green with a metallic blotch on the gill cover and red spots on sides and fins. The female is brown, with darker blotches on the flanks. The fish prefers slightly warmer water, 72–78°F. and some aquarists add sea water—one part in 200. Eggs are

laid on nylon wool or peat fibre and take ten days to hatch.

Fundulus heteroclitus **Zebra** or **Common Killie:** Very common down the Atlantic coast of North America, from Canada to Mexico, these fishes are often sold as bait for fishing. Males are green-brown with numerous blue bars on the sides, from which the name Zebra Killie is derived. The female is brown with many black spots on the side. They prefer brackish water though they are also found in land-locked fresh water pools. Add a teaspoonful of salt to every gallon of fresh water. Give them peat fibre clumps near the bottom on which to spawn. The incubation period is ten days at 70°F.

Jordanella floridae **American Flag Fish:** One of the more commonly kept of the North American Killifishes, from Florida, where it lives in ponds and marshes. The male grows to nearly 3″ in length, and when in good condition is a very attractive fish, though a fighter. The deep stocky body more resembles a Platy in shape than a typical Killie. Though the basic colour is brown-green, the sides vary considerably according to light—blue, green

Jordanella floridae American Flag Fish (to 3″)

Nothobranchius guentheri (to 1½″)

Nothobranchius palmquistii (to 2″)

Right: *Nothobranchius orthonotus* (to 2½″)

and red. The female is duller, with dark blotches on the flanks. Clumps of peat fibre on the bottom are best for the spawning medium, and the incubation period is five to ten days. Both young and adults eat algae.

The genus *Nothobranchius* from East Africa contains a number of species known to the aquarist and here again there are problems and doubts concerning the scientific names. These fishes seem to be particularly susceptible to Velvet disease.

Nothobranchius guentheri: One of the more common of these East African Killifishes, this egg burier grows to a length of 1½″. The basic impression of colour is green, but there are yellows and reds mingled with it. The caudal fin is red with a dark brown border. The female is a drab grey-brown. Both male and female dive into the peat when laying their eggs. Experience shows that drying out the eggs for twelve weeks gives best results. Growth after hatching is very rapid.

Nothobranchius orthonotus: An inhabitant of coastal areas and mangrove swamps, the male, as with others of this genus, is a splendid specimen, blue-green with a lavish sprinkling of deep red spots and specks. Breeding is not difficult, drying out the eggs giving the best results.

Nothobranchius palmquisti: This Killifish lives in pools which dry up in the summer months, and grows to 2″ in size. It is similar in appearance to *N. guentheri*, but the red caudal fin lacks the dark border. The female is brown to olive-green. It buries its eggs in

the peat and the best proportion of eggs hatching is obtained by drying out the eggs for twelve weeks.

Nothobranchius rachovi: A native of the Beira region in Portuguese East Africa, males of this species grow to 2″ in size. The basic colouration is orange-red, with numerous turquoise transverse stripes. The caudal fin is turquoise near the peduncle, shading to red, with a thick dark brown edge. The female is an undistinguished olive-brown. This species does not dive into the peat to spawn, laying the eggs just under the surface of the peat, or even on the bare glass base of the tank. The eggs, if dried out, hatch in four months at the earliest, the majority after six months' incubation.

Nothobranchius rachovii (to 2″)

KNAACK
NIEUWENHUIZEN

Nothobranchius taeniopygus (to 2¼″)

Nothobranchius taeniopygus: A synonym of *N. brieni,* this Killifish has a rounded caudal fin. Body colouration of the male is dark purplish-brown, with whitish bands across the anal and caudal fins. The female is lighter and more uniformly coloured.

Oryzias latipes **Japanese Medaka:** Although the most popular of this genus, *Oryzias latipes,* about 1½″ long, is not an especially attractive fish. Both sexes are pinkish-yellow, with a few iridescent blue spots on the flanks. In the male only, the dorsal fin is pointed and the anal fin fringed. It is an egg hanger and sometimes prefers to lay its eggs on floating peat fibres in the mid water of the aquarium. The incubation period is about twelve days. This species is not a robust one and any attempt to keep them in less than ideal Killifish conditions prevents them from spawning. Other members of the species, such as *O. celebensis, O. javanicus* and *O. melastigma* are rarely seen in aquarium tanks.

Pachypanchax playfairi: This fish lives in both brackish and fresh water in the wild, and is a fairly robust member of the Killifish family. The male is yellow-green with a dark back and rows of red spots on the sides. All the fins are yellow, spotted red. The female is dull olive with yellow fins. The males are heavy drivers and you must have three females to one male in the breeding tank. They are egg hangers, the eggs hatching in fourteen days.

Pseudepiplatys annulatus: This is a relatively new fish to aquarists and comes from Sierra Leone and Liberia, where it lives in swamp areas in open land. The fishes are small, males 1½″, females 1¼″. Both are striped brown and yellow, rather like the Bumblebee Fish. The male's caudal fin is red, brown and yellow, and the centre rays are extended. It is kept in the usual way and lays its eggs on nylon wool mops; the eggs hatch in two weeks.

CUPIT

Oryzias latipes Japanese Medaka (to 1½″)

NIEUWENHUIZEN

Pseudepiplatys annulatus (to 1½″)

Pterolebias longipinnis (to 3″)

KNAACK

KAHL

Pachypanchax playfairi (to 4″)

Pterolebias longipinnis: The males grow to 3″, females to 1½″. The characteristic feature of the male is his flowing scarf-like tail, with extended rays. His colour is brown, with green-yellow spots on the sides and on the pectoral fins. The female is brown, with smaller fins. It requires a typical Tooth Carp set-up for breeding but the depth of the substrate should be increased to allow the fish to dive deeply into the peat. Dry out the peat for twelve weeks.

Pterolebias peruensis: The other common member of the *Pterolebias* genus comes from Peru. The males grow to 3″, the female to 2½″. The male has an elongated flag-like tail, though not as long as *P. longipinnis*. He is generally pale brown, with a turquoise operculum. The dorsal and anal fins have turquoise stripes and there is also a turquoise patch on the caudal fin which has a thick orange lower border. The female is similarly coloured, but the hues are less bright and there is no extension to the caudal fin. Keep in the usual Killifish set-up with a temperature of 68°–74°F. They are relatively shallow egg buriers and a 1″ layer of peat is suitable. If the eggs are dried out, the incubation period is sixteen weeks. Leaving the eggs 'wet' in water, without drying out, results in an incubation period of seven months with far fewer eggs hatching.

NIEUWENHUIZEN

Pterolebias peruensis (to 3″)

97

Rivulus cylindraceus (to 2″)

Rivulus milesi (to 3″)

Rachovia hummelincki (to 3″)

Rachovia hummelincki: This fish from Colombia lives in temporary pools and ditches. The male which grows to 3″ long is brown-grey with about fifteen metallic blue transverse bars. The fins are metallic blue with dark grey blotches and the lower edge of the caudal fin has a white border. The fish is an egg burier and three females with one male will lay about a dozen eggs weekly. The eggs are dried out in the usual way and are said to need an incubation period of eight months.

Rivulus cylindraceus: This is the best known member of the genus *Rivulus,* which contains eight species well known to hobbyists. They are all egg hangers, do best at about 72°F., and are not as particular as other Killifishes about water conditions. Neither are they so attractive. *R. cylindraceus* comes from Cuba and Florida, and the male, who grows to $2\frac{1}{2}″$, is, like all *Rivulus* species, a good jumper. He is much the brighter of the two sexes, with a dark brown back, green-brown sides and an orange-yellow belly. His yellowish fins have dark spots and there are a number of red spots on the sides. The female is yellow-brown to reddish-brown, with dark spots on the sides and a dark spot on the upper part of

the caudal fin, where it joins the body. Some have the habit of laying eggs on the top surface of floating plants, almost out of the water. In bare tanks they dash around wildly, so floating plants and nylon mops for cover are helpful. It is easy to breed, the males being vigorous drivers. The large adhesive eggs, laid on the mops, hatch in ten to fourteen days at 78°F.

Rivulus milesi: Another popular species, the male is a bluish-grey fish, deepening to lavender-blue as it matures, with an overlayer of brownish-red spots. Dorsal, ventral and anal fins are yellow-green with black borders, and the end of the tail fin has a vertical white band. The female is predictably less colourful—a mottled grey.

Rivulus strigatus **Herringbone Rivulus:** The male has bright herringbone patterns along the sides and grows to $1\frac{3}{4}″$. The female ($1\frac{1}{2}″$) does not show this pattern but has a Rivulus spot. They do not breed easily but spawn best with one male to one female. Use the typical set-up for egg hangers. These fishes are good jumpers and must have a tight fitting tank top.

NIEUWENHUIZEN

Roloffia bertholdi (to 2½")

Roloffia bertholdi: A native of Sierra Leone, this variably coloured fish is generally greenish-blue with freely distributed red spots and blotches on body and fins. The outer fin margins are pale blue. It grows to about 2½" and lays eggs on the bottom of plants.

Roloffia occidentalis: This species has for many years been masquerading as *Aphyosemion sjoestedti*. Like the other members of the genus *Roloffia*, it comes from West Africa, west of the Dahomey Gap, and is very similar in appearance to the *Aphyosemions*. It is basically a brownish-yellow fish, the lower half of the rear end of the body appearing darker than the upper. The characteristic feature of the adult male in good condition is the dark royal blue of the lower jaw and operculum. The upper end of the dorsal fin, the lower end of the anal fin, and the lower edge of the lyre-shaped caudal fin, have a red band with an outer blue stripe. The female is bright brownish-orange, with hyaline fins. The caudal fin is rounded. It is an egg burier which requires an incubation period of sixteen weeks in the 'dried out' state. Males in breeding condition will fight, interlock jaws and do each other damage, so keep one male and three females for breeding. They are robust fish—the males growing to 3½".

Roloffia petersi: This fish, pink, with a light blue sheen, light blue fins and maroon spots, is rarely seen nowadays in aquaria, though once quite plentiful. It spawns on plants, usually close to the surface, and the incubation period is typical of the genus, twelve to sixteen days. It is found in the Ivory Coast and south-western Ghana.

KNAACK

Rivulus strigatus Herringbone Rivulus (to 1¾")

NIEUWENHUIZEN

Roloffia occidentalis (to 3½")

Roloffia petersi (to 2½")

KNAACK

99

Xiphophorus helleri Swordtail—red and green colour strains (to 5″). See page 111

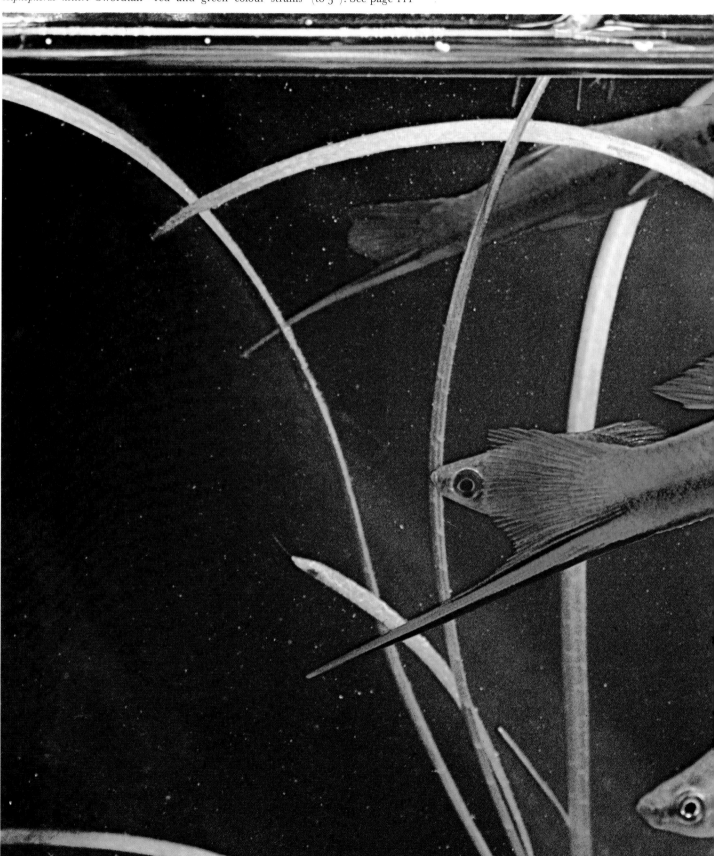

BURTON/COLEMAN

THE Live-bearing Tooth Carps are the most popular and interesting of all aquarium fishes. Not only, as their name suggests, do they produce live young, but due to the fact that they are readily bred and hybridised, many beautiful 'man-made' colour varieties are possible.

The family consists of about thirty different genera, all confined to the New World. Their range extends from the southern states of the U.S.A. through Central America and the West Indies down to South America as far as northern Argentina.

Certain species, notably *Gambusia,* because of their exceptional capacity for eating mosquito larvae, have been introduced to many other areas to help in malaria control.

Most Live-bearers grow to about 2"–3", the smallest species being the Mosquito Fish, which only reaches a length of $\frac{3}{4}$", and the largest the Giant Sailfin Molly, which grows to 6". Their life span is approximately two and a half years, the larger varieties tending to live longer. Although they are omnivorous—the exception being the voracious carnivore *Belonesox belizanus*—a small amount of green food in their diet is essential. This is naturally provided by algae, either in soft green form or as green water. To supplement their diet, small amounts of lettuce or spinach can be fed. This is particularly important when keeping and breeding Mollies.

In their natural habitats they live in quiet, well planted areas, often where there is little water movement. They prefer well matured water and fare considerably better in hard alkaline conditions. Some species are found in coastal regions, so that small traces of salt in the aquarium, simulating estuarine conditions, are beneficial. Others, notably Swordtails, are excellent jumpers and therefore tight-fitting lids should be used on all aquaria.

The reproduction pattern of this family is extremely interesting, since they are oviparous, that is, producing young by eggs which hatch within the body of the female, but do not obtain any nourishment from the parent.

Male fishes are easily distinguished for they possess a gonopodium. This is a modification of the fourth, fifth and sixth rays of the anal fin, forming a rod-like intromittant organ. The males too are much more colourful, so much so that they may appear at first glance to be a separate species. Some male Live-bearers have large extended finnage, a good example being the Swordtail. Females are generally much larger and a fish that is pregnant shows a large dark gravid spot, or peritoneum, just above the vent. Sometimes, shortly before birth,

the eyes of the unborn fish can be seen through the thin peritoneum wall.

The male is polygamous and will court numerous females. He chases the female and manoeuvres himself into a position where the tip of his flexible gonopodium just enters the vent. Spermatozoa are then injected and enter the oviduct. Eggs are fertilised in the ovarian cavity, where they develop exclusively on their yolk until they are ready for birth. With certain species, such as *Jenynsia,* the male's gonopodium is only capable of moving either to the right or to the left. The female's vent is also shaped so that mating is only possible from one side; thus the odd situation arises of 'right-handed' males mating with 'left-handed' females, and vice-versa.

Female Live-bearers are capable of storing sperms in the oviduct, so that from one mating may emerge four or five broods. A virgin female, therefore, need only be with an active male for a few minutes and yet produce large numbers of young, although any subsequent fertilisation tends to have dominance over the next brood.

The eggs take between thirty and forty days to develop before birth, but this varies slightly according to the species and climatic conditions.

The first brood is always very small, sometimes only two or three fishes, but the numbers increase with each brood, the fourth usually being the largest, the numbers then decreasing. Younger fishes also tend to have smaller broods.

With most species there is no breeding season, and young at various stages of growth can be seen all the year round. Some of the larger Mollies in their natural habitat, however, appear to have a resting period during the winter.

The young, though only $\frac{1}{4}$" long, are born fully developed. As soon as they are expelled from the female, usually tail first, they swim to the surface to fill their swim bladders, and then dart for cover from their hungry, cannibal-like parents. Fishes that are slightly premature frequently lie on the bottom for a time before filling their swim bladders, and often the remains of the yolk-sac can be seen. Normally these fishes recover, but a small trace of salt in the water often helps them.

Except for Mollies, it is advisable to trap gravid females in order to save the young. One method is to use a densely planted tank with heavy top cover, such as Duckweed. This method is only suitable if you are in constant attendance, and the use of a trap ensures that the young fishes are safe for much longer periods. The trap is really a scaled-down version of the one described for breeding Barbs (pages 117–19), and this enables a smaller breeding

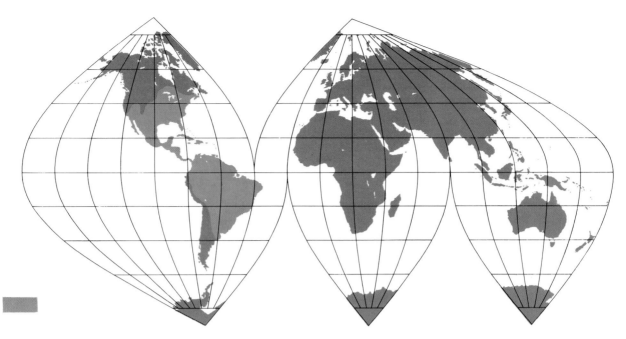

Distribution of Live-bearing Tooth Carps in parts of North, Central and South America and the West Indies

tank to be used (i.e. 12″ × 10″ × 10″). The gravid female should be introduced into the trap as soon as she appears to be pregnant, and it is useful to keep her fed with small quantities of daphnia. When the young are dropped, they fall through the base of the trap and swim away from it. Remove the female as soon as she has finished, and replace her in a quiet planted aquarium to recover. The young will start to take food immediately and should be given micro-worm or newly hatched brine shrimp. They grow rapidly and should be moved on to a larger tank as soon as possible. Small additions of green foods to their diet is beneficial. At this stage it is best to eliminate very small and poorly coloured specimens, giving the rest of the brood more growing space. When breeding a good strain of Live-bearers it is advisable to segregate the sexes as soon as they are apparent, for this allows you to practise selective breeding, aiming at good size, finnage development and deep, rich colours.

Due to the ease of hybridisation, many beautiful colour strains have been developed and established. Breeders are not only producing new finnage forms, but even cross-breeding fishes of separate genera, a particularly interesting subject for scientists studying genetics. But even a beginner can produce new varieties, provided he takes a few basic precautions.

There are two ways of producing a new colour variety or finnage development. One is to decide beforehand the strain you wish to develop and then by careful selection of the parent stock and planned cross-breeding, attempt to produce the desired fish. Several generations may have to be produced before the ideal form emerges and in the majority of cases there will be no signs of success.

Another method is to cross two distinctly different strains and see if the results show any interesting colour varieties. If some of the young look promising, carefully select them, separate them from the rest of the brood, and continue careful selective breeding. The outcome may be complete failure, but if and when you do manage to establish your new colour variety, all the hard work is well rewarded.

Cross-breeding between two distinct species has thus far successfully been achieved with the following fishes:

Poecilia latipinna x *Poecilia reticulata*
Xiphophorus helleri x *Poecilia reticulata*
Limia vittata x *Poecilia reticulata*
Limia nigrofasciata x *Xiphophorus helleri*

Another interesting and quite common phenomenon of the Live-bearing Tooth Carps is for sex changes to occur. Young Live-bearers at birth all resemble females, and not until they are several months old do some develop male characteristics. With some species, notably Red-eyed Red Swordtails and Sailfin Mollies, this may not occur until the age of nine to twelve months. Cases are also found of female fishes, having had several broods, suddenly developing male characteristics. A fish that has changed in this way can easily be recognised as the typical female body shape is retained and any male finnage development remains rather stunted. Changes from male to female are unknown, and 'reverted' males are always sterile. Swordtails are the most common sex-changers, but it is known among Mollies, Platies and Guppies.

103

Gambusia affinis: Although not a popular aquarium fish, it has a claim to fame as being the first live-bearing fish to be introduced to the public. Its popularity has since waned, due to the fact that it is a notorious fin-nipper, attacking not only other small fishes but also chasing and worrying species far larger than itself.

The economic importance of this fish lies in its remarkable capacity for gorging mosquito larvae. It is reported to be able to eat its own weight of larvae in one day. Consequently, they have been shipped all over the world, packed in polythene bags, and dropped from low-flying aircraft, over areas where malaria-carrying mosquitoes are a serious problem.

The female is dull grey, resembling a female Guppy, but with black spots on the caudal fin and sometimes on the body. She grows to $2\frac{1}{2}''$ and may have up to 60 young in a brood. The males are much smaller, only reaching $1\frac{1}{2}''$ and varying considerably in colour. Some specimens show such large areas of black markings over the body that attempts have been made to label them as two distinct sub-species.

Breeding this fish is simple, but a trap is advisable since the parents will often eat their young.

Heterandria formosa **Mosquito Fish:** This fish gets its common name not from its diet, but because of its minute size. The male only grows to $\frac{3}{4}''$ and the female is rarely seen over $1\frac{1}{8}''$ long. It is the smallest of the Live-bearers, and ranks as one of the smallest known vertebrates.

It is a delightful fish, best kept in a small aquarium on its own, for larger fishes either try to eat it or keep it away from the food. The basic colour is olive-green with a dark brown line running the length of the body. The fins are yellow and the dorsal has two spots, red above black. The males have a very large gonopodium in relation to their body size.

All other Live-bearers have numerous eggs fertilised at once, from which a brood develops to be born simultaneously. The Mosquito, however, develops several embryos of different ages and the young are born over a period of fourteen days. Thus the brood appears to be never ending, and brothers and sisters are always of different ages and sizes. The parents never touch the young and provided plenty of small food is given, it is safe to leave the fry in with the parents.

Poecilia reticulata **Guppy:** This is without doubt the most popular of all tropical fishes. Although discovered in 1859 it was first collected by Dr. R.

KAHL

Gambusia affinis (to $2\frac{1}{2}''$)

NIEUWENHUIZEN

Heterandria formosa Mosquito Fish (to $1\frac{1}{8}''$)

CUPIT

Poecilia reticulata Guppy ($1\frac{1}{8}''$–$2\frac{1}{4}''$). Young fish with tail not yet fully developed

Poecilia reticulata Exhibition-type Guppy, female

CUPIT

Poecilia reticulata Multicoloured Veiltail Guppy

Poecilia reticulata Snakeskin Guppy

Poecilia reticulata Red Veiltail Guppy

Guppy in Trinidad in 1866. This genus was originally classified as *Lebistes* but since 1963 the name of *Poecilia* has been internationally accepted. The name of Guppy will certainly remain in common use.

It is found in most areas of Central America, particularly in small streams and pools, where it withstands a wide temperature range and frequently stagnant, poorly oxygenated water. It is very hardy, eats most foods, and lives peaceably with other species. In the wild the females are olive-green, with a silver belly and clear finnage, growing to about $2\frac{1}{4}''$. The males are $1\frac{1}{8}''$ in length and exhibit several colours, dotted around the body, with finnage in no set pattern, though it tends to be extended. In fact no two males appear to have exactly the same markings, and it is this extreme variability of colour and finnage that has allowed aquarists, by careful selective breeding, to establish the many beautiful strains seen today.

On both sides of the Atlantic, standards have been produced and breeders aim at recommended

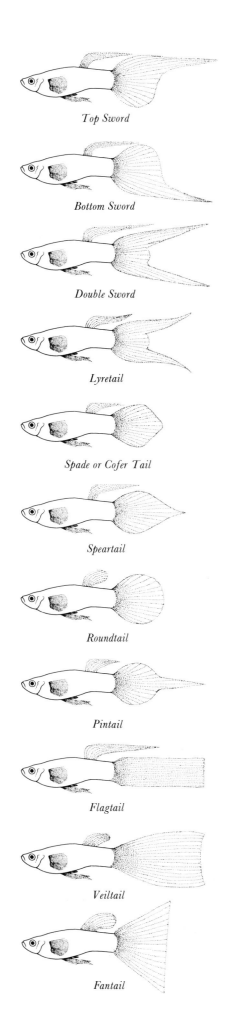

Top Sword

Bottom Sword

Double Sword

Lyretail

Spade or Cofer Tail

Speartail

Roundtail

Pintail

Flagtail

Veiltail

Fantail

finnage varieties, trying to introduce as many bright colours into the fish as possible. The names of some of these finnage varieties speak for themselves—Top Sword, Bottom Sword, Double Sword, Lyretail, Cofertail (named after the shape of a Welsh coalminer's shovel), Speartail, Roundtail, Pintail, Scarftail, Flagtail and Veiltail.

The modern trend is towards the very large Delta and Veiltail varieties, and the colours produced range from the beautiful Green Lace to the Red-finned Half-black Guppy. Breeders have even managed to produce females with long dorsals and shaped caudals, exhibiting colour not only in the body but also in the fins.

In several countries there are Guppy Societies whose members confine themselves to breeding *P. reticulata*. New strains are exhibited at the Societies' shows, and it is at these that the finest specimens can be seen.

Although establishing a new colour strain is not simple, breeding is straightforward. The females produce up to 100 young every four to five weeks and the young grow very rapidly and are extremely hardy. They take brine shrimp and dust-fine dried foods from birth, and quickly progress to grindal worms and chopped tubifex.

No fish has done more for the hobby and without doubt it will remain a firm favourite for many years.

Jenynsia lineata **One-sided Live-bearer:** A very unusual Live-bearer from the northern areas of Argentina. The male only grows to $1\frac{1}{2}''$ and is grey-green with dark horizontal bars on the body. The female is similarly coloured but grows to 4–5 ″. They require a certain amount of live food in their diet and older males can be quarrelsome.

The mating procedure of this species is unusually interesting, for the males are only capable of moving their gonopodium to one side. The direction of movement varies with individuals so that both dextral (right-sided) and sinistral males (left-sided) are found. The female's vent is covered by an enlarged scale which similarly moves only in one direction, so that dextral males can only mate with sinistral females, and vice-versa. In the wild, most males are found to be dextral and females sinistral.

The young, which normally number 30–40, are born fairly large $(\frac{3}{4}'')$, but since the female is very voracious, good cover or a trap must be provided.

Limia melanogaster **Blue Limia:** An extremely attractive Live-bearer that is not as popular as it deserves to be. It is found in warm water areas of Jamaica, where the females grow to 2 ″ and the males to about $1\frac{3}{4}''$. The back is olive-green, but the

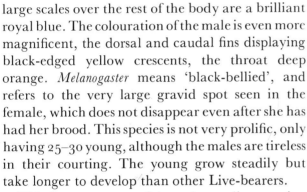

Top: *Limia melanogaster* Blue Limia, female (to 2″)

Below: *Limia melanogaster* Blue Limia, male (to 1¾″)

Top: *Limia vittata* Cuban Limia, female (to 5″)

Below: *Limia vittata* Cuban Limia, male (to 2½″)

large scales over the rest of the body are a brilliant royal blue. The colouration of the male is even more magnificent, the dorsal and caudal fins displaying black-edged yellow crescents, the throat deep orange. *Melanogaster* means 'black-bellied', and refers to the very large gravid spot seen in the female, which does not disappear even after she has had her brood. This species is not very prolific, only having 25–30 young, although the males are tireless in their courting. The young grow steadily but take longer to develop than other Live-bearers.

This is a very peaceful, undemanding species, and under good lighting is very beautiful.

Limia vittata **Cuban Limia:** As the common name suggests, this fish is native to Cuba, where the females are found up to 5″ in length, the males growing to 2½″. It is a pleasant, though not out-standing fish, the basic colour being olive-brown,

with a bluish sheen on the scales. The belly is a silvery pink and the fins pale yellow. The male has irregular dark vertical bars on the rear part of the body and black dots on the finnage. The female has four dark dotted lines running lengthwise along the body with fewer markings in the fins.

The Cuban Limia is undemanding, eats any-thing, but prefers to be kept at higher temperatures. It is very prolific; broods of 200 are common.

Poecilia formosa: This fish, found in various parts of Mexico, is interesting rather than beautiful, being a natural cross of *P. latipinna* and *P. sphenops*. It is a composite of both parents, both with regard to the numbers of rays in the fins and the position of the dorsal. Amazingly, only females are produced, which mate with a male of either of the original species. The colours are generally rather drab and the fish is rarely kept in aquaria.

Poecilia formosa Lyre-tail Molly (to 3¼″)

Poecilia formosa Albino Lyre-tail Molly

Poecilia latipinna **Sailfin Molly:** This very beautiful Live-bearer comes from the eastern states of the U.S.A. where it is mainly found in coastal or estuarine areas. For this reason a small amount of sea salt in the tank water is beneficial. It thrives on warm water, large swimming areas and green food. It is hardly surprising, therefore, that the best specimens come from the large outdoor fish farms of Florida, where all these amenities abound. Aquarium bred fishes, however carefully kept, never attain the size or splendour of finnage of these imported Mollies.

The fish is olive-yellow, often with bluish flecks. Several horizontal lines of brown dots, arranged in something of a zig-zag pattern, run the length of the body. The males often have five or six short, dark, vertical bars on the belly. The notable feature of this magnificent fish is the male's dorsal fin, which starts just behind the operculum and stretches almost the whole length of the body. In a good specimen it may stand $1\frac{1}{4}''$ high, and when fully displayed, exhibits flashes of red, yellow, blue and green. The female has far less colour and a smaller dorsal which starts farther back along the body. Both sexes, when fully grown, reach nearly 4".

Sailfin Mollies live for about three years and may not reach full maturity until they are eighteen months old. Indeed, the best males are those that develop their sexual characteristics late in life. A word of warning with regard to breeding. On no account should you attempt to trap a gravid female. In the wild they tend to breed only in the summer months and in aquaria they sometimes experience difficulty in becoming gravid. Give them plenty of small feeds, including algae or shredded greens. Dried food is readily accepted, and because of their large upturned lips, they feed naturally from the surface. A brood may number up to 150 young, which are fairly large when born. It is quite safe to leave the parents with the fry.

There are several colour varieties, and it was careful selective breeding that developed the famous Midnight Molly. This fish was originally produced by crossing a black Short-finned Molly with a Sailfin Molly. The body and finnage are velvet-black, and the large sailfin dorsal is edged with orange.

A recent change in nomenclature for Mollies from *Mollienisia* to *Poecilia* is now generally accepted.

Poecilia sphenops **Short-finned Molly:** This is one of the smallest of the Mollies, only growing to some $3\frac{1}{2}''$. It has a very wide natural distribution, ranging from southern states of the U.S.A., to Venezuela, and, as a result, a large number of

Poecilia latipinna Sailfin Molly (to 4")

Poecilia sphenops Short-finned Molly (to $3\frac{1}{2}''$)

colour variants are found. The Short-finned Molly is easily identified by its short, almost round dorsal fin. In the wild, the body colour is generally olive-green, with varying amounts of black blotches. It was from these darker fishes that the original Black Mollies were developed. Breeders selected fishes with the greatest areas of black, until, after many generations of selective breeding, they eventually established an entirely black fish, the 'Perma-black' Molly. This strain gives birth to black young, whereas with the original fishes the dark colours only developed as they matured.

The other well-known colour variety of this species is the Liberty Molly, from the Yucatan Peninsula of Central America. It has a steel-blue body and red fins, the dorsal having a yellow and

Poecilia velifera Giant Sailfin Molly (to 6″)

black crescent at the base. Unfortunately, inbreeding over the years has diminished these colours, and it has lost popularity. It is also rather a nuisance in a community tank, being apt to chase other fishes. Like all other Mollies, it is a vegetarian and requires algae or other green foods in its diet.

Be careful not to move gravid females, which may result in premature birth, and sometimes the death of the adult fish. Given a quiet, well planted tank, the parents will leave the young alone. The average brood is 40.

Poecilia velifera **Giant Sailfin Molly:** This lovely fish, the most magnificent of all the Mollies, but unfortunately rarely seen, is found only in certain regions of Central America, around Yucatan. It

Xiphophorus helleri Green Swordtail

Xiphophorus helleri Red Swordtail

has all the features of the Sailfin Molly, but on a much grander scale. For example, it grows up to 6″ long and the male's dorsal often reaches 1¾″ in height. This is set farther forward and the ray count is 17–18 as against 13–14 in *P. latipinna*. The colours are very vivid and the blues are usually well developed. The males often develop a spike at the base of the tail.

Care and breeding are the same as for the Sailfin Molly. Black specimens of this variety are very rare.

Phallichthys amates **Merry Widow:** An attractive small Live-bearer from Honduras. The male grows to 1″ and the females to 2″. The body colour is olive-green, fading to golden yellow on the belly. A dark vertical line runs through the eye, and the male has numerous faint dark vertical lines on the body. The outstanding feature of the male is the erect dorsal fin, bright yellow at the base, topped by a white-edged black crescent. The male has a very large gonopodium, turned down at the tip.

This species is fairly prolific, producing up to 40 young at a brood. It is advisable to use a trap, as the parents tend to eat their young.

The fry should be given brine shrimp and micro-worms, then dried food and chopped grindal worms.

Xiphophorus helleri **Swordtail:** The original Sword-tails, found wild in Mexico, were a drab olive colour, and the swords fairly short. Since then man has taken over and produced many beautiful colour and finnage varieties. This is a streamlined fish, adept at jumping and found in fast-moving shallow streams that have well planted inlets for cover and rest areas. The males grow to about 5″ and the females slightly less. The sword, a characteristic long extension to the lower edge of the caudal fin, is only seen in males. Swordtails tend to be bullies and do best in tanks with larger species. Hard water suits them best, with a temperature around 75°F. They are greedy feeders, eating most foods, and have been known to choke to death by trying to gorge over-large food. They are especially fond of tubifex but care must be taken not to give them too much.

The male Swordtail is an ardent courter and the females easily become gravid. Broods of over 200 are not unknown, but since they will readily devour their own fry, a trap must be provided. The fry grow very rapidly and require plenty of swimming space and food. The best specimens are those that develop their swords when already of a reasonable size. Cases of Swordtails changing sex are not uncommon and you must ensure that a late developer has not in fact changed sex, for it will then be sterile and useless for breeding.

There are a number of well-known established colour strains, the following being the most popular:

Green Swordtail This fish has a bright green body with a red zig-zag stripe running along the lateral line. The sword is yellow, edged with black.
Red Swordtail A bright scarlet fish with a yellow sword, edged with black.
Red-eyed Red Swordtail This fish has a deep scarlet body and fins, and as the name implies, a red eye. The sword is also scarlet. This variety is more difficult to breed and the males tend to be sterile.
Albino Swordtail A creamy white fish, the only other colouration being the typical pink eye and a faint zig-zag along the body.

Xiphophorus helleri Red Wagtail Swordtail

Xiphophorus maculatus Platy (to 3″). Red variety

Wagtail Swordtail This variety may be either red or green, with black fins. The lips are also black.
Black Swordtail This fish should be a shiny black all over. The scales glint and the throat is sometimes yellow. Breeding is difficult, the fishes often developing cancerous growths which result in death.

Recent work on the Swordtail has produced 'Hi-Fin' varieties exhibiting long, flowing dorsals. Many colour variants of this type are now being bred and established.

Xiphophorus maculatus **Platy:** Until recently this fish was classified in a separate genus, but later work established it as a member of the Swordtail family. This is borne out by the way that they readily cross-breed. Many of the colour varieties have some Swordtail origin and vice versa. It is a much deeper bodied fish than the Swordtail and the body shape should be almost circular. The fins are also rounded and the male lacks the extension to the tail.

The wild fishes are a dark olive-green with a bluish sheen. Two dark round spots, one above the other, are found at the caudal peduncle and the fins are almost colourless. They come from quiet water areas of coastal Mexico and Guatemala. A full-sized fish may reach 3″ in length but 2″–2½″ is more common. A good brood usually numbers about 100 and the fry are much smaller than Swordtails. They eat well, but not to the extent of gorging themselves. The young normally start to sex out at about eight weeks.

Man has again developed many colour varieties, all of which are hardy and peaceful.

Red Platy A deep scarlet fish which has good colour in the fins.

Moon Platy This is a yellow-bodied fish with a dark half crescent at the base of the tail. The dorsal fin is orange.

Blue Platy Although the basic body colour tends to be green, the scales reflect a metallic blue when shown under lighting. The fins tend to be clear.

Black Platy This fish has a good, even, black colour over the body, with clear finnage. The throat is often yellow or orange. It is not very easy to keep or breed, being far more delicate than other colour varieties.

Numerous other varieties, such as Sunset, Bleeding Heart, Spangled, Wagtail and Spotted Platies are frequently seen. Although some of them tend to be not very well established strains, they are undeniably beautiful.

Because of its bright colours and very pleasant disposition, the Platy is one of the most popular Live-bearers now kept and suitable for beginners.

Xiphophorus variatus **Variegated Platy:** The body of this Platy from southern Mexico is more stream-lined than *X. maculatus*, the dorsal longer and similar in shape to the Swordtail. It grows to 2″—the females being slightly larger.

There are many colour varieties, but the female is basically olive-green with a yellow belly, with two transverse dark zigzag lines on its side. The male has far more colour, exhibiting a brownish-yellow back and orange belly. Varying amounts of blue, red, brown and yellow dots are distributed over the body in different patterns, and the dorsal fin is often red.

Many beautiful colour strains have been developed from wild stock. They breed fairly easily, although the young have to be protected from their hungry parents. The fry grow fairly slowly and it

PENGILLEY

Xiphophorus maculatus Sunset Platy

CUPIT

Xiphophorus maculatus Black Platy

may be nine months before the glorious colours of the male are seen to their full advantage.

Dermogenys pusillus **Half-beak:** Although not strictly a member of the Live-bearing Tooth Carps, this very interesting species produces live young.

It comes from a wide distribution area around the Malay Peninsula, and is found in fresh and brackish water. A very slim surface-living fish that requires live food and plenty of swimming space, it is not very easy to keep in an aquarium as the males fight and the females are prone to lose their broods. They rarely have more than fifteen young at a time and the pregnancy lasts six to eight weeks.

This fish presents a challenge to the ambitious hobbyist and to raise a brood can be considered no mean achievement.

KNAACK

Xiphophorus maculatus Bleeding Heart Platy

CUPIT

Xiphophorus maculatus Red Wagtail Platy

NIEUWENHUIZEN

Xiphophorus variatus Variegated Platy (to 2″)
Dermogenys pusillus Half-beak (to 2¾″)

BURTON/COLEMAN

Rasbora caudimaculata (to 8″ in wild, approx half this size in aquaria)

CYPRINIDS

CYPRINIDAE, or Carps and Minnows, form the largest family of all freshwater fishes. From the aquarist's viewpoint they readily fall into two sections—Barbs in one group, Rasboras, Danios and Minnows in the other.

The family as a whole is represented over most areas of the globe, with the exception of Madagascar, Australasia, South America, Canada, Greenland and Iceland. Its members may be as small as 1″ or as large as 10′–12′, many of the larger species being caught as food fishes. Over 300 different species are known to have been kept by aquarists, most of them around 2″ in length, a popular size.

Fishes of the Cyprinidae family are fairly easily recognised by the following points. The body shape tends to be elongate-oval, ranging to slender, usually with rather large, well-pronounced scales. The finnage is generally small and the caudal fin on most species is forked. A large majority of the Carps and Minnows have barbels, either one or two pairs, which protrude from the lips and help them to grub and search for food. The dentition of the family is characterised by a lack of normal teeth, and all 'chewing' is done with large flat pharangeal plates situated in the throat. Although the colours of the individual species vary tremendously, most of them have areas of silver which reflect on their large scales. They are a very active family and most of them are fast swimmers.

BARBS

The Barbs have always been aquarists' favourites. They are active, yet peaceful, with bright colours, and most of them are fairly readily spawned.

They are found exclusively in the Old World and can best be divided into Asian and African. Of the several African species, very few are popular, mainly due to lack of bold colouration. The Asian species are found in most tropical areas ranging from India, through Malaysia, to China. Most of them come from fairly fast-flowing shallow streams, with a certain amount of plant cover. Nearly all Barbs are omnivorous but some, such as *Barbus schwanenfeldi*, have distinctly vegetarian tastes and should therefore be kept well away from planted aquaria.

They are not fussy about water conditions, hard or soft water being equally suitable, but, almost without exception, they prefer a well-filtered, aerated aquarium.

The smaller Barbs, which are the most commonly seen in aquaria, live for approximately two to three years, although some species such as the Nigger Barb (*Barbus nigrofasciatus*) have been known to live for seven to eight years, reaching sexual maturity at about eight months.

Barbs are definitely shoal fishes and are best seen when kept with several others of their own species. They are always on the alert for food and are most inquisitive. Their quick movements about the tank, large scales glittering in the light, make an extremely pleasing sight, and those aquarists who stock their large show tanks with shoals of three or four varieties are rewarded with an ever-changing spectacle.

Since they eat most foods, it is not difficult to get the fishes into a good spawning condition. Live foods are naturally preferred, but dried varieties are also eagerly taken.

To breed a species of Barb it is best to obtain six to twelve young specimens from two or three different sources to ensure unrelated pairs and grow them up to breeding size. When they are old enough it is essential to separate the sexes into different tanks. The reason for this is that many a pair have been observed spawning in community tanks, followed around by other fishes gaily consuming the eggs. It is very easy to tell when the fishes are in breeding condition, for the females 'roe-up' very easily and become very deep in the body. The males intensify their colours and in some cases develop distinct breeding hues. Male Barbs in spawning condition spar with each other and this playfulness may result in fin damage.

A shoal of Tiger Barbs, *Barbus tetrazona*

PENGILLEY

BREEDING

The Tiger Barb (*Barbus tetrazona*) is a typical and popular member of the family. Although not the easiest to breed, it sets a very general spawning pattern.

Barbs lay adhesive eggs, which are expelled by the female, about 8–12 at a time, following frantic chasing and nudging by the male. For this reason a tank not less than 24″ long should be used. Only 6″–8″ water depth is needed, so a tank measuring 24″×8″×8″ or larger is ideal. It should be glazed all round with plain glass, thoroughly cleaned out, and for complete safety, treated with a mild disinfectant such as Permanganate of Potash.

The next important consideration is water. Although Barbs can be spawned in hard water, success is more likely to be obtained by using filtered rain water. The best combination is two-thirds rain water, filtered through peat and topped up with fresh tap water. This gives a mixture which has a hardness reading of about 100–120 p.p.m. of Calcium Carbonate. Fresh tap water seems to give far better results than water that has stood for several days, probably due to a higher oxygen content which acts as a stimulant for spawning.

Fill the tank with about 6″ of water and then add one or two clumps of densely bunched plants or artificial spawning medium. If you wish to save a very high percentage of the spawning, however, a most effective breeding trap may be constructed in the following way.

For the base of the trap use a plastic mesh-netting with $\frac{1}{4}$″ holes, such as can be purchased by the yard in rolls two feet wide. Cut the base 3″ shorter than the length and 2″ shorter than the width of the tank. There is a 'right' and 'wrong' side to this material, so make sure that the smooth side is placed uppermost, otherwise the spawning pair may damage themselves on the rough surface. The sides and ends of the trap are made from nylon curtain material, with a very fine mesh. The depth of the material should be about the depth of the tank. It is advisable to stitch this all together with nylon or terylene thread so that it will not rot in use. The trap is then suspended into the breeding tank, using plastic pegs to support it at the top on the tank frame.

There are several advantages of using a breeding trap. One of the first difficulties a beginner experiences when breeding egg-layers is to know when the fishes have spawned. With this method the eggs are easily seen beneath the trap, and although they are adhesive, a large proportion will fall through the mesh, thanks to the wild flailing of the male. Furthermore, most of the spawning is protected from the greedy parents, who, when their spawning bliss is over, will not normally hesitate to devour all their eggs. Use of the trap also prevents the parents

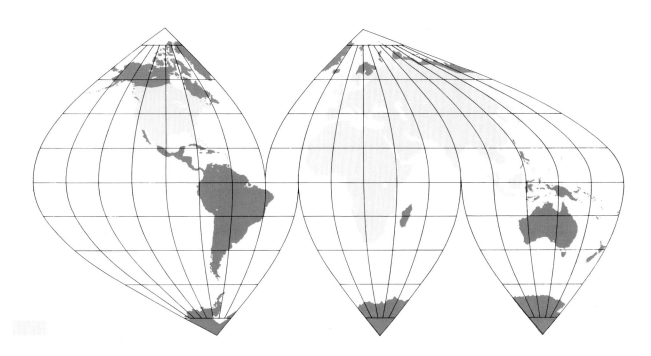

Distribution of Cyprinids in Europe, Asia, Africa and parts of North America

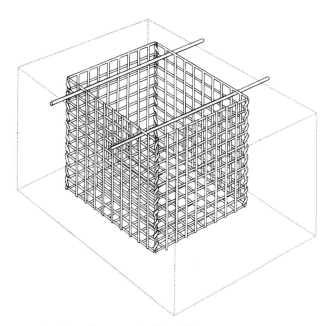

A typical breeding trap for Cyprinids

The fishes should be introduced into the tank early in the evening, and then left alone. This allows them time to settle in with the minimum of disturbance.

If the pair are in good breeding condition and the set-up is correct, they should spawn within the next thirty-six hours. Some take a little longer, but if nothing has happened after seventy-two hours, they should be separated and made ready for another attempt in about a week's time.

Assuming all goes well, fairly large amber-coloured eggs will be seen underneath the trap, not necessarily a large number, for most of them will still be hidden among the spawning medium. If the adults appear to have lost interest in each other, it is safe to assume that they have finished spawning. If, however, they are still chasing and the male is driving the female into the thickets, watch closely and you may be lucky enough to witness the actual spawning.

When all is over, remove the parents and wait for twenty-four hours. Make sure that all the eggs are free of fungus and start hunting for minute fry hanging on the glass. Most Barbs hatch in thirty-six to forty-eight hours but if you are not sure exactly when the spawning took place, you could be up to twelve hours adrift in your calculations.

As soon as you see the fry hanging on the sides of the glass, insert two or three pieces of crushed old lettuce leaves into the tank and introduce extremely mild aeration, preferably using a fine diffuser stone. This current of air should be just sufficient to create a slow circulation of the water. Any violent movement at this stage will harm the fry.

After two days of 'hanging on', the fry will leave the glass, their yolk-sac being absorbed, and start swimming around looking for minute food. By now the lettuce will be producing a fine infusoria, seen in the aquarium as a cloud of suspended matter, but actually composed of minute moving organisms, identifiable under a low-power microscope.

The Barb fry will live off these infusorians for about four days, when they will be large enough to eat micro-worms and newly hatched brine shrimp. Two weeks on this menu and they will be ready to take dust-fine 'dried food' and finely chopped tubifex. At this stage the trap may be removed.

If the spawning is a large one (up to 600 eggs are possible), you will have to move the fry carefully into larger tanks. To avoid large losses, care must be taken to ensure that the temperature and water conditions are similar. Netting must be done with a soft, fine mesh net to avoid any damage to the fry.

At this stage, aeration and filtration definitely increase the growth rate, and to raise the young

from seeing their own reflection in the glass base of the tank, a deterrent to the spawning process. Experience also shows that raising the fry to maturity is far more difficult when using gravel than with the aid of a simple trap in a plain tank.

Some form of spawning medium will be required to place inside the trap. Ideally, fine-leaved plants such as *Ambulia*, *Cabomba* or Hornwort should be used, though care must be taken not to introduce snails or disease. However, since the plant will almost certainly be of no further value once the fishes have spawned and the eggs hatched, it is preferable to use an artificial medium which can easily be scalded and used again later for another spawning.

There are many different materials available, weighted nylon wool being especially successful. This may either be placed on the base of the trap, using several strands of unravelled wool, or made into mops cut from short lengths—i.e. 2″–3″ long, and knotted to a strip of lead. When submerged in the trap, they resemble anemones.

Another very useful medium is coconut or similar fibre, which should be washed and scalded before use. Do not put too much spawning material in the trap or the fishes will not have enough room to chase each other.

The water temperature is not critical, but aim to set it at about 4°F. higher than the conditioning tank where the breeding pair are kept. This rise in temperature is often enough to trigger off the spawning. Placing the tank in a position to receive a little sunlight also seems to stimulate breeding.

Barbus arulius Arulius Barb (to 5″)

quickly to maturity it is advisable to change one-fifth of the water in the tank every other day. It is safe to top up with warmed tap water, thus gradually changing the water conditions from soft to natural tap water hardness.

A watchful eye must be kept on the fry since Tiger Barbs are susceptible to foul or unsuitable water conditions, and if the oxygen level falls they will crowd at the surface of the tank, gasping for air. When this happens you must change half the water and increase the aeration rate.

The growing Tiger Barbs will require considerable tank space. If this is not available, it is better to confine yourself to a modest number of fry, culling out the smallest ones as you go along.

Brief details and notes of interest follow about some of the more common varieties of Barbs.

Barbus arulius **Arulius Barb:** This is one of the larger Barbs, from Malaya, growing to 5″. Although it has been known since 1849, it has only recently been seen by aquarists in any numbers. Certainly it makes a striking addition to any large community Barb tank.

The young fish has fairly attractive markings and a pleasant overall hue. When mature, however, the male has extensions to the rays of the dorsal fin and the colour increases in intensity.

It is a very active yet peaceful fish. Breeding habits have yet to be fully investigated, but, apart from a larger tank, it is likely to require nothing different from the basic Barb set-up.

Barbus conchonius **Rosy Barb:** This fish from north-west India must rank with the Tiger Barb as the most popular member of the family and is ideal for the beginner because of its extreme hardiness. It will withstand wide temperature ranges and adverse water conditions and is resistant to most diseases. If lives for at least three years and grows to 6″.

The colour of the male is basically an olive-green with shiny, silver-green reflections. There is a black spot near the rear of the fish and the dorsal fin is heavily edged with black. In spawning condition he has a beautiful rosy hue all over the body. The female lacks these gaudy colours.

It is probably the simplest of all Barbs to breed. The fry are usually numerous and grow to maturity in approximately five months.

Barbus conchonius Rosy Barb (to 6″) 3″

Barbus cumingi **Cuming's Barb:** This delightful Barb comes from mountain forest streams of Ceylon and grows to 2″. The overall body colour is silver with a golden sheen. The two thick black bars on the body are very distinctive and the scales are edged with black. The fins of the male are orange and the female lacks the deeper colour of her mate.

They are very easy to keep, hardy, eating almost anything and apparently fairly immune to disease. Unfortunately, however, they seem reluctant to breed, and the few successful recorded attempts have made use of old, mature rain water, in subdued lighting. This fish is also found in two distinct colour varieties, the other having bright yellow fins instead of orange.

Barbus everetti **Clown Barb:** A colourful large Barb, the female growing to $5\frac{1}{2}$″ but the males only to $4\frac{1}{2}$″. The body colour is browny-orange and it has several broken dark bars. The fins are poppy-red.

It likes to eat soft-foliaged plants and should, therefore, be kept with *Cryptocoryne*-type plants. It

is one of the most prolific Barbs, especially for its size, capable of producing over 2000 eggs from one spawning.

Barbus fasciatus **Striped** or **Zebra Barb:** Sometimes called *B. lineatus*, but this only seems to be a local colour variant under an incorrect name. It is fairly large, growing to $4\frac{1}{2}$″, and comes from the Malay Peninsula. Its basic colour is silver, with several thin black stripes running horizontally along the body. The dorsal and anal fins are yellow, whereas the rest are colourless.

They are not as popular as most other Barbs, due partly to size and also to the fact that they appear to be rather prone to disease.

Barbus filamentosus **Filament Barb:** This fish from Malaya caused several headaches when it was first imported, for in its immature state it closely resembles *B. mahecola*, differing only in ray counts and lack of barbels. When young it is rather like an elongate Tiger Barb, with four thick dark bars. On maturing, the bars disappear and an oval black

Barbus everetti Clown Barb (to $5\frac{1}{2}''$)

Barbus fasciatus Striped/Zebra Barb (to $4\frac{1}{2}''$)

Barbus cumingi Cuming's Barb (to $2''$)

Below: *Barbus gelius* Golden Barb (to 1½″)

Above: *Barbus filamentosus* Filament Barb (to 6″)

Below: *Barbus hulstaerti* (to 1½″)

spot is left near the caudal peduncle. The males develop long dorsal extensions and make a fine picture, as they dart around the tank. Since they grow to about 6″, they require a large tank for spawning, and may lay over 1000 eggs. They prefer a vegetarian diet and eat quantities of Duckweed.

Barbus gelius **Golden Barb:** This is one of the smallest of the Barbs kept, being fully grown at 1½″. It is found naturally in quiet water areas of Central India. It is not as popular as it should be, perhaps due to lack of vivid colour, although given the correct surroundings, the golden hues of this diminutive fish make it an attractive addition to the tank. It is best kept in fairly well planted aquaria together with other small fishes. It is very undemanding and takes all small foods. Though not inclined to breed as readily as some of its relatives, given a tank with plenty of spawning media and soft, mature water, a pair can often be induced to lay up to 100 eggs. They are avid egg eaters, so care must be taken to remove them as soon as possible. The fry hide effectively, tending to remain on the underside of leaves or spawning material, or pressed against the tank glass.

Barbus lateristriga Spanner/'T' Barb (to 6″)

Below: *Barbus nigrofasciatus* Nigger Barb/Black Ruby (to 2½″)

Barbus hexazona **Six-banded Barb:** Although this extremely attractive fish is found in great numbers in its native Malaya, it is a very bad traveller. Since imported specimens either die immediately or rarely recover fully from their long journey, they are not often seen at their best.

It grows to 2¼″ and the body colour is a golden orange. The six black bars are evenly spaced, the first one running through the eye. It is rarely bred and requires very soft water. It is also an extremely avid egg eater.

Because of the high mortality rate, it is not frequently available and tends to be expensive.

Barbus hulstaerti: This is another of the small Barbs, only growing to 1½″. It was not discovered until 1945 and although still comparatively rare, is bound to grow in popularity. It is an African species, from the Congo, and at present very little is known about its breeding habits. It prefers to be kept in a shoal, losing both colour and energy if kept alone with other large fishes.

As yet this fish has no common name, but no doubt as soon as it is seen in numbers, a suitable one will be found. It is a very lovely species.

Below: *Barbus oligolepis* Checker Barb (to 2″)

123

Barbus lateristriga **Spanner Barb, 'T' Barb:** A fairly large Barb, growing to 6″, from the Malay Peninsula. The body colour is silver-grey, with two thick, vertical black bars on the front of the body, and a thinner horizontal line running from the last bar to the caudal peduncle.

Sexing is not easy and body depth is the only sure guide. It too is very prolific and requires a fair amount of swimming space.

Barbus nigrofasciatus **Nigger Barb, Black Ruby:** This is one of the old favourites, a very placid fish, not requiring any special conditions. It comes from Ceylon, where it inhabits sluggish water areas. It grows to about 2½″ and lives for several years. Two or more males in a tank provide a splendid spectacle, for the colours produced as they show off to one another frequently surpass even their breeding hues. The overall colour deepens to a beautiful purple, with a cherry-red head. The females are comparatively drab, with little or no colour in the fins. Breeding is simple and the fry take a little longer to reach full size than most other Barbs.

Barbus oligolepis **Checker Barb:** Another small Barb, only growing to 2″, this perky fish with its erect fins is very suitable for the beginner. The Checker Barb comes from Sumatra, and given soft lighting will show off his distinctive markings to full advantage. The males have the brilliant orange fins, edged with black, and their body markings are far more distinct than those of the females.

The fishes come into breeding condition very easily and the females are clearly distinguishable, full of roe. As soon as the males start to show off to one another it is time to attempt a spawning. They will not breed as readily as some other Barbs, but once a pair settle down in the spawning tank, there are no problems. They produce broods of 150–200 fry, which can be raised in the usual manner.

Barbus schuberti **Schubert's Barb:** This fish is one of the mysteries of the aquatic world, since it is not found in the wild state. It is certainly a man-made coloured fish, but of very obscure origin. Some say that it is a colour variation of *B. semifasciolatus*, others claim it to be a strain of *B. sachsi*. The first fish is believed to have come from an American breeder—Tom Schubert—hence the name, which, incidentally, is not scientifically recognised.

It is a bright yellow fish with deep orange fins. The male fish has a row of black spots on the body which are absent in the female.

Breeding is fairly easily achieved by using the usual Barb method.

Barbus schwanenfeldi **Tinfoil Barb:** Among the largest of the Barbs, when first imported they won rapid popularity with their large silver scales and orange, black-edged fins. These original importations, about 3″–4″ long, proved to be young specimens and adult fishes may grow up to 18″ in aquaria. This rather limits their use in ordinary tanks—a pity, for they are delightful fishes. A further problem is that they are both avid plant eaters and giant jumpers, so they require large, unplanted tanks with close-fitting lids.

Barbus semifasciolatus **Half-banded Barb:** One of the few fishes of Chinese origin kept by tropical aquarists, quite capable of withstanding fairly low temperatures. It is an elongate Barb, growing to about 3½″. The body colour is a greenish-gold with numerous thin, dark, incomplete bars. The fins are a rusty red with no dark markings. The male is a more colourful and slimmer fish. They breed fairly easily but are avid egg eaters.

Barbus stoliczkanus **Stoliczk's Barb:** An extremely beautiful Barb from Burma, growing to 2½″. The basic colour is olive, but it has large silver scales with dark edges. There is a black spot on the caudal peduncle which is surrounded by a golden 'halo'. The black, drop-shaped bar on the gill cover should be well pronounced. The male has a bright red dorsal fin edged with black and a black crescent in the centre.

This fish was at one time considered a sub-species of *B. ticto*, but is now thought to be a distinct species. It has a complete lateral line and no barbels.

It breeds very easily in typical Barb manner and

Barbus schuberti Schubert's Barb (to 3″)

PENGILLEY

Barbus schwanenfeldi Tinfoil Barb (to 18″)

Barbus semifasciolatus Half-banded Barb (to 3½″)

Barbus stoliczkanus Stoliczk's Barb (to 2½″)

KAHL

PENGILLEY

Barbus tetrazona Tiger Barb (to 2½″)

Barbus tetrazona Tiger Barb, albino

Barbus titteya Cherry Barb (to 2″)

can produce 300–400 eggs. The fry, greedy feeders, grow fairly rapidly. Again, plenty of space will be required to grow on a brood.

Barbus tetrazona **Tiger Barb:** Probably the most popular of all the Barbs, it comes from Sumatra and grows to 2½″. The body colour is basically a golden yellow, with four thick, distinct black bars. The males have deep orange-red fins and a bright red snout. The females are easily spotted by their comparative lack of colour and their deep, convex body shape.

The reputation these fishes have acquired for being fin-nippers and bullies is grossly exaggerated. Although the occasional trouble-maker is found, they are, on the whole, a peaceful species.

Lack of oxygen is harmful to them and the danger signal is when they are seen with their noses at the surface and tails hanging down. Immediate action must be taken to save fishes in this state. Fresh water or an aerator restores full health.

Breeding procedure for Tiger Barbs has already been described in detail. An albino form of *B. tetrazona* has become popular in recent years.

Barbus ticto **Ticto Barb:** A very common Barb from Ceylon and all parts of India. It resembles its close relative, *B. stoliczkanus,* but has certain distinguishing features—the lateral line is incomplete, it has a small black spot behind the gill instead of a bar, and the red and black colouration in the dorsal is much reduced. It has the same lively disposition but tends to grow a little larger, reaching full maturity at about 3½″.

When in breeding condition the males show an overall reddish hue on the body. All the comments on *B. stoliczkanus* regarding spawning and the rearing of the fry also apply to *B. ticto*.

Barbus titteya **Cherry Barb:** One of the favourite Barbs, the brilliant cherry colouration of the male in breeding condition being renowned. The Cherry, which comes from quiet, shady streams in Ceylon, only grows to 2″, yet is very hardy and long-lived. Apparently there are two distinct colour varieties found in the wild, one from the warmer lowland areas. In tank-bred specimens only one colour strain seems to prevail.

When spawning, the male fishes are very hard drivers and dense cover must be given for the female or she may be killed. It is often good practice to use two females to one male for breeding attempts.

Barbus vittatus **Silver Barb:** A hardy little Barb, coming from India and Ceylon. It grows to about 2″, the males tending to be smaller, and lives to a great age, specimens having been known to live and breed in aquaria for eight or nine years. It is distinctive, although not brilliantly coloured, with small black spots on the caudal peduncle and at the base of the anal fin. It also has a black bar on the dorsal. When in good condition, it exhibits a brilliant green line along the body, starting behind the gill cover and ending at the base of the tail. The fins are yellow and there are no barbels.

It is not fussy about water conditions and will spawn regularly.

Barbus viviparus **'Live-bearing' Barb:** This fish is included, chiefly because of its interesting background, as suggested by the common name. It is an African Barb, from Natal, growing to 2½″, basically a silvery, elongate fish, with two thin black lines running longitudinally. It also has a distinct black spot at the base of the anal fin.

When it was first dissected by Weber in 1897, he discovered young fry inside the body, and promptly named the fish *viviparus* (live-bearing). Much later these fry were identified as young Cichlids, obviously the last meal of the 'type-fish'.

DANIOS, RASBORAS AND MINNOWS

The Danios, Rasboras and Minnows form the largest division of the Cyprinidae family. There is great diversity in colour, shape and size within the group but most of them are shoal fishes found in vast numbers in their natural habitat. Unfortunately, several fishes in this family have proved extremely difficult to induce to spawn, and with the exception of the Danios, the few species that are bred are never very prolific.

DANIOS

This is an extremely active group of fishes found mainly in India, with some species extending their range into Burma. They are omnivorous, oviparous (egg-layers) and are ideal aquarium fishes, especially for the novice. They are very hardy, spawning easily and usually living for two years or more. When fed generously, especially with the occasional meal of daphnia and tubifex, they come into breeding condition very readily. Sexing at this time is simple, the females being generally larger and with very deep bellies. It is advisable to segregate the sexes prior to breeding, otherwise they will spawn in the community tank.

Very few special requirements are needed to breed these fishes. For the smaller species, an 18″ × 10″ × 10″ tank is large enough, but for such fishes as *Danio malabaricus*, a 24″ × 12″ × 12″ tank is necessary. All of them lay large numbers of small, clear, non-adhesive eggs, and a breeding trap, as described for Barbs, is ideal, though many aquarists still prefer the very simple device of covering the base of the breeding tank with glass marbles or round pebbles. Very shallow water, between 3″–4″ above the base of the trap, is sufficient; deeper water enables the parents, during the spawning chase, to eat vast numbers of eggs before they fall through the holes in the trap. Plants or other spawning media are really a hindrance and need not be included in the set-up. The water is relatively unimportant and except for the fact that it should be freshly drawn, the hardness or pH seem to have little bearing. A temperature around 78°–82°F. is ideal, but the essential point is to maintain it a few degrees above the temperature at which you keep your breeding stock.

If the breeding fishes are introduced in the early evening, they will usually spawn the next day. Trios or two pairs at a time can be spawned in the same tank if one requires large numbers of fry. Provided the fishes are in good condition, an early spawning is more likely by this method.

In order to protect the eggs from their ever-

NIEUWENHUIZEN

Rasbora daniconius Slender Rasbora (to 5")

Below: *Brachydanio frankei* Leopard Danio (to 1¾")

KAHL

Below: *Brachydanio nigrofasciatus* Spotted Danio (to 1½")

KAHL

hungry parents, some aquarists have installed a trap made of glass rods. This may well prove to be unsatisfactory; not only do the parents often get fatally wedged, but raising the fry is far harder.

The eggs hatch between twenty-four and seventy-two hours after spawning and the young 'hang on' to the glass for a further twenty-four hours. The free-swimming fry will require copious feeds of infusoria, either added regularly from an external source or created in the breeding tank itself by putting in crushed lettuce leaves immediately the first fishes hatch.

The fry grow fairly rapidly and are soon large enough to accept brine shrimp, micro-worm and dust-fine dried foods. Good aeration and filtration are extremely beneficial, and if large broods are to be raised, further tank space will be required. A good mixed diet and plenty of fresh water should result in their maturing in about eighteen weeks.

Because of their ease of breeding, natural hybrids have been produced and several other crosses have been obtained by hand-stripping. Unfortunately, these hybrids have proved to be both unattractive and sterile, so apart from academic interest, such methods have not provided the aquarists with any startling new fishes or beautiful colours.

Brachydanio albolineatus **Pearl Danio:** There are two distinct varieties of this fish, one showing the true pearl colour, the other with a golden sheen. In daylight their ever-changing colours are seen best.

Pearl Danios come from Burma and the Malay Peninsula, growing to $2\frac{1}{4}''$. They have a slightly deeper body shape than the Zebra and yet still maintain their streamlined contours.

They breed very easily, laying about 200–300 eggs. These hatch in three to four days and the fry 'hang on' for two more days. The young grow rapidly and at about four months the slimmer males can be easily distinguished from the females.

Brachydanio frankei **Leopard Danio:** This is a very recent discovery in the fish world, only being introduced to aquarists during the last ten years. It is an attractive fish, with a typical Zebra shape, the silvery-blue body being covered with small spots. Its requirements are typical of the genus, but although spawning usually produces large numbers of eggs, the degree of success appears to be much smaller. The percentage of fertile eggs remains low even by using two males to each female, and moreover, the number of 'runts' appearing in each brood is much higher than should be expected. The reason for this is not yet known, but it may be that special water conditions or food are essential.

Brachydanio nigrofasciatus **Spotted Danio:** A very close relative to the Zebra, but with only one horizontal blue stripe in the body and numerous small spots below this line. The fish comes from Burma and only grows to $1\frac{1}{2}''$. It is not as hardy as the Zebra and appreciably more difficult to spawn. Slightly higher temperatures should be used, but even then not every pair can be induced to breed. Keep several pairs and only attempt to spawn those that come into peak breeding condition.

Brachydanio rerio **Zebra Fish:** Certainly one of the most popular of all tropical fishes, the Zebra Fish comes from India, particularly the areas around Bengal, where it inhabits fast-flowing, shallow streams. The basic colour of the back is olive-green, and alternating blue and silver horizontal body stripes run from behind the head into the tail. The anal fin is also striped. The males, when in breeding hue, have a gold sheen over the body. The females grow to around $1\frac{3}{4}''$ and the males a little smaller. They live for about two years and can survive a range of temperature from $55°–100°$F.

Danio devario (to $4''$)

KAHL

Danio malabaricus Giant Danio (to 5″)

Although fairly immune to disease, the young fry seem very susceptible to Velvet and immediate treatment must be given at the first sign of trouble.

Danio devario: A large, chunky Danio, growing to around 4″, this is a native of northern India, but unfortunately is rarely imported. It is greenish-silver, with three blue stripes extending from the centre of the body, converging at the caudal peduncle and extending into the top fork of the caudal. The rear part of the fish has a bluish sheen. The dorsal fin is edged with white, whereas the anal and pelvic fins are tipped with blue.

Breeding is not quite so easy as with some of its closer relatives, but it has a wide temperature range and is very hardy. The sexes are best distinguished by the female's deeper body and paler colours.

Danio malabaricus **Giant Danio:** The Giant Danio comes from the Malabar Coast of India and parts of Ceylon. It grows to a length of 5″. The body colour is a silvery-blue, with several alternate blue and yellow horizontal stripes. The males are slimmer and the fins are a deeper red.

This fish lays adhesive eggs and will, therefore, need some spawning media in the trap to protect the majority of the eggs.

Although a large fish, it is very peaceful and ideally suited to the larger community tank.

RASBORAS

Although a few species are found as far apart as East Africa and China, most of the fifty or so known species come from the Malay Peninsula. They are definitely shoal fishes, found mainly in fast-flowing shallow streams where the water is fairly soft and slightly acid. The majority are slim-bodied fishes with forked tails and rarely exceed 7″. None of the Rasboras have barbels. They are very hardy and easy to keep, eating most foods, but not outstandingly spectacular. Yet although they lack vivid colouration, given the correct conditions of water and lighting, a shoal can be extremely attractive.

Unfortunately, breeding the smaller and more colourful species is much more difficult than some of their larger, less popular relations. Not every male and female form a 'pair' and one must either permute several fish or try flock spawning to get results. Some Rasboras spawn in very distinctive manners, but all require a long shallow tank with soft, slightly acid water. Large quantities of fine-leaved plants or nylon mops will be needed to protect the eggs, as the parents are avid spawn

Brachydanio rerio Zebra Fish (to 1¾″)

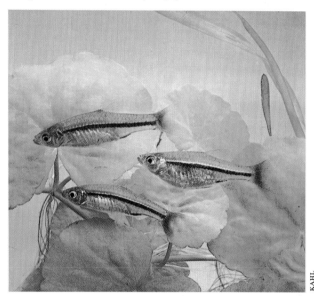

Rasbora borapetensis (to 1¾″)

Brachydanio albolineatus Pearl Danio (to 2¼″)

eaters. Driving is hard and often occurs at first light, when many semi-adhesive eggs are laid in the plant thickets. If the pair have not spawned within three days, either a change of partner will be necessary, or half the water should be replaced by fresh, well-oxygenated rain water.

The eggs hatch in two or three days and although the fry are small, they grow fairly rapidly, soon taking nauplii and brine shrimp. Aeration and filtration in Rasbora tanks ensures good health.

Rasbora borapetensis: This fish was only introduced to the aquarist in 1954 and thus far has no common name. Nor are its breeding habits yet known. It comes from Thailand, where it grows to around 1¾″, the males being slightly smaller and slimmer. The basic body colour is yellowish-green, with a broad, dark horizontal line running from behind the gill cover to the caudal peduncle. This line has a bright golden border and the fins are red-tinged.

Rasbora caudimaculata **Giant Scissortail.** This big cousin of the Scissortail grows to about 8″ in its native haunts of the Malay Peninsula. It differs

Rasbora dorsiocellata Eye-spot Rasbora (to $1\frac{3}{4}''$)   *Rasbora einthoveni* Brilliant Rasbora (to $3\frac{1}{2}''$)

from *Rasbora trilineata* not only in size, but also the lobes of the tail are gaudily daubed with red.

At this time there are no records of the breeding details of this fish, but it is almost certain that it closely resembles its relatives in this respect. A pleasant fish for the larger aquarium.

Rasbora daniconius **Slender Rasbora:** This is a much larger fish, growing to $4''-5''$. The basic colour is silver, with a thin gold-edged, blue-black line running the length of the body. The back has an olive-brown sheen, and the fins are delicate yellow.

A large tank is required for spawning as the chasing is very hard. They lay up to 500 eggs, but will quickly devour these unless adequate protection is given, and the spawning pair removed fairly soon after breeding.

Rasbora dorsiocellata **Eye-spot Rasbora:** A delightful little fish, which lacks bright colours but has very distinctive markings. It comes from Malaya and Sumatra, growing only to a length of about $1\frac{3}{4}''$. It is a very active fish, best seen in a shoal, where its bright green eyes glint in the light.

Rasbora elegans Elegant Rasbora (to 4½″)

The basic body colour is greenish-brown with a silver belly. It has a distinctive black spot in the top of the dorsal, forming a vivid contrast to the white lower edging of this fin.

The sexes of mature specimens can easily be identified, the males being smaller and slimmer in the body. Spawning is best achieved in very shallow water with masses of *Ambulia* or *Myriophyllum*. A layer of peat on the bottom of the aquarium is often found to be beneficial.

Rasbora einthoveni **Brilliant Rasbora:** A very similar fish to *R. daniconius* but noticeably more slender in the body. Found in the Malay Peninsula, it is not as outstanding as its common name might suggest. It grows to around 3½″ and although very peaceful, has not achieved much popularity. It spawns in typical Rasbora manner.

Rasbora elegans **Elegant Rasbora:** A rather attractive large Rasbora, from the Malay Peninsula, growing to 4½″. Although not vicious, it is advisable to keep it with larger fishes.

It is rust-coloured with two large black spots, one in the centre of the body, the other at the base of

the tail. It also has a black mark near the vent. Under the right light, the body takes on a purplish hue. The male is a smaller fish. Though not a ready breeder, it needs no special spawning conditions.

Rasbora hengeli : A very close relation of the Harlequin and easily mistaken for the same. It is, however, smaller, growing only to 1¼″, with a much slimmer body. The dark triangle is thinner and the colours are not nearly as intense. It was only identified in 1955 but is now often imported together with Harlequins.

Conditions for keeping and breeding are as for Harlequins, and it is believed that crosses occur not only in aquaria but also in nature.

Rasbora heteromorpha **Harlequin:** This is easily the most popular of the Rasboras, with a much deeper body shape than the others. It comes from the Malay Peninsula, where it is found in great numbers, growing to around 1¾″, both sexes being the same size. Sexing this fish is not always easy, but in a shoal, the males usually stand out with their brighter colours and slightly slimmer profiles. The Harlequin is rosy-orange with a very distinctive blue-black, triangle-shaped wedge which covers most of the hinder part of the body. The eye is a remarkable red and when in breeding condition the body takes on a violet sheen.

Spawning these fishes is something of an achievement and requires special preparation. A 24″ × 12″ × 12″ tank planted with numerous broad-leaved plants such as *Cryptocoryne* and containing mature, soft acid water, is essential. Diffused lighting should be used, and a temperature around 80°F. is required. It is a debatable matter whether it is better to attempt spawning in pairs or to put in six to eight fishes and let them choose their mates. The female lays adhesive eggs on the underside of broad leaves, three or four at a time. The male follows her and fertilises the eggs, and this process continues with short rests, until about 100 eggs have been laid. Once spawning is over, all fishes should be removed.

The young hatch after twenty-four hours and require very small food. Growth is not startling and the fry should be treated in the same way as other Rasboras.

These delightful fishes are always in demand and vast quantities are regularly imported. They travel exceptionally well and, with the aid of oxygen in the bags, withstand crowded conditions.

Rasbora jacobsoni **Jacobson's Rasbora:** A rather striking Rasbora from Western Sumatra, where it may grow up to 3″, though aquarium specimens are usually slightly smaller. The body is rusty-brown, becoming lighter in the belly areas. A dark black stripe extends from behind the eye down the length of the body, thickening considerably in the centre. There is a bright gold band immediately above this line. The dorsal and anal fins are yellowish-brown, fading towards the edges. A rather indistinct black line runs from the pectoral fins to the anal fin.

The females become very fat when in spawning condition and are easily distinguished from the brighter, slimmer males. Spawning habits are similar to those of the rest of the genus.

Rasbora kalochroma **Clown Rasbora:** A very attractive and peaceable new introduction to the aquarist hobby. It comes from Malaya and grows to around 3″. The fins are set well back in a slender body, which is a handsome red, with a small squarish dark spot just behind the operculum. There is another larger blue-black spot just above the vent. Sexing is very easy, for although both have bright red fins, the male has a black edging to the ventrals and anal.

Rasbora hengeli (to 1¼″)

Rasbora heteromorpha Harlequin (to 1¾″)

Rasbora maculata Spotted/Pigmy Rasbora (to 1″)

Rasbora kalochroma Clown Rasbora (to 3″)

Spawning is again in typical Rasbora fashion, requiring soft, slightly peaty water and masses of fine-leaved plants to achieve the best results.

Rasbora maculata **Spotted** or **Pigmy Rasbora:** One of the smallest of the Rasboras, and indeed, one of the smallest fishes in the world, only growing to 1″. Though large numbers are found in Malaya, especially in small pools, they are poor travellers and few survive the journey. Once established in aquaria, however, they do well and, because of their attractive colours and markings, are very popular.

The Pigmy Rasbora has a brick-red body, with a dark-blue blotch behind the gill cover, a small dot at the base of the tail, and another at the vent. The female has two spots near the vent, which on some specimens appear to merge and form an elongate bar. The fins are streaked with red and have minute black dots on the borders.

This is not an easy fish to induce to spawn — mature, peaty water being required. Often a pair will not spawn until they have been together for two or three days. Then the male drives hard and up to 100 small amber eggs are laid in the plant thickets. The fry need very small food at first, but their subsequent growth is very rapid.

Rasbora pauciperforata **Red-striped** or **Glowlight Rasbora:** A very slender fish which grows to $2\frac{3}{4}$″. It too comes from the Malay Peninsula, living in areas of shallow soft water with subdued light. It has an olive-brown back and a silvery belly. The outstanding feature is a brilliant copper-red line running the length of the body. This is edged below with a narrow black stripe, and above with a thin gold band. The eye is again brilliant red, and the fins are almost transparent.

Breeding is very difficult and attempts should be made using a tank with a peat base and numerous thickly rooted, broad-leaved plants. The fishes spawn among the roots. The fry are difficult to see but grow fairly rapidly, at first requiring fine infusoria but quickly moving on to brine shrimp.

Rasbora trilineata **Scissortail:** A well established favourite, which, although growing to 7″–8″ in its native Malaya, is rarely seen above 3″ in aquaria. It has a silvery, almost transparent body, with a thin black line running from the centre to the

Rasbora trilineata Scissortail (to 3″)

Rasbora urophthalma Tail-spot Rasbora (to 1″)

Rasbora pauciperforata Red-striped/Glowlight Rasbora (to 2¾″)

Tanichthys albunobes White Cloud Mountain Minnow (to 1½″)

Balanteocheilus melanopterus Silver Shark (to 7")

caudal peduncle. There is often a greenish sheen over the whole fish. The distinctively marked forked tail and its characteristic habit of opening and closing it in scissor-like manner, while remaining motionless, give the fish its common name. Each lobe has a black blotch with a white area below it. The rest of the fin varies from yellow to light orange.

The Scissortail will spawn at quite a small size in typical Rasbora fashion.

Rasbora urophthalma **Tail-spot Rasbora:** A very small Rasbora from Sumatra which only grows to 1″. It is not an outstanding fish, having a brownish back with a silver belly. A blue-black line, edged with gold, starts behind the eye and ends just before the caudal peduncle and a very distinctive black spot, surrounded by a brilliant golden 'halo', adorns the base of the tail.

This fish breeds in a similar manner to the Harlequin, laying its eggs on the underside of leaves as well as in plant thickets. So one must set up a tank suitable for both methods. The small fry require very fine infusoria as a first food.

Rasbora vaterifloris Pearly/Fire Rasbora (to 1½″)

Rasbora vaterifloris **Pearly** or **Fire Rasbora:** This is an attractive fish from Ceylon, similar in body shape to the Harlequin, but with longer and more pointed finnage. It grows to only 1½″. There are two colour varieties found, both having a pearly green body, but one with a pronounced reddish sheen in most of the fins.

MINNOWS AND OTHER CYPRINIDS

There are numerous fishes in this loosely termed group that are popular with aquarists, ranging from the tiny White Cloud Mountain Minnow to the giant Black Shark.

Aphyocypris pooni **Venus Fish:** This fish is so similar to the White Cloud Mountain Minnow that only a close examination will show the difference. The main distinguishing factor is the dorsal fin, which on the White Cloud is yellow at the base and edged with red, whereas the Venus Fish is red at the base, yellow outside and edged with blue.

Balanteocheilus melanopterus **Silver Shark:** A truly magnificent species, which has only recently been introduced from Thailand. It is seen in aquaria up to 7″ and has a fairly slim silver body. All the large fins are held erect and are orange in colour, deeply edged with black. It is a fast swimmer and often leaps out of the water when startled.

Breeding attempts have not been successful.

Epalzeorhynchus kallopterus **Flying Fox:** An attractive, distinctive fish from Sumatra where it grows to around 6″. Aquarium specimens rarely exceed

Epalzeorhynchus kallopterus Flying Fox (to 3½″)

Morulius chrysophekadion Black Shark (to 18″)

3½″ but are good community tank fishes. The body is slender, tending to be flat underneath. The top half is olive-brown, darkening to black. A bright golden stripe extends the length of the body, arching near the dorsal. The belly is yellowish-silver. The reddish dorsal fin is always erect and has a broad black bar. Although peaceful towards other fishes, it should not be kept with other specimens of its own kind. No breeding details available.

Esomus danrica **Flying Barb:** A misnomer since this fish is not a Barb at all. In shape it is like a Rasbora, yet it possesses two very large pairs of barbels. The back is olive-brown and the belly silver. A dark brown stripe runs the length of the body, with a golden band above. There is a red spot at the base of the caudal fin.

This fish grows to 4″ and spends most of its time at the surface. It has two well developed pectoral fins, enabling it to leap high above the water so a tank cover is necessary.

Breeding occurs in plant thickets near the surface, but since the eggs are non-adhesive, protection in the form of large pebbles on the bottom of the aquarium produces the best results.

Labeo erythrura Red-finned Shark (to 4½″)

Labeo bicolor Red-tailed Black Shark (to 7″)

Labeo bicolor **Red-tailed Black Shark:** By far the most popular of this group, a native of Thailand, well-known for its jet black body, and extremely brilliant red tail. Good specimens grow to 7″.

This fish is more active than *Morulius chrysophekadion*, and very quarrelsome towards its own species. Although spawnings have been reported, very few details are available.

Labeo erythrura **Red-finned Shark:** A smaller fish, also from Thailand, which only reaches a length of $4\frac{1}{2}$″ and has a slightly different shape from the rest of the family. The mouth is not situated so far underneath and the body is more streamlined. The basic colour is a brownish-grey and all the fins are bright red. This fish swims in the middle of the tank and feeds more off the plants than off the bottom. Again there is no record available of this fish having been bred in captivity.

Morulius chrysophekadion **Black Shark:** This fish from Thailand is the largest of the 'Shark' family, growing in the wild to 18″. When young it is jet black, but this colour fades with age. A harmless fish, it spends most of its life grubbing on the bottom, foraging with its barbel-covered mouth. It lives mainly on algae and is also known to remove soft growth from plants. As yet this species has not been bred in aquaria.

Tanichthys albunobes **White Cloud Mountain Minnow:** This fish is found in the White Cloud Mountain areas of Canton, China, where it inhabits fast-flowing mountain streams. For this reason it can endure a wide seasonal temperature range and may be kept successfully in outdoor ponds during the summer months. It grows to $1\frac{1}{2}$″ and lives for two or three years. This fish has an olive-brown back and a white belly. An iridescent blue-green band extends along the length of the body. Before reaching maturity it rivals the Neon Tetra for brilliance, at one time being known as 'the poor man's Neon'. Unfortunately, as the fish gets older and larger, the colours lose their glow.

Breeding is best carried out with a spawning trap and plenty of nylon mops. Several pairs or trios can be introduced as not all spawn readily. If well fed, the parents do not eat their eggs, and continue to breed over a period of days. The fry are easily raised, requiring no special treatment.

LABYRINTHS

FISHES of the Labyrinth or Anabantid family, together with their near relatives, Luciocephalidae and Ophicephalidae form an interesting group. They are remarkable for being air-breathing, having developed a special accessory organ which enables them to use atmospheric air to supplement the gills. They are not unique in this respect, for several groups of fishes have evolved different ways of utilising the atmosphere, but apart from the primitive Lung-fishes, few possess such an efficient apparatus. So dependent upon air have some of them become that they will actually drown if denied access to the atmosphere.

Because of this accessory breathing organ, these fishes are able to live in the dirtiest, muddiest waters, under conditions in which no fish dependent upon gills could survive. Some species are even able to leave the water and propel themselves overland to another pond or stream. This characteristic has given the name Climbing Perch to the fish known scientifically as *Anabas testudineus*, which is frequently found, particularly after rain, wriggling along on the ground. Indeed, there are reports of them being found up trees. These fishes have a very wide distribution, covering the whole of Africa south of the Sahara Desert region, while in Asia they occur from the Indian Peninsula through to China, extending south into the Philippines and the Malay Archipelago. No single species extends over this entire range, of course, and some are quite local in distribution.

The Anabantidae have the most highly-developed form of this accessory breathing organ.

This structure, known as the labyrinth, is situated on both sides of the gill chamber, and consists of plates covered by a layer of folded, wrinkled skin. It is a vascular organ, provided with many small blood vessels close to the surface, facilitating the gaseous exchange with the contained air. The fish visits the surface of the water from time to time to expel a bubble of spent air and gulp a fresh supply to refill the labyrinth. The inside of the organ is actually moist, for no breathing apparatus, be it lung, gill or labyrinth, can function without moisture, gaseous exchange only being possible when in solution.

The labyrinth is not present in the newly hatched or young fish and develops gradually during the first few weeks of life. As the fish matures, however, the organ becomes indispensable, normal gill breathing being inadequate to meet the oxygen requirements of the adult.

Fishes of this family are found in all kinds of water—in muddy drainage ditches, flooded paddy fields, irrigation channels, ponds, streams, weed-

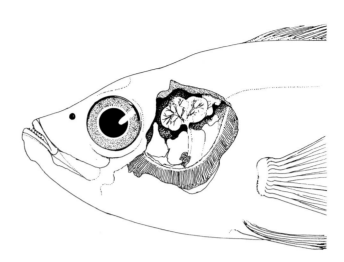

The labyrinth organ of the Anabantids enables the fishes to breathe atmospheric air and to survive in waters low in oxygen content.

choked rivers and swift-flowing mountain streams. Most species have no special feeding requirements and are quite prepared to take whatever is offered. As with most fishes, however, a mixed diet is best. The usual live and dried foods, sometimes with a vegetable supplement, are perfectly acceptable.

A temperature of 70°–75°F. suits most of them very well, although one or two species from the northern parts of China and Korea prefer a lower temperature, say 65°F. Yet most species can stand temporary falls in temperature down to as low as 55°F., and some, notably the Paradise Fishes and the Climbing Perch, can endure drops down to freezing point without suffering any harm.

Their accommodating habits make them, in most cases, ideal aquarium fishes. Many are long-lived and become very tame. But one or two species, being predators, are inclined to be snappish and are best kept alone, particularly when sexually mature. These will be mentioned later.

BREEDING

Breeding is usually not difficult. Most species of the Asiatic Anabantids are bubble-nest builders. The male fish constructs a foam nest by blowing bubbles, each of which is surrounded by a secretion from the mouth to prevent immediate collapse. The nest is usually constructed among floating plants and debris which help to hold it together. When all is

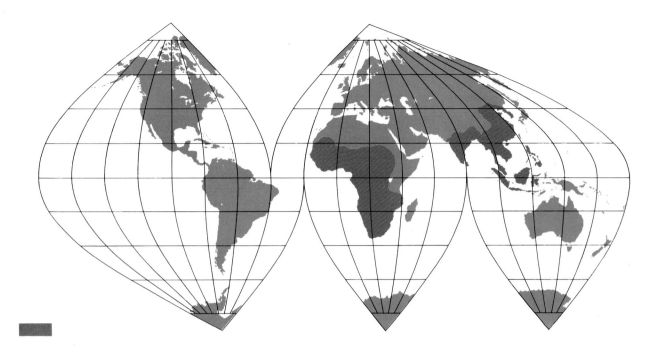

Distribution of Labyrinths in parts of Asia and Africa

ready the female is enticed to the nest and the male embraces her by wrapping his body right round her. Together they roll over, and as the eggs are extruded and fertilised, slowly sink through the water, separating just clear of the bottom. The male gathers the eggs in his mouth and blows them up into the bubble-nest. The whole procedure is then repeated until all the eggs are laid. In some species the eggs themselves, containing an oil droplet which gives them buoyancy, float. The eggs are usually very small and numerous, sometimes as many as 2,000 being produced at one spawning.

When spawning is completed the male takes complete charge, driving the female away from the nest. At this stage she should be removed in order to avoid her being damaged or even killed. The male then spends his time repairing the nest, replacing any burst bubbles with new ones, and catching and replacing any eggs or fry that may fall out of the nest. The young usually hatch within 36 hours and, depending on the temperature, are free-swimming in two or three days. It is best to remove the male at the end of the second day as his paternal instinct is short-lived and he may be tempted to eat the young. The tank should be kept closely covered during the period of nest building and afterwards, until the fry are about three weeks old, the atmosphere kept both moist and warm. The young fishes are particularly sensitive to both

Male *Betta splendens* building bubble nest

Fry of *Betta splendens* clinging to glass after leaving bubble nest

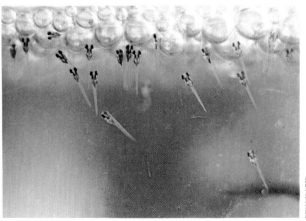

145

Above: *Belontia signata* Combtail (to 5″)   Below: *Anabas testudineus* Climbing Perch (to 3″)

draughts and chill and will succumb rapidly to either. Otherwise, though very small, they are quite hardy, and during their first few days require the very finest of ground food. Growth will be rapid provided there is a sufficient supply of the smallest infusorians and algae in the form of green water.

A few species do not construct the typical bubble-nest but lay their eggs at random in the water. These float to the surface to hatch; and of course there is no parental care. Other species, of the genus *Betta*, are mouth-brooders, this type of parental care also being found in the family Cichlidae.

The following few are the better known species.

Anabas testudineus **Climbing Perch:** This species is infrequently kept, for it lacks attractive colours, ranging from grey to silvery-green, lighter on the underside, up to 10″ in length, but in captivity rarely exceeds 3″. It has a wide distribution, being found in India, South China, Ceylon, the Malay Archipelago and the Philippines. The sexes may be distinguished quite easily, the female having a shorter anal fin and a soft dorsal fin.

It is a difficult fish to keep successfully in captivity, being very shy and rather pugnacious. It is virtually omnivorous but requires a supplement of vegetable food, shredded lettuce or spinach making a good substitute for algae.

A large, heavily planted tank, with many hiding places is required, closely covered at all times to prevent the fish leaping out from even the smallest aperture. It is usually seen resting on the bottom by means of its pectoral fins, on which, with the aid of its gill covers, it waddles along both under water and on dry land. According to Meinken it will breed at temperatures in the lower 70's F., laying eggs at random which float to the surface. These hatch within twenty-four to thirty-six hours, and are not eaten by the parents, who also ignore the fry. It is reported to burrow into the mud at the start of the dry season, waiting for the rains in similar fashion to the African Lung-fishes. Where found in large quantities as in India, it is used as a food fish, and even eaten raw.

Belontia signata **Combtail:** Another species rarely kept by the aquarist, probably because of its rather unexciting colouration. In young specimens green is the dominant colour but as the fish matures reddish hues develop until it may ultimately become a deep mahogany-brown colour with a poorly-defined pattern of lighter bars on the flanks. Its outstanding feature is the apparently ragged caudal fin, which, resembling a comb, gives it its popular name. The dorsal fin of the male is drawn out into a fine point extending over half the length of the tail, that of the female is rounded.

The forward rays of the pelvic fins are produced into points about twice the length of the main body of the fin. The dorsal and anal fins and the tail are of the same colour as the body, the pectoral fins being colourless.

In literature this fish is always reported to be savage and shy, generally an unsatisfactory aquarium inhabitant. Personal experience shows this to be an exaggeration. When kept in family groups or in the company of fishes of its own size, vicious tendencies are usually only seen at breeding time. A mixed diet is acceptable, which, as the fishes are by nature predatory, should be composed predominantly of meat. They are bubble-nest builders, breeding in the typical manner, the male taking charge. For general maintenance a temperature of 70°F. is satisfactory, but for breeding the temperature should be raised to 75°–77°F.

Natives of Ceylon, Combtails are reported to attain a size of about 5″ in the wild; in the aquarium, however, they seldom exceed 4″ from snout to caudal peduncle.

Betta splendens **Siamese Fighting Fish:** One of the most popular aquarium fishes, particularly with the beginner, intrigued at the idea of a 'fighter'. It is favoured by specialist breeders and domestic stocks have been bred, which, apart from the basic body structure, bear little resemblance to anything found in nature. From the wild stock, first bred in France in 1893, we now have varieties in a great range of colours, blues, greens, reds and black, with finnage so over-developed that when expanded, the shape of the fish sideways-on is almost a complete circle.

Many stories have been told of these fishes being kept and bred in Thailand for their fighting qualities, and of wagers being placed on such battles. These tales appear to have little substance. In fact, it is doubtful whether the fish is widely known in Thailand at all. Perhaps such contests do take place in Malaysia, where this fish is also found, for the Malayans are reputed to be great gamblers.

The males of this species are certainly aggressive, but normally only towards one another. The only time the female is liable to be attacked is if she is not ready to spawn when a nest is built, and if, after she is spent, she does not retire from the nest. Towards all other fishes, provided they are large enough not to be regarded as food, the Fighting Fish is peacefully inclined. It will, however, defend itself if attacked or annoyed, and is capable of

Betta splendens Siamese Fighting Fish (to 2½″), green variety

Betta splendens, blue variety

Betta splendens, long-finned 'phantom' variety

Betta splendens, red variety

inflicting considerable damage with its jaw teeth.

So many different descriptions of the native fish are to be found in the literature of the species, as to render them somewhat suspect. Since the wild stock is no longer imported into Europe, it is impossible to confirm any single report. All descriptions agree, however, on a size of 2″–2½″, bright red pelvic fins with white tips (which are still seen on the domesticated varieties), a sail-like dorsal fin, a long and deep anal fin and a rounded tail. The females possess smaller finnage.

In the wild it is reportedly found in ditches and ponds, usually dirty ones with a heavy growth of water plants. In captivity it is one of the easiest and least demanding of fishes, thriving in almost any

conditions at a temperature of about 70°F. and tolerating occasional drops of temperature down to 65°F. It does best, however, in a shallow (6″) well-planted tank of soft water with some floating plants and a soft peaty bottom, at a temperature of 75°–77°F. Whilst all kinds of food are readily taken, live foods should predominate. The fry particularly require large quantities of food, for they grow rapidly, reaching adult status in four or five months.

One sometimes sees male Fighters kept in bare jars, alongside one another, the idea being that this encourages them to keep their finnage spread, improving the colour and enhancing their development. This is a barbarous practice and much to be deplored. Colour and finnage are controlled

Colisa fasciata Giant Gourami (to 5″)

by genetic make-up and cannot be altered by such treatment. Only by selective breeding can stocks be 'improved' to meet the standards required by the judges on the show bench. This, coupled with the best of living conditions and ample live food will produce far better results than any practices based on ignorance of elementary biological facts.

The breeding behaviour of the Fighter follows the usual bubble-nester pattern. The male constructs a large, loose nest of bubbles, usually among floating plants. The female is embraced by the male and after two or three attempts the eggs are extruded, which float slowly upwards. Both sexes chase them and spit them into the nest. After several embraces, during which several hundred eggs are produced,

the male takes up his parental duties, replacing any eggs, and later fry, that may fall from the nest. The female should be removed immediately spawning is completed, as the male will attack her if she comes anywhere near the nest. The young hatch in about a day and at first are very small indeed. They must be fed with the finest of food, green water and small infusoria being best. At a pinch, boiled egg yolk squeezed through a fine cotton handkerchief may be substituted, but great care must be taken as too much yolk will rapidly decompose and pollute the water, with disastrous results. The male should be removed before the end of the third day as a precaution against waning parental instincts. The tank must be kept closely covered throughout the

Colisa labiosa Thick-lipped Gourami (to 2½″)

Right: *Colisa lalia* Dwarf Gourami (to 1¾″)

nest building and spawning and for at least the first three weeks of life of the young to retain the heat and humidity. Care must be taken when selecting a female for breeding, for if she is not ready to spawn the male may attack and kill her.

Betta brederi, Betta picta and *Betta pugnax* are very seldom seen in captivity, but are interesting inasmuch as they are mouth-breeders.

B. brederi, from Java and Sumatra, is a brownish fish, body length about 3″. The eggs are brooded in the mouth of the male. They hatch in about forty hours and remain in the mouth until able to swim.

B. picta is a smaller fish, only reaching about 2″, found in high mountain streams in Java, Sumatra, and Singapore. It is very variable in colour, according to geographical location. It is reported to be tolerant of low temperatures down to 65°F.

B. pugnax, from Penang Island, is a rather larger fish, growing to about 4″ in the wild. It too is variable in colour and Meinken describes an attractive reddish-brown specimen with a shining blue-green spot on every scale, and bright red fins. At the time of writing, it has not been bred in captivity.

Colisa fasciata **Giant Gourami:** Although this fish is known to aquarists by the name of Giant Gourami it is by no means the largest of the family, nor is it seen as frequently as some of its smaller and more colourful relatives. It grows to about 5″ and is widely distributed, being found throughout Bengal, Burma, Thailand and the Malay Peninsula. Colour is very variable, depending on locality, but is

generally green-brown, with a red eye. There is a brilliant green blotch on the operculum, sometimes with several smaller dots. Several narrow reddish bands cross the flanks and the fins are bluish, the dorsal with red spots, the anal with a red border.

The pelvic fins, which are produced into long feelers, have yellow-white bases with bright red tips.

These feeler-like pelvic fins are characteristic of the Gouramies and have seemingly evolved to assist the fish to live in opaque waters where the eyes are of little or no use. Yet instinct compels the Giant Gourami to use the feelers even in clear water, probing its surroundings like a blind man with a stick. The fins are of course articulated so that they may be moved in all directions, and the fish often swims with feelers extended straight forward.

Care and breeding follows the usual pattern for the bubble-nesters and they are seen to best advantage at a temperature of 73°–75°F. They will tolerate, however, falls of temperature down to well below 60°F. without coming to any harm. When bred they are usually very prolific, 600–1,000 eggs being produced at one spawning.

Colisa labiosa **Thick-lipped Gourami:** This fish, a native of Burma, especially the south, strongly resembles *C. fasciata,* so much so that for many years the two were confused by European fish-keepers. It can be distinguished by its smaller size, seldom reaching 3″ in body length, and by its much thicker lips. Its colour is brownish with an irregular pattern of blue-green and orange-brown bars on the flanks. The dorsal and anal fins are tipped with red and the anal also has a narrow blue line just beneath the red fringing. The tail is brown and the pelvic fins are red in the male, colourless in the female.

Osphronemus goramy Gourami (to 24″)

Also the rear of the anal fin is red in the female and blue in the male.

It requires no special conditions other than those for the family as a whole and seems quite happy in a range of temperature from 68°–78°F.

The eggs, which are lighter than water, are cared for by the male in the typical bubble-nest. This may be quite a ragged and diffuse affair, often little more than a thin layer among the floating vegetation.

Colisa lalia **Dwarf Gourami:** The smallest and most attractive of the three species of *Colisa*, whose native habitat is India, especially Assam and Bengal. It tends to be rather shy and is reported to be susceptible to Velvet disease *(Oodinium limneti-*

cum), though twenty years of personal experience with this species does not support this. The fish grows to $1\frac{1}{2}″$ to $1\frac{3}{4}″$ in the aquarium, and 2″ in the wild. The background colour is red and the flanks are covered with double stripes of bright pale blue and green. These stripes extend into all the vertical fins. The head and that part of the body immediately behind the operculum is a metallic blue-green, while the tail, the end of the anal fin and the pelvic fins are bright red. The females are less brilliantly coloured with the ends of dorsal and anal fins rounded, as against the rather pointed shape in the male.

This little beauty loves plenty of sunshine and thrives amid a heavy growth of algae. Peaceful by nature, it may be safely kept with other fishes of the

151

Helostoma temmincki Kissing Gourami (to 12″) Below: *Trichogaster leeri* Leeri/Pearl Gourami (to 4″)

same size provided it is not bullied. Its ideal medium is a heavily planted tank, kept in bright sunlight, at a temperature of about 72°F.

At breeding time the male constructs a bubble-nest, not very large, and fairly high above the water surface, usually in a corner of the tank among floating vegetation. The egg-laying pattern is typical of the family but the male seems much gentler with the female and never attacks her even when spawning is over. The female, however, should be removed to allow the male to care for his brood in peace. The eggs hatch in about a day and the male should be removed as soon as the fry are seen to be free-swimming. The babies are extremely small and require the very finest of foods. Care must be taken to keep the surface of the water free from chilling draughts. Provided they are well fed, the fry grow quite rapidly and a tank full of six-week Dwarf Gouramies is a most rewarding sight.

Sphaerichthys osphromenoides Chocolate Gourami (to 2″)

HARVEY

Helostoma temmincki **Kissing Gourami:** This fish, sometimes classified as *H. rudolfi*, is another large Gourami, growing to about one foot in length. It comes in two distinct colour varieties, the familiar form being an overall dull pink, with black eyes. The rarer variety is a greenish or yellowish-silver with a darker green back, sometimes with dark stripes on the flank. There are two short, dark vertical marks on the operculum and a brown edge on part of the dorsal and anal fins, which are otherwise greenish. The eye is yellowish-brown.

It is not possible to distinguish the sexes, nor are there authenticated reports of this fish breeding in captivity. It is believed that they lay floating eggs without a bubble-nest or any brood care. They require to be kept very warm and at no time must the temperature be allowed to fall below 70°F. The young fishes grow rapidly in captivity and have enormous appetites. They are predominantly vegetarian, consuming vast quantities of oatmeal or other vegetable flakes floating on the surface, but refusing to feed from the bottom.

The common name appropriately arises from their peculiar habit of coming together, mouth to mouth, and kissing. The significance of this is not known, but they will attempt to do it with other species if these are present. They are used as food fishes in Thailand, the Greater Sunda Islands and the Malay Peninsula.

Osphronemus goramy **Gourami:** This is the real giant of the family, a native of the Great Sunda Islands, and widely distributed throughout the East as a food fish. Since it grows some two feet long it is hardly a domestic proposition but it may

sometimes be seen in the larger public aquaria. Adult fishes are dull reddish-brown to black, but the young are more colourful, a light reddish-brown with a yellowish underside, and some irregular dark stripes and blotches. The fins are bluish, and the pelvics, typically elongated, are bright orange. The dorsal and anal fins of the male fish are pointed, those of the female being rounded.

The fish is a typical bubble-nest builder with the males undertaking care of the eggs and fry. It is essentially vegetarian and will grow rapidly if fed large quantities of foods such as oatmeal porridge or various kinds of cereal flakes.

Sphaerichthys osphromenoides **Chocolate Gourami:** Although known to science since 1860, this fish was not imported into Europe until 1933, and due to the difficulty of breeding and slowness in reaching maturity, wide distribution has been delayed. It is a mouth-breeder and produces very few young at each spawning. The sexes look alike and can only be distinguished when the female is ripe, full of eggs, and fatter than the male.

Native to Sumatra and the Malay Peninsula, these fishes grow to about 2″. The general colour is reddish to chocolate-brown, with a greenish sheen, a number of irregular white or yellow stripes sometimes being present on the flanks. The finnage is brown, often with a dark border and a yellow edge. The species is rather delicate and requires soft, slightly acid and well matured water, with a minimum of light. Live food is essential and a marked preference is shown for mosquito larvae.

Trichogaster microlepis Moonlight Gourami (to 6″)

Trichogaster leeri **Leeri** or **Pearl Gourami:** One of the most beautiful of the Gouramies, found in Borneo, Thailand, Sumatra and the Malay Peninsula. The body resembles mother-of-pearl, covered in small shining dots, and, when in good condition, overshot with orange-red. The pectoral fins, part of the anal fins, throat and breast are orange-red. The long, feeler-like pelvics are reddish, and the remaining fins yellowish. It grows to about $3\frac{1}{2}″$–$4″$ and does not become sexually mature until nearly full grown. The females may be distinguished by the more rounded form of the dorsal fin.

A well-planted tank at a temperature of 70°–75°F. seems to suit this fish well and it will eat most foods. It is not difficult to breed, the male building a large bubble-nest and caring for eggs and young in the typical Anabantid fashion. It has a peaceful temperament, only the males showing slight aggressive tendencies at breeding time.

Trichogaster microlepis **Moonlight Gourami:** This native of Thailand did not reach Europe until 1952 and is still something of a rarity. Whether further stocks have arrived since the original importation by McInerny or whether all present stocks are descendants of the original fishes is something of a mystery. In shape it is very similar to *T. leeri*, but somewhat larger and slimmer. Colour is a uniform bluish-silver with a reddish eye. The elongated pelvic fins are orange-red in the male only, thus forming a distinguishing feature. Breeding requirements are said to be as for the Leeri Gourami, a very large and shallow nest being built. In their native habitat, where they reach a length of 6″, they are used as a food fish.

Trichogaster pectoralis **Snakeskin Gourami:** Another large Gourami of fairly recent importation, coming from Vietnam and the Malay Peninsula. It is more popular than the Moonlight Gourami for it is very hardy, undemanding and prolific. Its colour is not spectacular, greenish with many irregular yellow or golden lines creating the snakeskin effect. The adults will not eat even the smallest of young fishes, so given sufficient room and food the whole of the large broods may be reared. A bubble-nest builder, it will become sexually mature and breed when only 3″ to 4″, although the full-grown fishes will reach about 10″ body size and have to be accommodated in very large tanks.

Trichogaster trichopterus **Three-spot Gourami:** This is an aquarist's favourite, popular because of its attractive mottled blue colour and the ease with which it may be kept and bred. The common name arises from the black spot on the caudal peduncle, another in the middle of the body under the dorsal fin, and the black eye.

A native of Thailand, South Vietnam, the Malay Peninsula and the Great Sunda Islands, it is reported to attain a size of 6″ in the wild. In an aquarium, $4\frac{1}{2}″$–$5″$ is a good sized specimen. It will become sexually mature at about 3″ and breed freely, but experience has shown that better results are obtained in breeding from larger specimens and from pairs matched for size and age. The females should not be prevented from breeding as they are prone to ovary troubles if unable to discharge eggs.

The sexes may be distinguished by the dorsal fin which is pointed in the male and rounded in the

Macropodus concolor Paradise Fish (to $3\frac{1}{2}''$)

female. The females also become excessively fat when ripe. They are bubble-nesters and should be cared for as in the family description.

Trichogaster trichopterus sumatranus **Opaline Gourami:** A variety or sub-species of *T. trichopterus*, with a darker blue colour and lacking the black spots, but sometimes with a diffuse dark marking along the body, seen especially in the males when breeding. Rather smaller than the Three-spot, $3''$ being a good average, it is reported to come from Sumatra, having arisen as a cultivated variety there. Care and breeding as given above.

Macropodus opercularis **Paradise Fish:** One of the most beautiful of all aquarium fishes, though, because of its very pugnacious nature, not seen too frequently. It comes from China, Korea, Vietnam and Formosa, and, like the Goldfish, is a popular aquarium fish in the Orient. *M. concolor*, a more recent introduction, is a closely related species.

This is most probably the fish mentioned by the diarist Samuel Pepys as 'living in a glass and will do so for ever'.

The Paradise Fish, which grows to some $3\frac{1}{2}''$, is vertically striped in brownish-red and blue-green, with black markings about the head and a black spot on the operculum. The pointed dorsal is black as is the lower edge of the anal; the caudal is brownish and drawn out into two points at its outer margins. The female is less colourful, lacking the blue striping, and has shorter fins. An albino

Macropodus cupanus dayi Brown Spike-tailed Paradise Fish (2¾″)

Ctenopoma ansorgei (to 3″)

Ctenopoma acutirostre Spotted Climbing Perch (to 6″)
Ctenopoma kingsleyi Tail-spot Climbing Perch (to 8″)

variety is sometimes seen—white with pink eyes. It is one of the hardiest of all the exotic fishes and will withstand temperatures down to freezing point.

For normal maintenance, it may be kept at a temperature of 55°–65°F., but for breeding this should be raised to 70°F. It is a bubble-nest builder and should be cared for as in the general description. The adults, particularly the males, must not be kept with other fishes, nor, unless in very large tanks where there are numerous hiding places, even with their own kind. They are very vicious and will attack and tear to pieces any intruders.

Macropodus chinensis **Round-tailed Paradise Fish:** A more peaceful relative of the Paradise Fish, less colourful and with shorter finnage. Coming from China and Korea they require a cool temperature, not over 70°F. Though fairly easy to breed in the bubble-nest manner, they are not prolific.

Macropodus cupanus cupanus **Spike-tailed Paradise Fish:** Another peaceful relative of the above, coming from India and Ceylon. The popular name is derived from the tail, drawn out into a single central spike. Care as for the preceding species.

Macropodus cupanus dayi **Brown Spike-tailed Paradise Fish:** A second sub-species of the above, coming from Burma, South Vietnam and the Malabar Coast. It requires the same care and treatment but should be kept at a somewhat higher temperature, say 68°–72°F.

The Paradise Fishes, apart from *M. opercularis*, are rarely seen nowadays in aquaria, which is a pity, for they are undemanding and easy to keep.

In Africa, the Labyrinths are chiefly represented by the genus *Ctenopoma*, known as the African Climbing Perches. These are almost unknown to the aquarist world, but the following species are said to have been imported into Europe.

Ctenopoma acutirostre, C. ansorgei, C. argentoventer, C. congicum, C. fasciolatum, C. kingsleyi, C. multispinis, C. nanum, C. nigropannosum, C. ocellatum, C. oxyrhynchus: All are apparently typical predatory fishes, feeding on small animals, insect larvae and other fishes.

Though rarely seen in aquaria, the family Ophicephalidae are interesting, for all possess an accessory breathing organ in the form of a simple diverticulum from the gill chamber. This permits them to breathe air and thus exist in the dirtiest and muddiest of waters, or even to wriggle their way

Channa asiatica Chinese Snakehead (to 12″)   Below: *Ophicephalus micropeltes* (to 35″)

overland. Indeed, the Chinese Snakehead, *Channa asiatica,* used as a food fish, is carried about in baskets or bags by local fishmongers and has to have several cuts taken from it before it dies.

This fish is occasionally seen in captivity, but in common with the other Snakeheads, members of the genus *Ophicephalus,* it is not a very satisfactory choice. The following Snakeheads have nevertheless been displayed in aquaria.

Ophicephalus africanus, O. lucius, O. marulius, O. micropeltes, O. obscurus, O. pleurophthalmus, O. striatus: All are large predatory fishes, the smallest reaching some 6″ in length and the larger growing to over 3 feet. All are edible and some are valued locally as food fishes. They require large quantities of live food, preferably fishes nearly as large as themselves. Only the young fishes will eat tadpoles or worms. Claims that some can be persuaded to eat meat appear doubtful. They are, of course, quite unsuitable to keep with other fishes, unless their companions are larger. They are reported to have bred in captivity, but the writer has no experience of this. The tank must be kept tightly covered at all times as they are expert jumpers and will also crawl out through quite small gaps.

CICHLIDS

CICHLIDS
OF AMERICA & ASIA

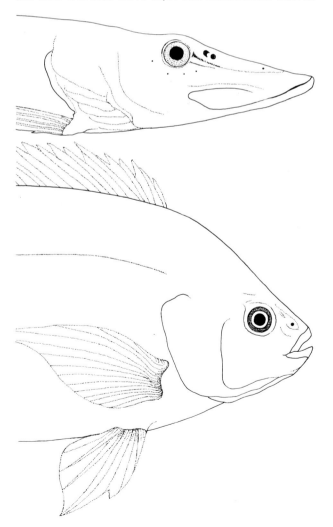

CICHLIDAE, better known to most aquarists as Cichlids, are a family of spiny-rayed fishes resembling the Perches, from which they can be distinguished externally by the presence of only one nostril on each side of the head, whereas the true Perches have two. See illustration below.

The body shape varies with genus from a Pike-like to disc-like form. Most species are usually deep, with a large head and eyes, fairly large scales, and a strong, jutting jaw with well-developed lips. The dorsal fin is long-based and single, the front part being spiny and usually larger than the soft rear part. The anal fin usually consists of at least three spiny rays, and a larger, soft after-part. In almost all species the male dorsal and anal fins are pointed, those of the female rounded. The lateral line is usually in two parts. The first part extends from the gill-cover to just below the soft-rayed part of the dorsal, and the second part looks as if it has been broken off and replaced at a lower level.

The Cichlids are distributed through Africa, including Madagascar, and Syria, with one genus only in southern India and Ceylon. In America they range from Texas, through Central America, including the West Indies, to Uruguay. They are found in still or slow-moving fresh waters with many hiding places, among tree roots, rocks, or under river banks among plant thickets. A few species are sometimes found in brackish waters.

AMERICAN CICHLIDS

The best-known genera found in America are *Aequidens, Apistogramma, Astronotus, Cichlasoma, Crenicara, Crenicichla, Geophagus, Herichthys, Nannacara, Pterophyllum* and *Symphysodon*. Except for the *Apistogramma, Nannacara, Pterophyllum* and *Symphysodon,* most of these fishes are inclined to be quarrelsome

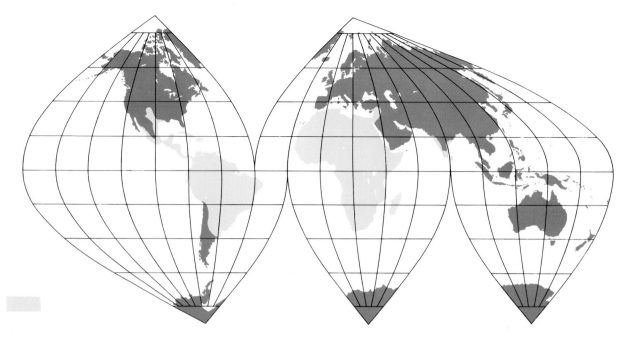

Distribution of Cichlids in Africa, Central and South America, and one genus only in southern India and Ceylon

with their own kind, as well as with other species. They are therefore unsuitable for a community aquarium, and are best kept as pairs in large, deep tanks.

The first requirement is a spacious aquarium, 36″ × 15″ × 15″, or larger. The bottom should be covered with 1″–2″ of medium-grade aquarium gravel, and filled with water. Most Cichlids are not particular about water composition, and tap water is usually suitable. (Exceptions to this rule are dealt with under individual species.) For general care a temperature of 72°–76°F. will suit most species. Heaters and thermostats used inside the aquarium must be securely fixed, because some large Cichlids have the habit of gripping the tubes with their mouths and shaking them vigorously. Water seeping into the tube could be dangerous.

Most large Cichlids like to dig in the bottom and do considerable damage to plants, so only tough, strong-rooted kinds should be used, planted in pots. The aquarium is best furnished with rockwork, and groups of stones. For breeding purposes, flower pots, laid on their sides to form caves, will provide suitable spawning places. Many species are territorial fishes and will defend and enlarge their territory especially when preparing to breed.

Cichlids do not like strong light, and shade can be provided by the use of floating plants. These also help to limit the growth of algae, which often develops in aquaria with such heavy feeders. The Indian or Sumatra Fern (*Ceratopteris thalictroides*) can keep blue-green algae, a common pest, under control. Because of the limited use of plants in these aquaria, however, filtration will almost always be necessary. A partial change of water at frequent intervals will also be welcomed.

Cichlids are not fussy about food, but they require a large amount to stay in good condition. Most of them are carnivorous, but they do like a small amount of vegetable food in their diet. They relish all types of large live foods, as well as crab meat, shrimps, liver and beef heart. Earthworms are ideal, and among suitable vegetable foods are lettuce, spinach, oat flakes and cooked green peas.

BREEDING

The breeding aquarium should be at least 36″ × 15″ × 15″ for the large Cichlids, and 18″ × 10″ × 10″ for the smaller species. Cover the bottom with about 2″ of aquarium gravel, and place in it three or four flat pieces of smooth rock, or large pebbles. Do not use plants, which will soon be ripped out during the spawning preparations. Maintain a temperature of 78°–82°F.

Cichlids are not always easy to sex. With young fishes it is almost impossible, but the mature male can usually be identified by the longer pointed dorsal and anal fins, and the intense colour. The large Cichlids are ready to breed at between one and two years, the smaller species, with a shorter life span, are ready at six months.

There are two methods of selecting fishes for breeding. One is to buy and raise half a dozen young fishes, preferably unrelated, and allow them to pair naturally. The others should then be removed, and the mated pair left in the aquarium. Do not move the pair as this may upset them and stop them from spawning. The second way is to select larger Cichlids which are already adult, placing them in a large aquarium with a glass

Aequidens curviceps Flag Cichlid (to $3\frac{1}{2}''$)

partition between them, and keeping them well fed. Watch them until they show clear mating signs. Often one partner is ready before the other and care must be taken not to remove the partition too early, as this may lead to a fight and even the death of one fish. If the female is ripe, however, and the partition is not removed sufficiently early, she will start laying eggs without the male. These, being unfertilised, will not hatch.

The usual sign that one of the fishes is ready is a darkening or intensification of colour patterns, accompanied by a spreading of the fins. When the other partner shows signs of acceptance, remove the partition, but observe them carefully to make sure that it is safe to leave them alone. If they are ready to spawn, they will face each other, spreading fins, and then, by interlocking their lips, grip and pull each other back and forth in a tug of war. If satisfied that they are equally matched, they will search for a place to spawn. If, however, during the tussle, one breaks off and retreats, the other may take this as a sign of weakness and set out to destroy it. Unless it is able to hide or is immediately removed, it may be killed.

Some days before spawning, the fishes dig pits in

the gravel bottom and start cleaning the rocks, in order to find the most suitable place on which to lay the eggs. They may even decide that the glass at the back or on the base of the aquarium is the perfect spot. Two or three days before spawning, a white protuberance appears at the vent of both fishes. This develops into the breeding tube, and is a positive sign that they are ripe. The fishes usually spawn early in the day, for they will not normally lay their eggs on a site which is too bright or too dark. The female starts the spawning with one or two trial runs over the selected site. She then begins to deposit her eggs, the male following close behind and fertilising them. A few eggs are laid at intervals over a period of up to three hours. From the moment the eggs are laid, both parents take turns at guarding and fanning them. The fanning is to prevent dirt settling, and to provide a circulation of fresh water over the eggs. The parents continually pick the eggs up in their mouths, destroying any that are attacked by fungus.

The fry hatch in two to four days. At first they are not fully developed and are stuck by their heads to the breeding site. The parents then move them to one of the pits they have already dug, picking them

Aequidens itanyi Dolphin Cichlid (to $5\frac{1}{2}''$)

up from time to time, cleaning them with a chewing action and spitting them back into the pit. They frequently shift the fry to other pits, an interesting procedure since at no time is any part of the brood left without a parent in charge. The fry are free-swimming in four to eight days, first appearing as a shoal, swimming under the parents close to the bottom. Any that stray away are picked up in the mouth and shot back into the shoal. These young fishes are quite large, and there is no need of infusoria as a first food. Newly hatched brine shrimp, micro-worms, and sifted live daphnia, are all suitable and should be fed plentifully and often. If they are over-crowded or under-fed when young, they will never grow into well proportioned, full sized specimens. The adults must also be kept well fed. Sometimes they will take this food into their mouths, chew it over and spit it out into the shoal for the young to eat.

From the time the eggs are laid, and long after the fry are free-swimming, the parents will make certain that nothing comes near the brood. If you approach the aquarium, one fish will come forward to defend the eggs or brood, the other carrying on with its duties. A planting stick or finger inserted into the water will invite attack. Any disturbance is resented, especially in the evening when they are settling the young for the night, and this may result in their losing interest and devouring the brood. Leaving them in peace is more likely to ensure success.

Once the fry are free-swimming the parents can be removed, although they will care for the brood until they are ready to spawn again, usually in six to eight weeks. This can be a dangerous time for the fry, as sometimes the parents see them as a threat and start to kill them off. To be on the safe side, it is wise to remove the fry to new quarters within three weeks of their hatching.

Some young fishes spawning for the first time have no parental instinct and eat the eggs. Should this happen repeatedly, exchange the culprit. Sometimes two female fishes will spawn together to get rid of their eggs. These eggs will of course be infertile and will be attacked by fungus. Should this fungusing occur with consecutive spawnings of fishes thought to be a pair, it is advisable to exchange the fish you have taken to be the male. Cichlids mate for life, although if one of the pair dies the other will usually accept a new partner.

163

Aequidens maroni Keyhole Cichlid (to 5″)

The larger species have a life span of about ten years, but begin to show signs of age when they are about five years old. The scales become coarse, the colour remains subdued, a hump develops just behind the head, in front of the dorsal fin, and the fish is unable to close its mouth completely.

The genera *Apistogramma*, *Pterophyllum* and *Symphysodon* have a slightly different breeding behaviour. The first two are described individually. The *Symphysodon* or Discus Fish forms the subject of a separate section.

The following list is a representative selection of American Cichlids, most of them freely available.

Aequidens curviceps **Flag Cichlid:** This fish from the Amazon Basin grows to $3\frac{1}{2}″$. It is grey-green, with a brown back and pale yellow belly. The scales have dark edges. Blue spots adorn the caudal and anal fins. The Flag Cichlid is a peaceful member of the genus, will not rip out plants, and will eat all foods. An occasional change of one-third of its water is recommended. It breeds in large Cichlid manner, but parents are prone to eat their eggs. They are ready to spawn at six months, when $2″$ long, and lay about 200 eggs, which hatch in three days and are free-swimming three days later. Fry should be fed infusoria for the first week, then put on to fine live foods.

Aequidens itanyi **Dolphin Cichlid:** A native of north-eastern South America, $5\frac{1}{2}″$ long, the Dolphin Cichlid has a light brown body. The young have a broad dark stripe from the eye to the base of the dorsal fin. In adult fishes this is broken into six patches. The male has a more pointed tip to the anal fin, and the tip of the dorsal extends beyond the caudal fin. It is kindly disposed towards other fishes, but will dig in the bottom compost and uproot plants. Live and dry foods are acceptable, and its breeding habits are as for large Cichlids.

Aequidens maroni **Keyhole Cichlid:** This Cichlid comes from Guiana and Venezuela, and attains a length of $5″$. Its body colour varies from cream to light brown. A dark brown band extends over the head, with rows of dark spots on the lower side of the body. Young fishes have a dark keyhole-shaped patch on their side, but in adults this is more of a dark blotch. The upper edge of the dorsal and caudal fins of older fishes have white edges.

The Keyhole Cichlid is a very peaceful species, never destroying plants. The male, with a life span of about seven years, is not aggressive towards his mate. This fish likes to hide among plants, and resents being moved from place to place. It will eat most foods as long as they are not too large.

Aequidens portalegrensis **Brown Acara:** This fish from southern Brazil and Bolivia has a large head with a blunt nose. Young specimens are green to brown with a blue or red sheen by reflected light. The adults are brown with a large dark patch on the side, and grow to $9″$. Dorsal, caudal and anal fins have light green flecks. One of the easiest of the genus to breed, it will stand temperatures down to $60°F$. It is fond of digging, especially during the breeding period, and will eat all foods. At breeding time a broad dark stripe appears along the side.

Aequidens pulcher Blue Acara (to 7″)

Aequidens pulcher **Blue Acara:** The Blue Acara comes from Trinidad and Venezuela, and grows to 7″. Its body colour is olive-green to grey. Young fishes have eight dark bands and numerous stripes, while the adults have light blue spots, with bars less evident. This is an easy species to breed, digging a lot during the breeding period, and often cleaning the bottom gravel away from large areas.

The genus *Apistogramma* are the small fishes of the family, and their requirements are slightly different to those of their larger relatives. They can adapt themselves to a smaller aquarium, 18″ × 10″ × 10″, and different species can often be kept together. The aquarium should be well planted, and provided with secluded places—plant thickets,

rockwork or flower pots—where the fishes can hide. They are not as hardy as the larger Cichlids, and are easily affected by chemicals, if used to treat water or disease. The water should be soft and slightly acid, a hardness of 100–150 p.p.m. and a pH of 6.8–7.0 being acceptable to most species. The temperature should be 76°–80°F. and up to 82°–84°F. for breeding.

There is usually no need to make special breeding arrangements, provided the fishes are well fed. The choice of spawning sites varies, some fishes choosing the underside of a large stone or the inside of a flower pot, others a large plant leaf. The male usually cleans the breeding site, and then invites the female to lay her eggs, which he immediately fertilises. The eggs are darker than those of the

Apistogramma agassizi Agassiz's Dwarf Cichlid (to 3″)

Apistogramma borelli Borelli's Dwarf Cichlid (to 2¾″)

large Cichlids, usually yellow or light brown. The care of eggs and brood is done by the female, who drives the male away if he attempts to go too near the breeding site. At this stage he should be removed for his own safety. Such an attack by the female on the male may be the first signal of a spawning, but the fishes also show brighter or darker colours at this time. The young hatch in three to five days, and are shifted to a pit or gap between the rocks or stones. Four to six days later they are free-swimming. The fry are much smaller than those of their larger relatives, and need infusoria for the first week or so. In many species, until the young are about three weeks old, any unexpected noise or intrusion near the tank will alarm the mother, who, by movements of body and fins, will transmit her apprehension to the fry. They will then freeze and drop to the bottom, or close up into a tight shoal underneath their mother. With young fishes, the eggs of the first spawning are usually devoured. If this should persist with following spawnings, the eggs may be removed and artificially hatched in the manner described for *Pterophyllum*. *Apistogramma* species have a life span of approximately two years. In most cases the female is not as large as the male, although she can hold her own in skirmishes.

Apistogramma agassizi: A native of the Amazon Basin, the male attains a length of 3″, the female 2″. It is yellow-brown with a dark brown back. A dark brown stripe runs from the mouth to the tip of the caudal fin. The dorsal fin of the male is orange, the caudal fin is pointed, pale orange with a blue edge. In the female, the caudal fin is rounded and the body colours are less bright. This is a very attractive fish, fond of all small live foods. It is ready to breed at six months, but the female is a poor mother and usually eats her eggs, so that artificial rearing is the best choice. Curiously, there always seem to be more males than females from a spawning.

Apistogramma borelli: This fish comes from central and southern regions of South America, the male being 2¾″ long, the female 2¼″. Its body colour is olive-brown with a blue sheen, and the throat and belly are yellow. In the male, the caudal fin has a straight rear edge and an extended point top and bottom. The caudal, anal and ventral fins are pale blue with a dark edge and white tips. The third and fourth rays of the dorsal are elongated and bright red in colour, the rear tip elongated and pointed. The female's fins are rounded.

These colourful, fairly aggressive fishes are best kept as pairs on their own. They eat dry and live foods, and are ready to breed at six months, the female clearing the breeding site and coaxing the male to spawn. She usually takes good care of the eggs and fry, and artificially hatched eggs never seem to give as good results.

Apistogramma commbrae: Coming from the upper Parana Basin, males of this species are 2″ long, females 1½″. The colour is yellow-brown with a green sheen on the back. A broad dark stripe runs from the mouth through the eye to the base of the caudal fin. There are also six to seven bars on the side. The colouration of this fish is very variable, although it closely resembles *Nannacara anomala*. Dry and live foods are eaten, and they are ready to breed at six months. The eggs are yellow-brown. After spawning, the female is very aggressive and the male should be removed as soon as possible.

Apistogramma ornatipinnis: A native of Western Guiana, whose length is 2¾″ in the male, 2″ in the female. The body colour of this fish is yellow-brown with a rusty brown belly and small dark blue patches on the side. There is a dark band from eye to throat, a dark spot in the middle of the body and another to the base of caudal fin. A double row of spots extends below the lateral line. The male's dorsal fin is orange with a black edge, the caudal fin is concave, orange with a red edge. The first ray of the ventral fin is red. This fish likes plenty of live foods. The best way to breed it is to buy six young fishes and let them choose their partners. The initial squabbling will not last long. Spawning is preceded by much digging, resulting in many patches of untidy floating plants.

Apistogramma ortmanni: The colour of this fish from Guiana and the middle Amazon is brown to grey, and its size ranges from 2″ in the female to 3″ in the male. The male dorsal and anal fins are long and pointed, and the caudal fin has a square rear edge, with a slight point top and bottom. The female dorsal, anal and caudal fins are rounded and they become bright yellow when she is ready to spawn. This fish will eat all types of food, but particularly enjoys small worms. Though not one of the bright, showy members of the genus, it is well worth keeping for its easy breeding, and the female's careful treatment of her young.

Apistogramma pertense: **Yellow Dwarf Cichlid:** This fish, 2″ long, is native to the Amazon, between Nanaos and Santarem. It is brown, with a wide dark stripe from the eye to the caudal fin base, and a dark band from eye to throat. All the scales have dark edges. The male caudal fin has a concave rear

edge, the top and bottom points being well extended and coloured orange. The dorsal and anal fins are pointed, the rear edge of the dorsal fin being orange. The female dorsal, caudal and anal fins are rounded, with a row of dark spots on the side; the fins are yellow. This fairly peaceful fish, which prefers only live food, poses no problems for the breeder. It is ready to breed at six months, and does not often eat the eggs. The belly of the male turns orange at breeding time.

Apistogramma pleurotaenia **Checkered Dwarf Cichlid:** Native to the Amazon Basin and southeast to Bolivia, the length of this Cichlid is 3″ in the male, 2″ in the female. The body colour is yellow-brown, and a wide, dark stripe runs from the gill

NIEUWENHUIZEN

Apistogramma ortmanni Ortmann's Dwarf Cichlid (to 3″)

Apistogramma ramirezi Ram Cichlid (to 2½″)

CUPIT

Apistogramma reitzigi Dwarf Yellow Cichlid (to 2″)

Apistogramma reitzigi **Dwarf Yellow Cichlid:** The Dwarf Yellow Cichlid, from the middle Rio Paraguay Basin, varies in length from $1\frac{1}{2}$″ (female) to 2″ (male). It is grey-brown with green spots on the gill covers. The belly and caudal fins are pale yellow. The male ventral fins are pointed, with the dorsal and anal fins reaching almost to the end of the caudal fin. The dorsal and anal fins of the female are shorter and turn brighter yellow at breeding time. The males fight with one another but seem to have great respect for the females. Eating both dry and live foods, they are ready to breed at six months, the male alone doing all the preparatory work. Once the eggs are laid, however, the female keeps him at a distance, and he is best removed for his own safety. The eggs are often laid on a plant leaf. The female chews these in her mouth and spits out the young. Partial changes of fresh water are recommended.

cover to the base of the caudal fin. There are six bands on the side, and blue-green spots on the gill covers. The male shows a checkered pattern on the base of the caudal fin, and also on the rear of the dorsal and anal fins. In the female the dorsal and anal fins are shorter, with no pattern and the body colour is more subdued. It will eat all foods but likes small worms and daphnia. During the breeding period the fish displays a beautiful colour pattern of yellow, orange and black. It is inclined to dig in the bottom and uproot plants.

Apistogramma ramirezi **Ram Cichlid:** This fish, $2\frac{1}{2}$″ in length, comes from Venezuela, its colour being pink with multi-coloured reflections along the sides according to the light. There is usually a blue sheen with dark bands. In the male, the second and third rays of the dorsal are well produced, while the female dorsal fin rays are not as long, nor the colour as bright. This is one of the most popular of the small Cichlids, and a very handsome fish. It enjoys sunlight and revels in a high temperature. Though ready at six months, it is sometimes a very difficult fish to breed. Both parents take an active part in the breeding care, so there is no need to remove the male after spawning. About 150 eggs are laid, often on a broad plant leaf. They hatch in two days and are free-swimming in another four. If the spawning pair proceed to eat eggs or fry, the next batch should be removed and hatched artificially.

There is a golden variety of this fish, which has a yellow-orange sheen. It only reaches a length of 2″, and is very shy, breeding in the same manner, and having the same bad habit of eating the eggs.

Astronotus ocellatus **Oscar, Marble** or **Velvet Cichlid:** This Cichlid is a native of eastern Venezuela and the Amazon Basin to Paraguay. A distinctive feature is that the scales are not visible, so that it has the texture of velvet suede. The colour pattern of the young fish, brown with irregular yellow barred markings, is reminiscent of marble. Adult fish are grey-green to black with red-orange markings. There is an eye spot at the base of the caudal fin and sometimes another at the base of the dorsal. This is a very hard fish to sex, but adults that have small spots at the base of the dorsal fin are usually males. This Cichlid glides rather than swims. It is not an aggressive fish but tends to be greedy, regarding any smaller fish as fair game. It is easily tamed and can be hand-fed. Ready to breed at 4″, it spawns in the large Cichlid manner, but attempts may not invariably be successful. Fed well in large aquaria, these fishes grow fast and can reach a length of 6″ or so by the time they are a year old, while specimens approaching twice that length are not uncommon in the large tanks of public aquaria.

Cichlasoma aureum: This fish, 6″ long, is found in southern Mexico and Guatemala. Its body colour is green-brown, with a golden sheen on the sides of the male. There is a large dark spot on the body under the dorsal fin, and several bands, particularly noticeable when the fish is excited. The dorsal and anal fins are edged red, and in the male have long extensions. A fairly peaceful fish when young, it is liable to become very aggressive, especially with its own kind as it matures. It will eat all foods and likes plenty of vegetables in its diet.

Astronotus ocellatus Oscar/Marble/Velvet Cichlid (to 12″)   Below: *Cichlasoma bimaculatum* (to 8″)

Cichlasoma biocellatum Jack Dempsey (to 8″)

Cichlasoma bimaculatum: Native to northern South America, the body colour of this 8″ fish is grey-brown with a darker back and silver belly. Young fishes are barred, but as they get older the bars disappear and the adults have two spots, one on the middle of the side and a smaller one on the upper base of the caudal fin. At spawning time the silver on the belly becomes pale yellow and the throat is silver blue. It is usually quite peaceful with its own kind, provided of equal size. All live meaty foods are taken but it is not fond of dry food. They breed in large Cichlid manner and usually take good care of their young.

Cichlasoma biocellatum **Jack Dempsey:** The Jack Dempsey, named after the famous boxer, is an 8″ fish from the middle Amazon Basin and Costa Rica. The colour varies with age, young fishes being grey with seven or eight dark bands, adults grey-black with shining green scales and peppered all over the body and fins with blue spots. At breeding time the body colour is a deep blue, with red edges to the dorsal and anal fins. The female has fewer blue spots on the sides. The fish has a strong head that bulges with age.

The Jack Dempsey likes to dig and will often clear the gravel from the bottom and pile it up the sides of the aquarium. It is easily tamed and will take food from the fingers—any meaty and live food will do, especially earthworms. Ready to spawn at 3″, it breeds in the large Cichlid manner, laying about 400 eggs that hatch in four days, and are free-swimming in eight. Be careful, however, as the male will often attack the female after spawning. Despite this pugnacious streak, true to its name, it is a very popular fish.

Cichlasoma coryphaenoides **Chocolate Cichlid:** A native of the Amazon Basin, the colour of the young fish is dark olive to brown with a black spot on the middle of the side. The adult is brown with a 'W' marking behind the eye and a red sheen on the sides. This species, which grows to 10″, is very difficult to keep, being extremely shy and fond of hiding among plants. It requires a high temperature of 78°–80°F. to be kept in good condition, and may be fed on most live and meaty foods.

Cichlasoma facetum **Chanchito:** The Chanchito, 12″ long, comes from southern Brazil, Paraguay

Cichlasoma facetum Chanchito (to 12″)

Cichlasoma festivum Barred/Flag Cichlid (to 6″)

Cichlasoma meeki Firemouth (to 5″)

and northern Argentina. The colour varies from green to yellow with several dark bars, sometimes almost black. Sexing can be determined with certainty during the breeding period by the shape of the breeding tube, which is pointed in the male and blunt in the female. Apart from this, the male usually has more yellow on the back, between the bars. This is a very aggressive fish, fond of digging, with a long life and large broods. It will eat most foods, though not fond of dry types.

There is a pink colour variety of this fish, on which the bars can hardly be seen. It is not quite an albino as the eye pupil is black, not red. It does not seem to grow as large as the original type, 5″ being a large specimen; nor is it as pugnacious or as busy a digger.

Cichlasoma festivum: This Cichlid, 6″ long, comes from western Guiana and the Amazon Basin. It is grey-green with a yellow tinge, easily identifiable by an oblique stripe that runs from the mouth, through the eye to the rear top edge of the dorsal fin. Adult specimens have long, thread-like ventral fins. Sexing is only possible at breeding time, the breeding tube of the females being blunt; but adult males do have a longer dorsal fin and their markings are darker.

In its native habitat it is found with *Pterophyllum*, and these make suitable companions in the aquarium. But it is a shy fish, needing a large well-planted aquarium with plenty of hiding places. It swims near the surface of the water, which should be well aerated and warmer than that required by most of the genus. Not an easy fish to breed, it is usually a poor parent and best results are obtained by artificial rearing of the fry.

Cichlasoma meeki **Firemouth:** The Firemouth, from Guatemala and Yucatan, is a grey fish, 5″ long, with a green-edged black spot on the gill plate. Its belly and throat are red. It is a very popular fish, not disturbing plants outside the breeding period, and usually making a very good parent. The occasional pugnacious specimen is found, but this is rare. When kept in aquaria with other fishes of the same size, they have been known to spawn and rear their young without causing any harm to the other inhabitants. They thrive on live foods, particularly earthworms. General care is the same as for the large Cichlids.

Cichlasoma nigrofasciatum **Convict Cichlid:** This silver-blue fish from Guatemala, Salvador, Costa Rica and Panama, grows to 6″. The young have as many as ten dark convict-like bars, but as they get older the bars diminish and the adults have only seven or eight. During the breeding period, the bars on the male become metallic and the female is more colourful with gold spots on her sides.

True to its name, this is a very aggressive species, not to be trusted with other fishes, for it will attack with lightning-like swiftness. All rockwork must be well seated in the gravel, as the fishes will dig under rocks and displace them. At breeding time plants will be dug up and reduced to shreds, so flower pots laid on their sides are a useful addition. Although they eat all foods, they should be given some vegetable foods to keep them in prime condition.

Cichlasoma severum : A native of the northern Amazon Basin and Guiana, the colour of this 8″ fish is very changeable, pale grey to deep green, brown or black. Young fishes have eight or nine dark bars on the sides, and at this age look very much like *Symphysodon discus*. Adults have a black bar linking the dorsal and anal fins just before the caudal fin. The male has regular rows of red spots on the sides, the female has only a few spots and shorter dorsal and anal fins. Though very peaceful when young, it becomes more pugnacious as it grows. All live foods and some vegetables are taken and earthworms are especially recommended. Breeding tends to be difficult as they are not easy to mate. Avoid plants in the breeding aquarium.

Crenicara maculata **Checkerboard Cichlid:** This Cichlid from the middle Amazon is yellow with two rows of dark spots. The male grows to 4″, the female only to 2″. Though the young fishes are not very colourful the adults are beautiful. The pointed male dorsal fin has a red edge, the anal and ventral fins, also pointed, have blue and orange stripes. The Checkerboard Cichlid will eat all live foods, although it is not very fond of tubifex. It is a reasonably peaceful species that is reported to breed as the genus *Apistogramma*.

Crenicichla dorsocellata **Two-spot Pike Cichlid:** Native to the middle Amazon Basin and Rio Parahyba, this 8″ fish has a Pike-like body shape, its colour being dark blue-green. The young have seven to nine dark bars on their sides, fading as they mature, but replaced by a large dark spot with a white and red edge in the middle of the dorsal fin and a smaller dark spot on the tail, just in front of

Cichlasoma nigrofasciatum Convict Cichlid (to 6″)

PENGILLEY

Cichlasoma severum (to 8″)

the caudal fin. The fish behaves like a Pike too, lying in a plant thicket until an unsuspecting fish swims near, then darting out, quick as a flash, to catch and eat it. It will, in fact, eat almost anything, including fishes nearly as large as itself.

Crenicichla lepidota **Pike Cichlid:** This is another Pike-like fish from the Amazon and northern Argentina, 8″ long and grey-green. There is a large dark spot behind the gill cover and a smaller one at the base of the caudal fin. The top edge of the dorsal fin and the lower part of the caudal fin are red. The female sometimes has brighter colours. It will eat all large live foods and is said to breed in the large Cichlid manner, with the male looking after the eggs and young.

Crenicichla saxatilis **Ring-tailed Pike Cichlid:** Another very pugnacious species, not safe with other fishes, is this 12″ fish from Trinidad and the central and eastern Amazon Basin to southern Brazil. It has a dark olive, Pike-shaped body and a yellow-white belly. A dark stripe runs from the mouth, through the eye to the caudal fin and there is a large dark brown spot, yellow-edged, in the

caudal fin. The dorsal fin has a white stripe below a black edge. This species eats all live foods.

Geophagus brasiliensis: Found in eastern Brazil, often in brackish waters, the body colour of the young fish is olive-brown with some faint bars. The adults, 12″ long, are grey-green with a dark spot on the centre of the side. Smaller pearly spots are dotted all over the sides. The only sure way to sex this species is during the spawning period, by the shape of the breeding tubes. It will take all live and meaty foods and is reported to breed in the large Cichlid manner, though the adults are not good parents.

Geophagus jurupari **Earth-eater:** This pale yellow fish from north-eastern Brazil and Guiana grows to 9″ in length. The young have bars on their sides and adults are covered with pearly blue spots. Unlike its fiercely predatory relatives, it is a peaceful member of the genus, deriving its name from a habit of using its mouth as a shovel, scooping up the bottom sand in its mouth and spraying it out through the gills, retaining any food that it finds. Because of this habit of sifting the bottom sand for food, only the smallest grained sand should be used

PENGILLEY

Crenicichla saxatilis Ring-tailed Pike Cichlid (to 12")

Crenicara maculata Checkerboard Cichlid (to 4")

NIEUWENHUIZEN

as a bottom compost. It will eat dry and live foods but they must not be too large. The eggs are carried in the mouth of the female.

Herichthys cyanoguttatum **Texas Cichlid:** A large Cichlid, 12" when full grown, from north-east Mexico and Texas, this is the most northerly of the American Cichlids and the only one native to the United States. The young are light green-brown with dark bands. The adults' bodies have a light green base colour, thickly sprinkled with many bright green spots that go right into the dorsal fin. This is a very difficult fish to sex. Males, when

about three years old, develop a hump behind the head, in front of the dorsal fin. This is not seen in the female nor are her spots as bright.

Although pugnacious and fond of uprooting plants, this is a very beautiful fish. It emphatically dislikes water that is too old and this should therefore be changed at frequent intervals. Fortunately, it can stand temperatures down to 56°F. At first it eats all foods, but as it gets older it will only take live and meaty foods. When preparing to breed they will often clear half of the aquarium bottom, on which the eggs are later laid. They are often poor parents, neglecting the eggs, which should be removed and artificially hatched. Two females will frequently spawn together to get rid of their eggs and these will naturally be attacked by fungus. *See illustration on pages 158–9.*

Nannacara anomala **Dwarf Golden-eye Cichlid:** This species, ideal for anyone who wants to try breeding Cichlids in a small aquarium, comes from western Guiana. The body colour of the male is brown with a green metallic sheen under reflected lighting, and two broad dark stripes along the sides. The eye is orange, and dorsal and anal fins are

Geophagus jurupari Earth-eater (to 9″)

large and pointed. The dorsal fin is edged with orange. The female is lighter brown, with rounded dorsal and anal fins. The male grows to $3\frac{1}{2}$″, the female to $2\frac{1}{2}$″.

If kept in a well-planted aquarium with flower pots and rocks, this peaceful species will need no special set-up for breeding. It will eat all live foods and limited amounts of meaty ones. Ready to breed at 2″, it lays about 60 eggs, usually inside a flower pot. These hatch in three days and are free-swimming in another five. Fry are small and need infusoria for a week; they can then go on to brine shrimp and micro-worms.

Nannacara taenia **Dwarf Lattice Cichlid:** Very similar to *N. anomala,* but with a lattice pattern on the sides, the male of this Amazon species grows to $2\frac{1}{2}$″, the female to 2″. The male is yellow-brown with a broad black stripe from the eye to the base of the caudal fin. The dorsal has a red and black edge. The female is lighter in colour and usually has stripes. This very peaceful fish is almost as easy to breed as *N. anomala,* but less frequently seen. It will eat all live and meaty foods and a small amount of dry.

Nannacara taenia Dwarf Lattice Cichlid (to $2\frac{1}{2}$″)

Nannacara anomala Dwarf Golden-eye Cichlid (to $3\frac{1}{2}''$)

The popular genus *Pterophyllum* consists of fishes with a disc-like shape and well extended dorsal and anal fins. The ventral fins are very long and look like feelers.

Pterophyllum altum : This fish from the Orinoco River has an extra long dorsal and anal fin. Growing to 4″, its body is silver with four dark brown bars. There are brown spots between the bars across the top half of the body. The species requires slightly acid water and should only be kept with slow-moving fishes.

Pterophyllum eimekei **Angel Fish:** The body colour of this Angel Fish from the middle Amazon is also silver, but with four distinct black bands. There is a yellow-brown tint over the back and a light blue sheen over the lower part of the body. There are a number of red-brown spots on the sides and the ventral fins are blue. The fish grows to 5″.

Pterophyllum scalare **Angel Fish:** Another native of the Amazon, this Angel Fish, which grows to 6″, has a silver body, tinted grey-green, with four black bands, as well as three shorter, less distinct ones.

The fifth band runs from the tip of the dorsal fin across the body to the tip of the anal fin. The ventral fins are yellow-green.

The original Angel Fishes were difficult to breed because they needed special water requirements. Over the years *P. eimekei* and *P. scalare* have been interbred and the fishes seen today are hybrids of these two species. Locally bred, as against imported specimens, are easy to breed, being quite satisfied with the water conditions supplied to their parents. Because of their tall shape, however, they do need deep aquaria, which should be well planted, with a high temperature of 80°F. The only sure way to sex these fishes is during the spawning period, by observing the shape of the breeding tube, pointed in the male and blunt in the female. But there are other pointers which may serve as sexing guides.

1. The fin spines at the leading edge of the dorsal fin are more irregular and jagged in the male than the female.
2. The space between the base of the ventral and anal fins is longer and less curved in the female.
3. The lower jaw of the male overlaps the upper jaw, and vice-versa in the female.

177

4. The black stripe that passes through the eye is straighter in the male. The top of the female's stripe curves towards the dorsal fin.

5. Looking head-on at the fish, the female is thicker behind the ventrals and below the pectoral fins.

Angel Fishes eat all live foods and some dry foods, but it is best to keep changing the type of food or they may go on a hunger strike. They will breed at 2″, often choosing a plant leaf as the breeding site. Eggs hatch in two to three days, and the fry start to swim in short curved hops in about four days, though it is six days before they are swimming properly. The fry need infusoria or newly hatched brine shrimp as a first food.

Adult fishes do not always make good parents and you may have to rear the young artificially. To do this you can put a strip of glass, plastic, slate or cane in the breeding aquarium on which they will lay their eggs. After spawning, remove the eggs to another aquarium, with the same kind of water as in the breeding aquarium. The water should be about 6″ deep and at a temperature between 80°–84°F. Add five drops of a five per-cent solution of methylene blue to every gallon, to prevent fungus attacking the eggs. Place the glass or plant leaf with eggs upright in the aquarium and allow a slight aeration of fine bubbles to rise up past them but not actually to touch them. This serves to keep water passing over the eggs in the same way as when the parents fan them. Once they are free-swimming, rearing is easy. For the first couple of weeks they look like ordinary fishes; they do not develop the characteristic Angel shape until they are about four weeks old.

There are many colour varieties of this fish. One of them has a pale blue body colour, another pale yellow. There is also a black variety which is black all over, and a Black Lace, which is grey-black with a black lace pattern on the fins. The Veiltail Angel has a much longer caudal fin and the dorsal and anal fins are also more developed. The latest colour variety is the Marbled Angel, where all the bars are well broken, with brown-black patches on a silver-yellow background. Owing to the very many different finnage forms that can be produced by selected breeding, the Federation of British Aquatic Societies have published a standard drawing of what they consider to be the ideal type.

Symphysodon: For details of this popular genus, see pages 191–7.

Uaru amphiacanthoides: The body colour of young fishes of this species from the Amazon and Guiana

Pterophyllum eimekei Angel Fish (to 5″)

is dark brown. The adults are yellow-brown with three black patches on the side. The eye is orange. Adults grow to 10″. In the wild this fish is found with *Pterophyllum* and *Symphysodon*, so that it needs the same water requirements as these genera. This rare fish is quite peaceful, and will eat live, dry and vegetable foods.

ASIATIC CICHLIDS

There are only two Cichlids from the Far East known to the aquarist, *Etroplus maculatus* and *E. suratensis*, both from India and Ceylon, the latter being of little interest since it is not particularly colourful and prefers very brackish water.

Uaru amphiacanthoides (to 10″)

Etroplus maculatus **Orange Chromide:** For some reason this beautiful little Cichlid, which never exceeds 3″ in length, is not as frequently seen today as it was in the early days of the hobby when its cheerful golden-yellow colouring and peaceful nature earned it a place of honour in many a community tank. Its appearance is further enhanced by three large black spots of varying intensity on the flanks, while rows of small bright red spots extend over most of the body.

Breeding care follows the general pattern for the family, though the eggs are attached to stones or tree roots by a short thread. Both parents undertake diligent brood care but the young fry demand a very plentiful food supply and, being susceptible to impurities in the water, are not as easily reared as most of their relatives.

Etroplus maculatus Orange Chromide (to 3″)

Tilapia melanopleura (to 16″)

CICHLIDS
OF AFRICA

GENUS *Haplochromis* is found in various parts of Africa and is known as a mouth-breeder or mouth-brooder, the latter term being the more accurate. The commonest and most popular species is the Egyptian Mouth-brooder.

Haplochromis multicolor **Egyptian Mouth-brooder:** Widely distributed in East Africa and northwards into Egypt and the lower Nile, it is a peaceful fish and does well in community tanks. Attaining some 3″ in length, it does not reach its full colour range until in breeding condition, when the males are particularly attractive. The grey-brown body colour takes on varied hues of blue, green and gold, according to the lighting, while the vivid green gill covers are edged with black. The dorsal and anal fins are rust-red with pale green rays, bordered in blue and edged in black. The caudal and pectoral fins are yellowish.

The general rules for Cichlid tank-breeding apply to this species. The males may be rather aggressive in their courtship and the pair dig small pits in the gravel, in which the female eventually lays about 50 eggs, the male following and fertilising them. The female then takes the eggs into her mouth and throat pouch, which becomes very distended. It is wise to remove the male at this stage to keep conditions peaceful. The female keeps the eggs in her throat for the entire ten days incubation period, not feeding during this time but moving

Haplochromis multicolor Egyptian Mouth-brooder (to 3″)

NIEUWENHUIZEN

Haplochromis philander (to $4\frac{1}{4}''$)

the eggs around in her mouth. She releases the fry only for very short periods at first—during which time both she and they feed. Newly hatched brine shrimp and fine particles of hard-boiled egg yolk are used as a first food. After five days or so the young shelter in the mouth of the female, at first nearly all the time, but later only at night or when endangered. After ten days the female may safely be removed.

Quite a number of other species of *Haplochromis* are available to the aquarist, but it should be borne in mind that positive identification can be extremely difficult because of the very considerable variation in form and colouring within a single species, according to its origin, condition or environment. Indeed, a single specimen can display so bewildering a change from one day to another as to appear a totally different fish; and these changes are not necessarily associated with breeding condition.

One of the species frequently available to the aquarist, *Haplochromis philander*, has been found to have several forms or racial characteristics, some of them being introduced to the hobby under separate names.

Hemichromis bimaculatus **Jewel Cichlid:** This is one of the most popular of all Cichlids, neither a dwarf nor a large species, the maximum aquarium length being about 5″. On the whole they are peaceful, especially if kept on their own. As they mature they select mates and establish a part of the tank as their own territory. They do a great deal of digging and are best provided with half a plant pot, which both fishes will clean and where the female will lay the eggs, to be fertilised by the male. During breeding, the female is more brightly coloured than the male —unusual in tropical fishes. The eggs are laid at intervals in a circular pattern on top of the plant pot, where they are guarded and fanned in turn by both parents. If any other fish in the tank intrudes into the parents' territory it is chased off very rapidly. The eggs hatch after a few days and the fry are removed by the parents to a small depression they have dug in the gravel. At this stage they are extremely difficult to see and the only evidence of their existence is the presence of the parents, still in glorious breeding hue, apparently guarding this depression in the gravel. About a week after spawning, the fry become free-swimming. As they make their first attempt to leave home they are picked up in the mouth of one or other parent and 'spat' back into the middle of the rest of the brood. Eventually the whole brood is taken for a swim— the parents keeping them together as a very tight shoal and rounding up any stragglers. The parents will look after the young until they feel the urge to spawn again, sometimes a fortnight after the original spawning, at which point they should be removed to another tank. Newly hatched brine shrimp, followed by the usual larger foods, causes rapid growth among the fry. It is particularly important when the fry get to the 1″ stage to give plenty of food, otherwise they may try to eat one another, starting with pieces of the caudal fins.

Long study by the British Aquarists' Society has indicated that this is one of the easiest fishes to breed, hence its popularity.

Hemichromis fasciatus **Banded Jewel Fish:** A large Cichlid (12″) living in West and Central Africa. This fish is basically a brownish-yellow, with about eight transverse darker bands, and a greenish blotch on the gill cover. During breeding, the fish takes on a more shining appearance. The blotch on the gill cover is edged with gold, each scale develops a red spot, and the iris turns bright red. The female is drabber than the male, but similarly coloured.

Nannochromis nudiceps: This dwarf Cichlid is not often seen in aquaria, despite its pleasant colouration. The body is blue and the dorsal fin orange, with a white line along its free edge. The upper half of the caudal fin is striped. It does well in soft water and spawns on a bisected plant pot like *Hemichromis bimaculatus*.

The genus *Pelmatochromis* is West African, extending from Liberia southwards to the Congo. There are several species known to aquarists, of which the gloriously colourful *Pelmatochromis kribensis* has become by far the most popular. All these fishes live in coastal regions where the water may occasionally receive mixtures of salt water; some authorities often recommend one tablespoon of salt to every two gallons of water.

Pelmatochromis arnoldi **Arnold's Cichlid:** This rather aggressive fish grows to 4″. It is grey-yellow, with five large blotches on the side. In breeding condition, the male shows bright red or orange on the lower parts. Given a tank to itself with plenty of live food, it grows well and spawns vigorously, a plant pot being the best medium for this purpose. Broods may be large. To ensure raising the fry, remove the adults and use aeration to replace the

Hemichromis bimaculatus Jewel Cichlids (to 5″) spawning

Parents fanning the eggs

Parents spitting back fry
Three-day-old free-swimming fry

NIEUWENHUIZEN

Hemichromis fasciatus Banded Jewel Fish (to 12″)

Below: *Pelmatochromis arnoldi* Arnold's Cichlid (to 4″)

PENGILLEY

Below: *Pelmatochromis kribensis* (to 4″)

NIEUWENHUIZEN

parents' care, as they occasionally eat the fry. It is believed to be synonymous with *P. annectens*.

Pelmatochromis kribensis: A fish from the delta of the Niger, the male is 4″ long, the female 3″. The basic colour is bluish-violet with a bright red area at the most convex area of the belly. The male has up to five spots on the upper half of the caudal fin. The female is often as bright as the male. At breeding time, in both males and females, the area of the abdomen around the vent becomes an intense reddish-purple. These fishes are terrific diggers and when put into an aquarium lined with say, 2″ of gravel, they will be down to the bottom glass within forty-eight hours. Soft acid water suits them well but any gravel must be lime free. Ordinary aquarium gravel is unsuitable as it contains calcium salts which makes the water hard.

These fishes like flower pots—either half of a 5″ pot or a whole 3″ pot will do equally well. Courtship and cleaning of pot and gravel goes on for days. Increasing the temperature to 80°F. is a useful stimulus to promote spawning. The young hatch after three days and are then kept in a depression in the gravel for another three or four days before they become free-swimming. At the free-swimming

Pelmatochromis subocellatus (to 4″)

stage they should be given brine shrimp and the parents should be removed. Some aquarists prefer to remove the newly laid eggs from the plant pot to a bare tank, thus giving them good aeration in place of the parents' care. In any event, these fishes are not prolific and often the average brood of 25 may well turn out mainly of one sex. Exchanges can of course be made with aquarists whose broods show an opposite tendency.

Pelmatochromis subocellatus: The normal colour of this Cichlid is greyish-green with a reddish lower part. A dark band runs from the nose to the caudal peduncle, and the fins are yellow with blue lines and spots. An interesting feature of this fish is that the female becomes more brilliant than the male during the breeding season—velvet-black except for the dorsal fin and adjoining parts of the body, which are pure white. It breeds in the same way as *Pelmatochromis kribensis.*

The species in the next three genera, *Labeotropheus*, *Petrotilapia* and *Pseudotropheus* are known, together with *Haplochromis callipterus*, as the Lake Nyasa Cichlids. Lake Nyasa has recently become a source of a number of new and colourful aquarium Cichlids. Since the lake water is hard and alkaline,

Labeotropheus fuelleborni Fuelleborn's Cichlid (to 5″)

these fishes must be kept in hard (200 p.p.m. calcium carbonate) and alkaline water. The temperature should be 75°–80°F. In their natural habitat they eat algae as well as live foods, but many will also eat dried foods. They are not recommended for the community tank as they will eat species smaller than themselves. In the aquarium they all grow to 4″–5″ and all are mouth-brooders. In most of the species there is great sexual dimorphism—one would hardly think that the female and male belonged to the same species.

185

Pseudotropheus auratus Golden Lake Nyasa Cichlid, male (top) and female (to 4″)

Labeotropheus fuelleborni **Fuelleborn's Cichlid:** This species grows to 5″ in size. The male is bright blue in colour with bright yellow spots on the anal fin. They eat algae as well as live foods and the female mouth-broods the eggs.

Labeotropheus trewavasae **Red-finned Cichlid:** The blue male with his red dorsal is very striking compared with the 'mottled' female. They are aggressive and best kept in large tanks with rocks for hiding places. They grow to 4″ in length, and, in their natural habitat, eat algae and plants. The male digs a depression in the gravel and the female lays the eggs in this. Fertilisation then takes place and the female picks up the eggs and mouth-broods them for about thirty days.

Petrotilapia tridentiger **Blue Petrotilapia:** This fish has a dark blue body with eight indistinct, transverse blue bars. The male has a small number of yellow spots on the anal fin. These highly colourful mouth-brooders require the normal Lake Nyasa water conditions, with algae or substitute (spinach) as well as live foods. They grow to 4″ in size. The male, like most of these mouth-brooders, has spots on the anal fin.

Labeotropheus trewavasae Red-finned Cichlid (to 4″)

Pseudotropheus auratus **Golden Lake Nyasa Cichlid:** This fish exists in two colour varieties. Normally it is yellow, the male becoming dark blue and striped at breeding time, the female being striped longitudinally in black and yellow. The other colour variety has a black and white female, and a male which becomes bright blue in breeding condition.

In both varieties the male grows to 4″ long and is very aggressive. Newly bought pairs should be

Pseudotropheus zebra Zebra Nyasa Cichlid (to 4″)

separated by a sheet of glass and the tank should contain plenty of rocks as hiding places for the female. When spawning, the male makes depressions in the gravel and the female lays the eggs, where they are fertilised by the male. She then picks up the eggs, at which stage the male should be removed. The eggs are brooded by the female for three or four weeks: the fry are ¼″ long when born.

Pseudotropheus zebra **Zebra Nyasa Cichlid:** These fishes are blue with seven to eight darker blue transverse bands on the body and two incomplete transverse bars on the head. The anal fin of the male has a number of bright yellow spots. They grow to 4″ in length and spawn in the usual manner of Lake Nyasa Cichlids. The female broods the eggs. A highly colourful fish, aggressive, quarrelsome, and a great defender of his territory.

The genus *Tilapia* contains the most important Cichlid fishes in the world—though not from the aquarist's viewpoint. They are, in fact, valuable food fishes in many regions and are being actively spread by governmental and international agencies interested in improving nutrition in developing tropical countries. If young *Tilapia* (fingerlings)

are deposited in rice paddies at the time of planting, they can be harvested as 5″ fishes together with the rice, providing a useful source of animal protein. As dams are built in many tropical areas, and as rivers give way to lakes, it is expected that this type of Cichlid will become even more common. Experiments have already been made to breed them in heated ponds in the U.K. and it is suggested they might be acceptable as a food fish.

Many *Tilapia* grow too large for aquaria, and only *T. mossambica* is really popular.

Tilapia must be kept in large tanks with 2″ of gravel on the bottom and a number of rocks which can form territorial bases. They will eat plants so do not provide them with expensive varieties. Some species need plant material—algae or spinach or lettuce substitutes—for proper growth.

Tilapia guinasana: From Lake Guinas in Southwestern Africa. Grows to 6″ in length. Like *Tilapia mossambica* it exists in pale and dark forms. The fishes spawn in pits and are not mouth-brooders.

Tilapia guineensis: Growing to 10″ in the wild, these fishes live in brackish as well as fresh water. There are a number of colour variations, some being

Tilapia guinasana (to 6″)   *Tilapia mossambica* Mozambique Cichlid (to 14″)

PENGILLEY

Left: *Tilapia nilotica* Nile Mouth-brooder (to 20″)

Tropheus duboisi White Spotted Cichlid (to 2½″)

CHLUPATY

green with a metallic hue, others silvery-grey with a greenish hue. Eggs are laid on a flat rock which is cleaned up before spawning by both parents. The fry, as soon as they are hatched, are put in pits dug in the gravel; the parents remove them when they become free-swimming and form shoals. They like plants and will eat algae, spinach or lettuce.

Tilapia melanopleura: Another large member of the genus, from the Congo. The colour is grey-green with seven or eight indistinct, darker transverse bands on the body. The fins are hyaline with a faint suggestion of red. When breeding, the fish is said to develop a bright red abdomen. *Illustration page 180*.

Tilapia mossambica **Mozambique Cichlid:** Although this fish comes from East Africa, its wide distribution as a food fish has given rise to such exotic names as Hawaiian Mouth-brooder. There appear to be a number of colour varieties of this fish, some black, others black with iridescent blue areas. Some specimens in breeding trim can hardly be recognised as the same fish. If a number of mature fishes are kept together in a tank, each male takes up a territory which he guards aggressively, finally enticing a female into his 'den'. The eggs are laid on flat rocks, the male closely following the female to fertilise them. The female immediately takes the eggs into her mouth. Some authorities claim that the female, in lifting the eggs, collects sperm so that fertilisation actually takes place in her mouth. The young hatch in about ten days and are gradually released from the mouth for longer periods. Remove the male after spawning and the female when the young become free-swimming.

Tilapia nilotica **Nile Mouth-brooder:** This is the biggest of the Mouth-brooders known to aquarists, 20″ in the wild, though rather smaller in tanks. They do not become mature until they are 12″. The colouration is variable, usually greyish with white undersides. There are a number of indistinct, darker transverse bands and a black spot on the gill cover. The female mouth-broods the eggs.

Tropheus duboisi **White Spotted Cichlid:** A native of Lake Tanganyika, which prefers hard alkaline water. This is a dwarf Cichlid, growing to 2½″. The young are black with white spots, the adult males are black with a yellow vertical band, whereas the females are black with white spots.

The fishes spawn on a flat rock and only a few large eggs are laid at a time. The female mouth-broods the eggs.

CICHLIDS: THE DISCUS FISH

SINCE their introduction in 1933 the keeping and breeding of Discus fishes has been the ambition of many aquarists throughout the world. There were occasional reports of spawnings, chiefly from America, but never in complete detail. In 1956, following intensive research and ultimately the successful breeding of the species, the first full account of the reproduction of these fishes was published by the author of the following article. In giving the requirements of these fishes readers may be reassured by the fact that the author is still breeding the species in the manner described.

Symphysodon discus, **Discus** or **Pompadour Fish,** a Cichlid from the Amazon region, has often been described as the king of freshwater tropical fishes. In fact, one common name in the United States describes him simply as the King.

The Discus is a real show fish, large—maximum 8″ long—and brilliantly coloured. The colours, as will be evident, vary enormously, with the basic body hues ranging from orange to russet-red and blue-green. Distinctive features are the discoid body shape, similar to the Angel Fishes, but without the high, soaring dorsal and anal fins; and the patterns of undulating lines, vertical through the eye and throat, horizontal on head, nape and gill-cover. But no written description can convey the variety and beauty of this wonderful fish.

The classification of the genus *Symphysodon* by certain American ichthyologists has led to much controversy in the fish-keeping world. Moreover, the use of popular names or descriptions helps not at all; if anything, it makes matters more confusing.

At the present moment, according to the afore-mentioned American source, there are two species of the genus *Symphysodon,* with three sub-species of one of these.

Other specialists, with whom I would agree, argue that there are only two species and numerous colour varieties of these two.

The common Brown Discus, formerly genus *Discus* (Heckel), now bears the unwieldy scientific name of *Symphysodon aequifasciata axelrodi* (Schultz), but since personal preference has been expressed for the two-species classification, the following suggestion is made in order to simplify the issue.

Symphysodon aequifasciata **Common Brown Discus:** available in the following colour varieties: Blue—additional horizontal blue veining and general blue body colouration; Red—red body colouration; Rainbow or Seven-colour—additional yellow in the body and yellow, red and blue in the dorsal and anal fins.

Symphysodon discus (Heckel), which has become commercially available only in recent years, has been generally accepted, by British aquarists at any rate, as the 'Heckel'. It is easily distinguished from the Brown and its varieties by the overall blue and red horizontal veining. Unfortunately, further confusion arises when certain South American exporters use the term Blue Discus in describing this fish, whereas English importers use the name Red Heckel. A green colour variety of the Heckel is sometimes available, the colour coming from the horizontal veining, which is lighter than the normal blue variety.

Perhaps the simplest solution would be to use Heckel and Schultz as follows:
Brown Schultz Discus
Blue Schultz Discus
Red Schultz Discus
Rainbow Schultz Discus
Red Heckel Discus
Green Heckel Discus

There are other beautiful variations, often having both Heckel and Brown characteristics, confirming the generally accepted view that these different species and sub-species readily interbreed.

The rarer colour varieties, Blue-Brown, Green-Heckel and Seven-colour are expensive to acquire, costing three to four times as much as the commoner types.

One thing is certain; whatever species, race, variety or strain we are dealing with, colour will change with environment. Changes from brown to red and brown to green can be brought about simply by adjustment of the pH and hardness of the aquarium water. Colour changes have also been observed through diet; for example, broods of Browns attain red body colouration through almost exclusive feeding with *Daphnia pulex*. So it will be appreciated that it is extremely difficult to identify these fishes either by colour or pattern. An additional headache is the fact that young fishes of about 1″ body size give no indication as to what their adult colouration will be.

Unfortunately, no hard and fast method of sexing Discus can be offered, for even adult fishes show no positive distinguishing signs. For this reason, before purchasing pairs of these fishes, it is advisable to ask whether they have already had a fertile spawning. An even more satisfactory way to obtain a breeding pair is to buy several young fishes and raise them to maturity. The males and females will sort themselves out soon enough, provided, of course, the conditions in the tank are right.

Do not be afraid to shop around and take a long hard look before purchasing your Discus. Ideally, Discus should be kept on their own, both in the shop and in your aquarium. The reason is simple—why risk infecting these valuable fishes with disease from commoner and cheaper specimens? Avoid dark-coloured fishes, any that skulk in corners and any that are thin above the eyes. Discus abhor dirty tanks and suspended matter in the water, so that if your fishes come from clean, well-filtered tanks they are much more likely to prove healthy. The water condition can easily be checked and you can then make sure that the water in your reception tank matches it. Some far-sighted dealers do take the trouble to provide Discus with nature water, i.e. water known to be similar to that in which the fishes are found naturally. If this is the case, try to remove as much water as you can when taking the fishes and use it as a basis for your own aquarium. This will be of very low mineral content and a pH content varying from acid to very acid.

If you are seriously considering breeding Discus you must provide water of similar quality, i.e. low in minerals—under 100 p.p.m. and pH6 for rearing only, and around 10 p.p.m. and more acid, pH5, for breeding.

SOURCE OF SOFT WATER

Some aquarists are fortunate in having access to suitably soft water. But if you live in a hard water district you will have to look elsewhere. There are several alternatives:

Rain water. This is only suitable if collected in clean air districts, and then only *after* heavy rain has been falling for ten to fifteen minutes. The water must then be collected from newly exposed clean surfaces, as, for example, polythene sheeting. Winter rainfall will seldom produce clean water. A pH check of suitable rain water should show a near neutral reading, an acid reading almost certainly indicating the presence of sulphuric acid, which is unacceptable. Water samples, whatever their origins, should be aerated before testing, as dissolved carbon dioxide in the water will give an acid reading.

Distilled water. This is an expensive way to achieve 'Discus water' but very suitable provided the manufacturer does not store it in lead or copper vats. Distilled water, before use in an aquarium, must be aerated until a pH reading of neutral or near neutral is obtained.

Demineralised water. By a system of exchange resins, pure (mineral-free) water is achieved. This is the water sold by chemists as pure water, and again must be aerated before use.

Boiled water. It is possible to boil out temporary hardness from a domestic water supply, leaving water with permanent hardness. Before using this method, check with the chemist of your local water supply authority. If the permanent hardness is greater than 150 p.p.m., the end product will not be worth the effort.

The procedure entails placing the tap water in a stainless steel, glass or clean enamel vessel and boiling for five minutes. Allow the water to cool and then syphon it into the storage vessel, taking great care to avoid disturbing the precipitated mineral. Aerate as before.

Water from domestic water softeners. This is not suitable as it stands, but can be rendered so by adding sufficient hydrochloric acid until a reading of pH4 is achieved. This water must then be vigorously aerated until a neutral pH reading is reached.

Very soft water, whatever the origin, must be stored in vessels made from non-toxic material.

Polythene water containers, of the type used for camping, are suitable, as too are any made from stainless steel or glass.

A monthly change of one-quarter to one-third of the bulk of the aquarium water is good practice. The fishes show their appreciation by displaying good colouration and it helps to maintain a good feeding rate. The water used may be pure water of no hardness and of neutral pH.

ACHIEVING DESIRED pH

Assuming that soft water is available, it is a relatively simple matter to make it acid. My own preference is for the natural way, using sphagnum moss peat in an air-operated or motor-driven outside filter.

The peat is first washed under the tap in a net or sieve to remove peat dust and then, if the tap water is hard, steeped in soft water, squeezed out and placed in the filter between two layers of filter wool.

The speed with which the desired pH is reached is of course dependent on (a) the softness of the water to be acidified, and (b) the relationship between the bulk of peat and the bulk of water. The peat can be dispensed with when the water issuing from the filter has the same pH reading as the bulk of the water in the aquarium.

It will probably be found that to maintain a certain acidity some peat will be required in the filter at all times. Having achieved a suitable water condition, do not be tempted to use a charcoal filter. Activated charcoal (unless it is supplied matched by the manufacturers to a certain pH) will undo all the good work and bring the water back to neutral. Nowadays, filter resins that have good filtering action and no effect on the pH can be obtained from aquarist shops.

One further point about filters—remember to switch off when feeding swimming live food, and to screen the filter intake with stainless steel mesh when newly hatched fry are about.

SETTING UP A DISCUS AQUARIUM

Size of aquarium. The recommended minimum size for an adult pair is 30″ × 15″ × 15″. For raising a small shoal of six young Discus of 1″ body size, start with a 30″ aquarium, at 2″ change to 36″ and at 3″ to 48″. This is ideal for them to reach maturity and pair off.

An aquarium constructed of any of the orthodox materials will be found satisfactory but preferably, where a traditional glazing medium is used, a filter of siliconised rubber sealant (of a type marketed expressly for aquarium use) should be run around all glass, and glass to angle junctions.

Preserving character of water. Any rocks and gravel and plant containers must be lime-free. A simple test can be made by pouring hydrochloric acid over a sample, any effervescence being an indication of unsuitability. It is not practical to render gravel lime-free by soaking in acid. Discus seem to appreciate the security of largish rock formations in the aquarium—again, such rocks should be lime-free. Slate is reasonably easily obtained and is excellent for the purpose. Other rocks should be acid checked as with gravel.

Planting. Most of the larger species of *Echinodorus* grow well in soft acid water, and the cover afforded by these large-leaved plants seems to be appreciated. Some surface plants are beneficial, *Salvinia*, or even common Duckweed being quite suitable.

Temperature. Discus can be successfully raised and bred at temperatures around 78°F. It is written elsewhere that higher temperatures, up to 90°F., will make for healthier fishes, but there is no conclusive evidence to prove this. These high temperatures do not occur in the wild and it is probable that if prolonged, such temperatures will accelerate the metabolism, shortening the life span.

Feeding. Discus can be finicky with their food. They are definitely moderate feeders—being equipped with small mouths they cannot gorge like other Cichlids. What they need is a little food, rendered small, and fed at frequent intervals.

Of live foods, earthworms, gnat larvae, glass worm and daphnia are recommended. *Enchytrae*, dwarf white worm and micro-worm may be fed in limited amounts, Live brine shrimp is most suitable for very young Discus.

Among the dead foods, raw ox heart and freeze-dried foods are satisfactory. Ox heart can be cut to suitable size by scraping with the edge of a sharp knife or razor blade. This produces a fibrous puree and should be stored in a refrigerator when not being used.

Discus can very easily become addicted to a particular food, and this should be avoided at all costs by keeping a variety of foods going. I belong to the anti-tubifex school, however, and although this is by no means conclusive proof, have raised wild baby Discus to maturity, bred them and raised subsequent broods to maturity without the use of tubifex, and without a single occurrence of Discus disease. The problem with tubifex is that it is impossible to sort out tubifex species from other tubifids, some of which can be predatory. Granted that certain chemical treatments can be used to 'clean' the tubifids, but predators, clean or unclean, are just as dangerous.

Lighting. The best form of all is natural lighting, and here the owner of a fish house has an advantage. But even so, some shading will be necessary, for Discus fishes dislike strong light. The glass roof should be shaded and floating plants introduced.

Artificial lighting, whether incandescent or fluorescent, is satisfactory, something like 40 watts of fluorescent lighting for an aquarium 60″ × 18″ × 18″ being about right.

Location. Ideally, the aquarium should be placed with the base no lower than 36″ from the floor, and in a place where there is not too much domestic disturbance. When the fishes are spawning, some additional cover will be necessary.

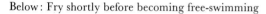

Below: Fry shortly before becoming free-swimming

Above: Discus with eggs, day of spawning

Free-swimming fry, seven days old

Left: Parent Discus transferring hatching fry

Below: Fry feeding from parent fish

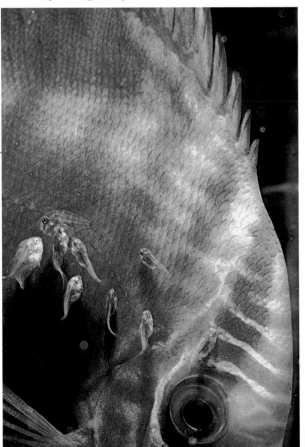

BREEDING

The most active breeding period appears to be between October and April, although odd spawnings do occur at other times of the year.

Assuming there are a number of mature specimens in an aquarium and that feeding and environment have been maintained to an exacting order, the first signs of a pair wishing to spawn will be a cleaning of surfaces and an odd convulsive shudder from both fishes.

The cleaning-up action is not very vigorous and can easily be overlooked. Neither sex engages in showing off, but some typical Cichlid jaw-locking does occur during this period. Naturally, all other fishes in the Discus aquarium must be removed at this stage.

The actual spawning occurs, almost without exception, during the early evening and may be on any vertical surface, be it plant leaf, rock or the aquarium glass. It is not unusual for the parents to eat the first spawning raised, so be prepared for this early disappointment.

The eggs hatch in four days and for the following three days the fry are very vulnerable and care should be taken to see that the aquarium is not unduly disturbed. This is *not* the time to invite strangers to witness your prowess as a breeder!

During these first seven days from laying the eggs, the parents are very busy fanning and cleaning the fry.

Since their appetites are not good, make sure that introduced food is only as much as the parents will eat, for the disturbance caused by the removal of uneaten food may spark off cannibal instincts!

Once the fry are free-swimming, you can, with a degree of assurance, relax. At this time you will be rewarded with the sight of the babies feeding from the bodies of the parents. This unique habit continues for thirty days and you will marvel at the amount of food the parents produce. No other type of food could induce the same growth rate during these first few weeks. This natural food is exuded

Hybrid Discus with slight Heckel characteristics

Blue Hybrid Discus

by both parents through the scales and has nothing whatever to do with the slime and mucus protective coating that all fishes produce. Both parents will take turns in feeding and when one has been 'cleaned' of food he or she will dash off unceremoniously, leaving a cloud of fry to swarm immediately round the other parent.

There is no point in introducing other food until seven days after the fry become free-swimming; then a little newly hatched brine shrimp can be given and if seen to be taken can be fed at frequent intervals throughout the day. At this point a good supply of brine shrimp must be kept going. A medium-sized brood of 80 fish will require a battery of at least three one-gallon jars of regularly hatching brine shrimp to maintain a good growth rate.

To guard against a build-up of salt in the brood tank, it is essential to rinse the brine shrimp in fresh water before feeding. Follow-on foods must of course be of gradually increasing size—screened daphnia, cyclops, micro-worm and dwarf white worm all being suitable. But the sooner the babies are able to take shredded earthworm, the better.

When it is obvious that the parents are producing little or no food, usually when the babies have been free-swimming for about thirty days, they should be removed to another aquarium. Great care must be taken to ensure that temperature and water conditions are exactly matched to the brood tank. Ideally, the growing-on tank should be alongside the brood tank. The water from each tank can then be interchanged via a filter and this ensures that any difference is gradually equalised. It is important for the fry to be given plenty of room to grow. A 50-gallon aquarium is not too large for a start; at approximately two months, they will need double the space and at approximately 3″ body length, not more than six should be accommodated in a 30-gallon tank.

Fishes of equal size should be kept together, but remember that a given number of one brood of equal size could turn out to be of the same sex, a point worth considering when buying small stock.

Pair of Schultz-type seven-colour Discus

SKIPPER

Synodontis angelicus (to 8″)

CATFISHES

THE Catfishes are an extremely varied and primitive group, some of them very specialised. Many have remained suspended in an evolutionary back-water, unchanged in appearance or behaviour for millions of years.

The different species of this large group continue reproducing successfully and show no signs of becoming rare or extinct. The only threat to them is where chemical pollution, introduced by man, has poisoned their natural habitats. But in general the Catfishes can endure far worse natural conditions than most other species. They do not insist on the clear, well-oxygenated running water essential to the Trout and Salmon, but manage quite well in water that is muddy, short of oxygen and suffused with bacteria. Being bottom feeders, they have this built-in ability to withstand conditions which are untenable to other species.

One of the specialised features of some Catfishes is a curious mouth development. In these species the mouth is adapted to form a sucker, enabling them not only to feed on algae but also to cling to stones or rocks when at rest in running water. It also helps them to negotiate steep rock faces and waterfalls, nibbling their way along the wet, algae-covered stones, and often appearing in the most unexpected places.

The many species of Sucker-mouthed Catfishes are of great interest and value to the aquarist. As algae eaters, they help to keep the tank clean and tidy. They also assist the growth of aquatic plants by removing algae from the leaves, allowing the aquarium to take on that sparkling appearance that can only be achieved with well grown plants in good condition.

Among the most important families are the Bagridae (Naked Catfishes from Africa and Asia); Callichthyidae (Mailed Catfishes from South America, chiefly represented by the well known *Corydoras* genus); Clariidae (from Africa, India and the Malay Archipelago): Doradidae (Thorny Catfishes from South America); Loricariidae (Suckermouthed Catfishes from South America); Malapteruridae (Electric Catfishes, represented by one African species only); Mochokidae (exclusively African); Pimelodidae (a large family from Central and South America); Pygididae (worm-like Catfishes from South America); Schilbeidae (from Africa, India and the Malay Archipelago); and Siluridae (Old World Catfishes of Europe and Asia).

The following species are just a few of the many interesting Catfishes suitable for freshwater aquaria. There are, in fact, well over a hundred species classified.

CALLICHTHYIDAE

Brochis coeruleus: The mingled and contrasting yellows and greens of this 3″ Mailed Catfish give it a strikingly beautiful appearance. It differs physically from the *Corydoras* species in that the snout as well as the body is armour plated. Temperamentally, however, it resembles other members of the family, responding to the same general care and feeding. Unlike *Callichthys callichthys*, it has not been known to breed in captivity.

Callichthys callichthys: This Mailed Catfish from eastern Brazil is larger than all the *Corydoras* species, growing to about 7″. It has a long body, a broad head with two pairs of barbels, and two neatly overlapping pairs of scutes on the flanks. The body colour is dark grey or dark green with a bluish sheen on the flanks; the belly is greyish-brown and the grey fins show dark spots.

Care and feeding in the aquarium is as for most *Corydoras* but the breeding procedure is individual. A bubble nest is constructed beneath large floating leaves or plants and the male is responsible for guarding the nest and eggs. The young respond to the same form of care as *Corydoras* fry.

The Catfishes most frequently kept in aquaria are the various species of the genus *Corydoras*. Some of the most popular members of this genus are discussed on pages 203–4, but the following comments are generally applicable.

Brochis coeruleus (to 3″)

NIEUWENHUIZEN

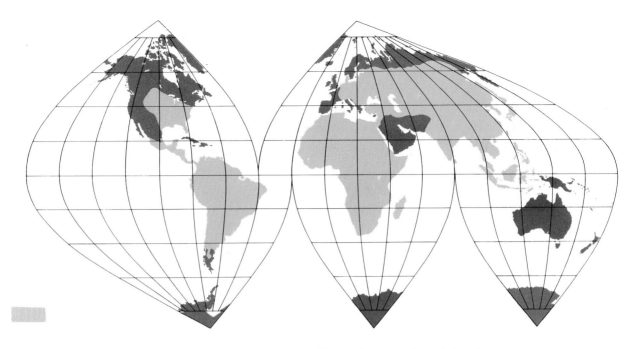

Distribution of Catfishes in parts of Europe, Africa, Asia, and North, Central and South America

Callichthys callichthys (to 7″)

PENGILLEY

As with the two previous species, the scale arrangement of these fishes is reminiscent of a medieval suit of armour. The bony plates, or scutes, on the flanks are arranged in two series that overlap like armoured elbow joints. The *Corydoras* show these characteristics very clearly, but differ from other members of the family in having much shorter bodies in relation to head size.

Occasionally these fishes leave the shallow waters and move out on to the mud banks in search of food. Provided the atmosphere is sufficiently humid, they can cover considerable distances on land, propelled by their rigid pectoral fin spines. In foul water, or water low in oxygen, they are able to breathe atmospheric air, by means of a specialised respiratory system, enabling them to live and feed in conditions where other fishes could not survive.

Most of the *Corydoras* species make excellent aquarium fishes and are good scavengers and tank cleaners. Provided they are well fed and not overcrowded, their inquisitive nature makes them far tamer and easier to handle than most other species. On the whole they are beautifully marked and patterned. Their colours, though not bright, are always well defined and show best in water which is not too acid. They are tolerant of most water conditions, but are adversely affected by salt, even in moderate concentration. A neutral pH reading in old, soft water is best for them.

Their feeding requirements are simple, good dry and live foods of all kinds being acceptable. But they prefer to chew around in the mulm on the bottom, finding food that has been overlooked by other fishes.

To bring them into spawning condition, special feeding is recommended—small or chopped earthworm, white worm and tubifex are all excellent.

The sexes in adult fishes are not difficult to distinguish, the females usually being larger and much broader around the belly. The ventral fins and dorsal are rounded at the tips in the females— more pointed in the males.

The *Corydoras* species are not particularly easy to breed in captivity. Among the few that have been propagated in the aquarium are *C. aeneus*, *C. paleatus*, *C. hastatus*, *C. julii*, *C. melanistius*, *C. rabauti*, *C. schultzei* and *C. reticulatus*. Of these species, *C. aeneus* and *C. paleatus* remain the most prolific.

The first requisite for successful breeding is, at minimum, a 12-gallon tank with old, mature water and a muddy or mulm-covered bottom. Soft neutral water is essential, with plenty of cover in the shape of smooth rocks, but nothing of a calcareous nature such as shells, marble, alabaster or limestone. The rocks must be of a hard dense kind, for the fishes to

clean before and during spawning. A rise in water temperature or even a fluctuation to a cooler temperature will often stimulate the process: the range should be from 70°–82°F. Very bright light may be detrimental as it is possible that in a wild state these fishes are semi-crepuscular, feeding and breeding at night and early first light.

It is usual to use a trio, two males and one female, as the breeding subjects. The beginning of the spawning or courtship act is unmistakable. The males swim around the female, caressing and prodding her with their mouths and noses. This continues until she joins with the males in swimming around, all pausing at intervals to clean stones and plants. Either of the males then presents his ventral side to the mouth parts of the female and the pair cling together for some time, this act being repeated many times with one or both males. It is not known for certain whether or not the sperm from the male is taken into the mouth of the female, who is meanwhile depositing her eggs. If this is the case, sperm lost through the gills would flow over the eggs and fertilise them. Some authorities believe that when the male is induced to release his sperm by the sucking action of the female, it is simply lost in the water and fanned over the eggs by the fin and body movements of the fishes.

During short rests from the spawning act, the fishes will feed; so it is important to keep food available, otherwise they will consume the eggs. The parents should be removed immediately the spawning is completed. They are in no way necessary to the hatching and will, if left, certainly eat the eggs.

Healthy eggs are of a pale shade and very slightly opaque. As the time for hatching approaches, they become darker.

A well conditioned pair, or trio, will continue spawning at intervals over a period of five or six days, giving perhaps 20 batches of eggs, obviously with slightly different times of hatchings, but averaging between five and ten days. The temperature should be maintained at 75°–80°F. A good hatching may yield 250 fry.

If the fry are left in the spawning tank, a partial change of water may be necessary every three days to keep down heavy bacterial concentration; alternatively the fry can be removed to a clean-bottomed tank, provided clean, old water is used. The fry will prosper on paramecium, rotifers and other infusorians, and soon go on to the nauplii of cyclops and sifted daphnia, and eventually chopped tubifex, white worm and other standard large foods.

The breeding and rearing procedures described above may be applied to the following species:

Corydoras aeneus Bronze Catfish (to 3″)

Corydoras arcuatus Arched Catfish (to 2″)

Corydoras hastatus Dwarf/Pigmy Catfish (to 1½″)

Corydoras julii Leopard Catfish (to 2½″)

Corydoras aeneus **Bronze Catfish:** This handsome little Catfish from Venezuela, Trinidad and the River Plate is distinguished by its delicate reddish-brown colouring, uniformly distributed and enhanced by a greenish metallic sheen on the sides of the head and body. Its character and requirements are typical of the *Corydoras* species.

Corydoras arcuatus **Arched Catfish:** The body colour of this Catfish is grey-green. This is embellished by one broad dark band which starts at the corner of the mouth, takes a curved course to the dorsal, travelling parallel with the curve of the body, and then downwards to the tail, where it continues into the lower rays of the tail fin. The tail fin is also marked with fine dark spots and a dark upper edge.

Corydoras hastatus **Dwarf** or **Pigmy Catfish:** A small and elegant Catfish, very pleasing in all aspects, handy and simple to keep under standard *Corydoras* conditions. If kept in quantity, they will shoal and swim quite freely around the aquarium. This species does quite well even in very small tanks.

The common name aptly describes this fish which is rarely more than 1½″ in length. The overall colour is green to golden yellow, dark olive-green back and yellow flanks. A black band runs from the back of the gill cover to an oval-shaped mark at the root of the tail. This mark has a surrounding yellow margin. All the fins are grey, except the base of the caudal, which is blackish.

Corydoras julii **Leopard Catfish:** This species comes from the lower Amazon and tributaries and is easily identified. It is about 2½″ long and is distinguished by a light grey and black body pattern. The silver-grey takes on a metallic green appearance in a side light, and is sprinkled with numerous black dots which develop on the gill plates and head into black etched lines. Laterally, down the body, there is a broad black band edged with silver. The fins are grey, except the caudal, which is spotted, and the dorsal, which is tipped with solid black.

This is the original Leopard Catfish, although this common name has since been given to quite a few other spotted *Corydoras* species. The fish known as *C. leopardus* is perhaps merely a local variety of *C. julii*.

Corydoras melanistius **Black-spotted Catfish:** This spotted *Corydoras* from the northern part of South America is often mistaken for *C. julii*, though it is by no means as strikingly marked. It reaches about 2¾″ in length, and its colour is brassy silver to grey, with a faint pink tinge, sprinkled with small dark brown dots. A wedge-shaped black band runs from the nape across the eye to the lower edge of the cheek. Another black band runs from the base of the pectorals to the base of the dorsal. The tail and anal fins are spotted, with very small fine dots of dark brown, the rest of the fins being hyaline. It is not a delicate species and can be kept in the same manner as other *Corydoras*.

Corydoras myersi **Myers' Catfish:** This 2½″ fish is possibly the most brilliantly coloured of all the *Corydoras* species, bright orange, red, shading in places to almost black, and pale yellow on throat and nape. The gill plates, and the area behind them, are iridescent green, the area around the eyes dark brown. A dark brown, almost black, band runs from in front of the dorsal fin direct to the upper root of the tail. All the fins are hyaline.

These vivid colours are only all present in healthy, fully mature fishes kept at correct temperatures in suitable water.

Corydoras nattereri **Blue Catfish:** The common name of this small Catfish from eastern Brazil, which grows to approximately 2¾″, is derived from the glowing green-blue colour of the flanks. The back is brown, the belly pale orange or pink. A dark stripe extends from the gill cover to the root of the tail, and the fins are grey.

Corydoras paleatus **Blue Leopard Catfish:** This species from the La Plata basin of Brazil, is a very old favourite with aquarists, hardy and easy to keep. The overall colouration is dark olive-green, with a metallic sheen, and the belly is yellowish-white. There are large blue-green blotches, irregular and often bar-like in arrangement, on the sides and back. The entire body is also overlaid with small dark spots. All fins are grey and hyaline, with rows of dark spots.

Corydoras reticulatus: A strikingly marked little fish, approximately 3″ when adult. The reticulated markings resemble a dark brown net lace, laid over an orange-green background. The band along the back, from the base of the dorsal, is a beautiful ochre. The dorsal fin is dark at the base with dark brown spots, and the caudal fin has wide rows of dark spots. There are also dark blotches on the anal fin.

The baby fishes, up to about six months of age, have a different colouration—grey, with dark reticulated markings.

Again, this is a good aquarium fish, which should

Corydoras melanistius Black-spotted Catfish (to 2½″)

Corydoras myersi Myers' Catfish (to 2½″)

Corydoras nattereri Blue Catfish (to 2¾″)

be given the same conditions as all the Amazonian *Corydoras* species.

Corydoras schultzei: The back of this species carries a dark ridge, the area below being golden, the middle of the flanks deep green to black. The belly and underside are bright yellow, head and operculum dark brown. All fins are hyaline.

Corydoras paleatus Blue Leopard Catfish (to 3″)

Corydoras reticulatus (to 3″)

Corydoras schultzei (to 2½″)

LORICARIIDAE

Farlowella acus : Native to Venezuela and southern Brazil, this Catfish, like others of the genus, has a slim, elongate body and head. The dorsal fin is situated immediately above the anal, and both the ventral and upper surfaces are covered by over-lapping scutes. The fish attains a maximum length of 6″. Colour ranges from olive-green to brown, the belly being much paler. A dark broken band runs from the head to the root of the tail. The rays of the hyaline fins are spotted.

Otocinclus flexilis : Very closely resembling *O. affinis,* this fish from the La Plata region is pale green to yellow, darker on the back and fading to creamy white on the underside. The fins are green or white, the vertical fins showing rows of spots. There is a dark but broken lateral line from the gill cover to the root of the tail. This is another species which is fully covered by rows of scutes. The female is fuller in body than the male. Like other Loricariidae, it feeds voraciously on algae and is best kept in numbers.

Plecostomus punctatus : Another Sucker-mouthed fish from southern Brazil, growing to 12″ in the wild, though appreciably smaller in captivity.

The dorsal fin, when held erect, stands very high in the centre of the body. Adult specimens are brownish, with numerous black spots and, when fully grown, five dark transverse stripes. The colour of both sexes is similar.

It is a fairly easy species to keep, provided the aquarium is well established, full of mature water, plant life and some algae. If they prove difficult to acclimatise, as is sometimes the case when received directly from their natural habitat, add sea-salt in the ratio of one teaspoon to five gallons.

Algae is essential in the feeding of this species, but they will eat other organisms as well—small crustacea, tubifex worms, shrimp and water lice. The best substitute for algae is soft peas, split and dropped into one section of the tank.

This is a rewarding fish to keep, improving in appearance as it grows. It thrives best at 75°–82°F.

Xenocara dolichoptera : A native of the Amazon and Guiana, this is a dark brown fish with a dark blue sheen and bluish fins. Dorsal and anal fins have white spots. This species grows to about 5½″. It is distinguished from the *Plecostomus* species in that the lower part of the gill cover is flexible and inward-turning. A number of long forked tentacles

NIEUWENHUIZEN

Farlowella acus (to 6″)

Plecostomus punctatus (to 12″)

NIEUWENHUIZEN

Otocinclus flexilis (to 2½″)

Plecostomus punctatus, showing sucker mouth attached to glass

CUPIT

CUPIT

206

protrude from the snout and forehead. The ventral surface lacks scutes. General care is as for *Plecostomus*, and like them they are efficient algae devourers.

MOCHOKIDAE

Synodontis angelicus: A representative of the most common genus of Naked Catfishes from Africa, this species is crepuscular by nature, hiding during the day, often in an upright position against a river bank or beneath branches and roots. The body colouration ranges from grey to black or violet, with a number of circular red-yellow blotches. There are transverse bars on all the fins. In young specimens these blotches are pure white against a uniformly violet background. Fully grown fishes may grow up to 8″ in length. Like other members of the family, it has a thickish body, spines on dorsal and pectoral fins, and three pairs of barbels. It is a peaceful fish, readily eating plants and small live foods, and is best kept in dimly lighted surroundings. The ideal water temperature for all *Synodontis* species is 70°–78°F.

Synodontis nigriventris **Upside-down Catfish:** This amusing small Catfish from the Congo and tributaries is literally able to swim upside-down. Consequently, although it is ideally built for bottom feeding, it has evolved into a surface-feeding fish because of its odd swimming habit. The colour pattern also differs from that of other Catfishes, for the belly is dark brown, almost black, and the back much lighter, the very opposite of the normal fish's natural camouflage system.

The overall colour is pale grey or cream, with dark brown dots and blotches. The fins are colourless, with a number of dark spots.

Some algae is necessary in feeding although they will take almost any food, and the water temperature should be as for most Catfishes.

The mature females are easily identified, being very deep in the body. This species has been bred in the aquarium and is not considered difficult to propagate.

Synodontis nummifer: Growing up to 7″ long, this species is basically grey in colour, darker on the back and paler underneath. There are several black blotches on the flanks, the largest one over the ventral fins. The maxillary barbels are fairly short and the adipose fin longer than in the very similar *S. notatus*. There is no external sex differentiation.

NIEUWENHUIZEN

Xenocara dolichoptera (to 5½″), small specimen

KAHL

Synodontis nigriventris Upside-down Catfish (to 2½″)

PIMELODIDAE

Pimelodella gracilis **Graceful Catfish:** This fish from the Orinoco and Amazon basins is a good representative of the large family Pimelodidae, distributed over Central and South America.

This species is recommended for the larger aquarium, acting as an excellent scavenger and posing no threat to other fishes. It is quite striking in appearance, with a very long pair of maxillary barbels and two pairs of shorter mandibular barbels. The colour is whitish-green to blue-grey, the back being dark and the belly white. Young fishes have a black band from the gills to the root of the tail. The fins are transparent; the anal fin is rounded and the tail fin deeply forked, with the upper lobe a little longer than the lower. The pectoral fins carry toothed spines and there is a shoulder girdle with a protruding, thorn-like process, used only for defensive purposes.

The fish is happy in old water at a temperature of 72°–82°F. It does not like bright light, so give it a well planted tank with plenty of shade. There is no known method of sexing—both look alike. They have not yet been bred in captivity.

Sorubim lima: This rare Catfish, from the Rio Magdalena and tributaries, is not remarkable for colour, blue-grey, darker on the dorsal fin, with a silver-white belly; but the shape of the spatulate head and the slender body make it an attractive aquarium member. The barbels are remarkable for their length and placement about the mouth. A rather large fish, suitable for the specialist, it has a peaceful temperament but will readily eat smaller fishes. Temperature requirement 75°–78°F.

SCHILBEIDAE

Etropiella debauwi: This African species from the Congo closely resembles the Indian Glass Catfish *Kryptopterus bicirrhis*, but is a member of the *Schilbeidae* family.

It is an active shoaling fish, which positively demands the company of others of the same species. Single specimens tend to sicken (the sign is when it rests on the bottom) and die.

The body is elongated and very compressed. There are three pairs of short barbels. The very small dorsal fin is set far forward almost on the head. The tail is forked and the anal fin extends almost the full length of the body. The translucent, silvery-white belly has three well defined blue-black stripes on the flanks, darkening and becoming more prominent with age. The males are more strikingly marked than the deeper-bodied females. As yet, they have not been bred in captivity although the respective sexes can be easily determined. They show a preference for live food, but will also take floating dry food.

SILURIDAE

Kryptopterus bicirrhis **Glass Catfish:** This is one of the few Catfishes which spends most of its time in mid-water, rather than on the bottom.

A native of India and neighbouring islands, it is almost as transparent as polished glass, with a yellowish hue and, in reflected light, a rainbow-like iridescence. The body is very compressed and slender, the spine being visible along the lateral line of the body. All the internal organs are contained in a small silver sac under the fish's head. The dorsal fin at first glance seems to be non-existent, but closer observation reveals a single first ray remaining. The large anal fin reaches almost the full length of the body. The caudal fin is deeply forked, the lower lobe being somewhat larger than the upper. There is one pair of long maxillary barbels.

Pimelodella gracilis (to 6½″)

Etropiella debauwi (to 3¼″)

Sorubim lima (to 24″)

These fishes are at their best when kept in a roomy well-planted aquarium with well aerated water, at a temperature of 72°–82°F. Water conditions are not important, but they are seen to better advantage in small shoals of four or five, rather than singly. They are not happy with very lively fishes such as Tiger Barbs, Zebras etc.

Any small live food such as daphnia, tubifex etc. is essential, but they will take some dry foods.

At the time of writing no noticeable sexual difference is known, and they have not yet been bred in captivity.

Kryptopterus bicirrhis Glass Catfish (to 4″)   *Synodontis nummifer* (to 7″)

MISCELLANEOUS

SPECIES

Botia macracanthus Clown Loach (to 12″). See page 215

THIS CHAPTER is devoted to a number of species which, though not all suited to the community tank, are well worth consideration. It should be made quite clear that these species, arranged for convenience under families, in strict alphabetical sequence, are in no way related to one another. They are included here because they cannot properly be classified under any of the main headings dealt with elsewhere.

Some of these fishes, notably the Archer Fishes, the Scats, the Gobies and the various Finger and Puffer Fishes, require a certain amount of salt content in their water and are sometimes classified as 'brackish water' species. In nature they are often found in mangrove swamps and river estuaries, and can survive in both fresh and sea water. For such fishes, provide old, mature fresh water, which must be clean and aerated with the aid of a simple filtration system. Sea salt may then be added, in the proportion of 2–3 teaspoonfuls to one imperial gallon of water.

The aquarium for these fishes should be furnished as for a marine aquarium, with hard sea sand, large pebbles or pieces of rock. Tree roots or sea-washed, sun-bleached driftwood may also be used to good effect.

ATHERINIDAE

Most members of this family are marine fishes and are closely related to the Grey Mullet. The true freshwater species – the Rainbow Fishes – are found in Australia, Madagascar and the Celebes Islands. All species seen in aquaria possess double dorsal fins. They make ideal community fishes, tolerating a wide range of water conditions but preferring hard, slightly alkaline water.

Bedotia geayi **Madagascar Rainbow Fish:** Closely related to the Australian Rainbow Fishes, but smaller (about 4″ fully grown), and more iridescent. It has the same type of separated dorsal, but not quite such an elegant manner of swimming.

The body colour is somewhat variable but often a brilliant beige with a dark lateral line. There is a touch of blue on the operculum. The caudal fin is tipped with strong red in adult males and white in immature males and all females. The dorsal fin is lined with white, but pink to red in mature males.

Spawning procedures are the same as for the Australian Rainbows, except that eggs hatch at 77°–80° F. within two or three days.

Bedotia geayi Madagascar Rainbow Fish (to 4″)

Melanotaenia fluviatilis **Australian Pink-tailed Rainbow Fish:**

Melanotaenia maccullochi **Australian Black-lined Rainbow Fish:**

Melanotaenia nigrans **Australian Red-tailed Rainbow Fish:**

All these species are recommended for the community tank, *M. maccullochi* and *M. nigrans* being especially popular. Although the young fishes show little promise of the colours to come, adults in good condition fully justify their common name. Growing up to 5″, they are active and undemanding, thriving in water with temperatures ranging from 60°–80° F.

It is not difficult to distinguish the sexes, the male fish possessing stronger colours. Nor is breeding a great problem. Given some natural light on the breeding tank, the fishes will spawn readily at 75°–77° F. The eggs are adhesive and are not usually eaten by the adults, hatching in seven to nine days at the above temperature. A successful spawning will yield 100–300 fry.

Telmatherina ladigesi **Celebes Rainbow Fish:** This fish is not so easily spawned as the genus *Melanotaenia* and is therefore not so readily available. When mature, the second dorsal and anal fins of both sexes are bright yellow, the leading rays being black and the tail also showing a faint yellow hue. The body has little background colour but a blue stripe commences behind the gills and extends to the caudal peduncle.

M. fluviatalis Australian Pink-tailed Rainbow Fish (to 5″)

PENGILLEY

M. maccullochi Australian Black-lined Rainbow Fish (to 5″)

CUPIT

Melanotaenia nigrans Australian Red-tailed Rainbow Fish (to 5″)

PENGILLEY

Telmatherina ladigesi Celebes Rainbow Fish (to 3″)

Chanda ranga Indian Glassfish (to 2″)

CENTROPOMIDAE

These are commonly known as Glassfishes, the majority of which inhabit either marine or brackish water. Those species suitable for freshwater aquaria come from South-east Asia and prefer hard, slightly alkaline water, to which 2–3 teaspoonfuls of salt per gallon have been added. As the common name suggests, they have very transparent bodies, with the spinal skeleton and swim bladder clearly visible. Most species are difficult to breed.

Chanda ranga **Indian Glassfish:** This, the most frequently seen of the Glassfishes, comes from India, Burma and Thailand. It grows up to 3″ in nature but only about half this size in captivity. The background colour of the body is pale gold with two faint vertical bars. The dorsal fin is deeply split, giving the impression of two fins. Both the dorsals and the anal fins are dark, edged with pale blue. The fishes are rather timid until they become accustomed to their surroundings.

Chanda wolfii: This species reaches 6″–8″ in its native Thailand, Sumatra and Borneo, but considerably less in aquaria. Not nearly as colourful as *C. ranga*, the body is silver with an iridescent horizontal line. It has the same type of split dorsal fin.

Gynochanda filamentosa: A comparatively recent discovery, this fish resembles the members of the genus *Chanda*, having the typical split dorsal fin. Growing to about 2″ in length, the male has very long extensions to the anal and second dorsal fins, making it a rather striking fish.

Chanda wolfii (to 6″)

Gynochanda filamentosa (to 2")

COBITIDAE

The commonest members of this family, whose natural distribution extends from Asia to Europe (including the British Isles) and into North Africa, are the Loaches. All are timid fishes, tending to hide under rocks in the aquarium. It is best to keep a number of these species together and provide flat stones or rock arches as hiding places. Most prefer soft, fresh water but are not too particular as to diet, taking most live or prepared foods.

The genus *Acanthophthalmus* comprises a number of species, all with long, slender bodies, and distinguished by variations in their body patterns.

Acanthophthalmus kuhli kuhli **Coolie Loach:** This is a typical member of the genus, growing to about

$3\frac{1}{2}$". The body colour is pale gold, with numerous vertical dark brown bars. Its unusual appearance has earned it considerable popularity.

Members of the genus *Botia* also have a common body shape. The two following species are often imported, both reaching about 4" in aquaria.

Botia lohachata: This fish has a very variable body pattern of dark bars and circles across the back, on a greyish-silver body. The bars are also visible, though fainter, in the dorsal and caudal fins.

Botia macracanthus **Clown Loach:** This is the best known member of the genus and a brilliantly coloured fish. The background colour is orange-red, with three vertical dark brown bars, one through the eye. The dorsal and anal fins are brown and the others bright red. *Illustration pages 210–11.*

Acanthophthalmus kuhli kuhli Coolie Loach (to $3\frac{1}{2}$")

Botia lohachata (to 4")

CERATODONTIDAE & LEPIDOSIRENIDAE

The Lung-fishes of the Order Dipnoi are often described as 'living fossils' and are survivors from a very early period of the earth's development. They make an interesting group, although because of their size they are unsuitable for home aquaria.

Their natural habitat is usually water of low oxygen content which completely disappears during the dry season. At such times the fishes hibernate in cocoons at the bottom of holes in the mud, using their lungs to remain alive. With the return of the water, the fishes break out of their burrows.

There are two separate families of Lung-fishes. The Ceratodontidae comprise the single genus *Neoceratodus* from Australia; the Lepidosirenidae include the genera *Lepidosiren* from South America and *Protopterus* from Africa.

Neoceratodus forsteri **Australian Lung-fish:** This rare species has large, pronounced scales with near-normal rather than rudimentary anal and pectoral fins. It is the largest of all the Lung-fishes, adult specimens attaining a length of almost 6 feet.

Protopterus annectens **African Lung-fish:** A good deal smaller than the preceding species, at around 20″ this is a much more frequent inmate of public aquaria. Though sluggish by nature, like all Lung-fishes, it still requires plenty of room, and although it can endure dirty conditions in nature it must have clean water in captivity. Its normal diet may include fishes, small reptiles and amphibia, and raw meat. Water temperature can vary from 60° to 90°F., for it is extremely hardy.

Neoceratodus forsteri Australian Lung-fish (to 6′)

PENGILLEY

Protopterus annectens African Lung-fish (to 20″)

ELECTROPHORIDAE

This family is represented by one member, again not suitable for most private aquaria, both because of its size (up to 7½ feet) and its dangerous habits.

Electrophorus electricus **Electric Eel:** Found in many parts of the Amazon and Orinoco rivers, this fish possesses organs capable of discharging powerful, often lethal, electric shocks.

It is a predatory fish, very tough and long-lived. In captivity an adult specimen requires an 8-foot tank, 2–3 feet wide and at least 2 feet deep. The water must be kept at temperatures ranging from 60°F. to 82°F., and must be clean and slightly acid. Droppings are copious when the fish is feeding well, and plenty of food is needed to keep it fit, including live or freshly killed fishes, large earthworms, ox heart, raw liver and indeed any fresh or dried meat. Above all, handle this fish with the utmost care for even a mild shock can be unpleasant.

Electrophorus electricus Electric Eel (to 7½′)

GOBIIDAE

The little banded Gobies of the genus *Brachygobius* from Thailand, Malaysia and Indonesia, are almost impossible to distinguish from one another so the two commonest species are discussed together.

Brachygobius nunus, Brachygobius xanthozona **Bumblebee Fish** or **Wasp Goby**: Growing to about $1\frac{1}{2}''$–$1\frac{3}{4}''$ in length, these are chunky, cylindrical-shaped fishes, with rounded heads and slightly compressed tails. In good condition the ground colour is clear yellow with a variable pattern of four broad black bands, slightly thicker in *B. nunus*.

They are not good community fishes, often ripping the fins of other species, and should be given a separate tank with plenty of hiding space. Although very hardy, and able to survive for some time in fresh water they are better kept in slightly salty conditions. Once they have overcome their initial shyness they become quite active and make an attractive picture.

Feeding may be a problem, as they thrive best on a varied live food diet, some eating nothing else. Spawning may be encouraged by placing a small flower pot, laid on its side, in the aquarium. The 100–200 eggs are fairly large in comparison with the parents' size. They hatch in four days at a temperature above the 75°F. mark. The male guards the eggs and the young, which should be fed on the usual paramecium and rotifer infusoria.

Brachygobius nunus Bumblebee Fish (to $1\frac{3}{4}''$)

KAHL

GYRINOCHEILIDAE

This family, from Thailand, contains only three species, of which the following is the best known.

Gyrinocheilus aymonieri **Sucker Loach**: This fish is a useful member of the aquarium, being the most efficient of all algae eaters, more reliable than the *Otocinclus* Whiptails or the *Plecostomus* species.

The body is elongate, rounded and not compressed. It is not unlike the European Minnow (genus *Phoxinus*), apart from the head which, with its prominent lips and sucker mouth, is quite Loach-like.

Although they grow to about 19″ in the wild, 5″ is a good size for an adult aquarium specimen. The females may be distinguished by their deeper bodies, and the males have a greater number of tubercles on the head. The colours are unremarkable, brown to fawn with dark blotches on the back, a dark lateral band with lighter blotches, and a silvery belly.

Sucker Loaches respond to well planted conditions and good aeration. They are fast, elusive swimmers, difficult to net even in small aquaria. They have not been known to breed in captivity.

MONODACTYLIDAE

The Finger Fishes found off the coasts and in the estuarine waters of Africa, southern Asia and Australia, are typical 'brackish water' residents. They are quite at home with *Poecilia* species or with other community fishes enjoying similar water conditions, and may even be kept under full marine conditions, making good companions for the smaller coral reef fishes. Though they may seem shy at first, they gain confidence and are seen to best advantage when kept in shoals. In fact, single fishes often tend to become morose, either hiding or bullying other species. They can stand fairly cool water but for good colour and rapid growth, a temperature of 77°F. is desirable. Neither of the species described below has been bred in captivity.

Monodactylus argenteus **Finger Fish** or **Malay Angel Fish**: This beautiful fish, ranging in nature from Malaysia to the east coast of Africa, will grace any brackish water aquarium. In good health, the colour is a strong silver with black striping. One stripe runs through the eye from the top of the head, a second starts at the front of the dorsal,

Gyrinocheilus aymonieri Sucker Loach (to 5″)

Monodactylus sebae (to 8″)

crosses the body and then runs back along the edge of the anal fin. The dorsal and anal fins are a beautiful golden-orange with black tips when in the peak of condition.

Monodactylus sebae: This West African Finger Fish is distinguished from *M. argenteus* by its very deep body, high curving dorsal and long anal fin, and a single body stripe from the tip of the dorsal across the body to the tip of the anal fin. There is an extra black stripe across the caudal peduncle and the fin colouration is generally a lighter yellow than in *M. argenteus.* Care and provision are basically as for the related species but it is less hardy and being rare, it tends to be somewhat expensive.

Monodactylus argenteus Finger Fish (to 8″)

MORMYRIDAE

The eleven known species of the family Mormyridae are all freshwater fishes from Africa. Strangely shaped, they make interesting aquarium inmates and are avidly sought after by connoisseurs. Their popular name is Elephant Fish or Elephant Trunk Fish, some of them having an elongated proboscis, others a finger-shaped proboscis on the lower jaw functioning as a feeler. These are all bottom feeders, occupying still, muddy water. A few species have electric organs capable of giving out weak discharges.

The Elephant Fishes are not fussy about aquarium conditions, but they dislike new, immature water and should therefore be housed in established tanks with soft mulm on the bottom. Plenty of cover in the form of cave-like rockwork should also be provided. The temperature has to be carefully watched, however. Ideally it should be between 75° and 80°F. Lower temperatures are dangerous and rapid cooling of the water may prove fatal.

The fishes should be fed on the usual live foods, especially tubifex worms, and will also take dried foods (dead daphnia, cyclops, etc.) and plant detritus. It is important to keep them feeding. Disturbance or water cooling may cause them to go off their food and it is essential for them to recover their appetites before they lose too much weight. Often a rise of a few degrees in water temperature will do the trick.

The following three are good community fishes.

Gnathonemus macrolepidotus: Like other members of this genus, the body is elongate and compressed. The chin protrudes slightly but there is no suggestion of a snout. The body colour is brown, the belly pale, often silvery, while some have a sprinkling of small black specks on both body and fins. Not yet bred in captivity.

Gnathonemus petersi: Again the body is flattened and rigid in appearance, the mouth small and rounded, the trunk appendage curving from the lower jaw. The dorsal fin starts well behind the anal fin, the caudal is small and deeply forked. The colour varies from dark brown to brownish-violet, and two ragged transverse bars are visible between the dorsal and anal fins. It is a peaceful fish and somewhat playful. Like other Mormyrids, it has not thus far been bred in aquaria.

Gnathonemus macrolepidotus (to 12″)

PENGILLEY

Gnathonemus petersi (to 9″)　　　　　　　　　　*Marcusenius longianalis* (to 6″)

Badis badis (to 2½")

Badis burmanicus (to 2½")

Marcusenius longianalis: This long, slender fish from the lower reaches of the River Niger, markedly different in shape to its stocky relative *M. isidori*, grows to approximately 6". The anal fin is significantly longer than the dorsal. The body colour is light brown, irregularly marked with black spots; the belly is appreciably paler and the back considerably darker. It is reputed to be somewhat pugnacious towards those of its own species although not outstandingly aggressive towards other species. Like other Mormyrids, there is no record of it being bred in captivity.

NANDIDAE

Of the eight known species of this family only three are normally available to the aquarist.

They are predatory fishes, with vicious temperaments hardly equalled by any other families. Most of them are quite capable of devouring fishes up to three-quarters of their own body size. They also have tremendous appetites and unless kept well fed will soon lose condition, languish and die.

The only safe community fish in the family is *Badis badis*. None of the others can be trusted with species smaller than themselves, although a few fishes of equal size and condition may be kept together. Nevertheless, they make interesting aquarium inmates, provided they are given plenty of live foods, raw meat, etc. They dislike strong light and must be afforded adequate shade in the form of plants and rocks. The majority spawn on the bottom, with the males caring for the young.

Badis badis: This is a charming little fish from India, about 2½" in length. Because of its changing colour pattern, it was once known as the Chameleon Fish. Within a few minutes, in fact, these colours can range through blue, grey, green and even light pink. Eight to ten transverse bars are often visible in young fishes, not present in the adults. A black line runs from the start of the dorsal fin across the eye to the mouth, and some males may show a checkered pattern on the flanks. The dorsal fin is usually marked with red or greenish longitudinal stripes. The body is flattish in shape but longer than it is deep. Females are deeper in body and slightly less colourful.

Spawning procedures are as for dwarf Cichlids. A plant pot laid on its side is generally used as a spawning base, the male guarding eggs and fry. The water temperature should be from 78° to 82°F.

A reddish-brown variety with lines of dark spots, from Burma, but seldom seen, is *B. burmanicus*.

Polycentropsis abbreviata African Leaf Fish (to 3¼″)

Monocirrhus polyacanthus **South American Leaf Fish:** This is by far the most convincingly leaf-like of the three contenders to this name; indeed this inhabitant of the Amazon and the Rio Negro may be cited as a perfect example of camouflage.

The body is flat and leaf-shaped, the head pointed and a short barbel on the lower lip of the protrusible mouth looks exactly like a leaf stalk. Colouration is variable, changing according to the conditions of background and bottom.

The fish maintains an oblique, head-down attitude among plants like a drifting leaf. It is an extraordinarily predatory species, feeding almost exclusively on fishes and capable of consuming the equivalent of its own weight daily. It can, however, be induced to take scraped meat, garden worms etc. It prefers very soft, slightly acid water at a temperature in the 72°–76°F. range.

Polycentropsis abbreviata **African Leaf Fish:** This fish from West Africa differs from other members of the family in that it is a bubble nest builder. Its colouration is very variable, to such an extent that an accurate description is difficult. In general, the colours are dark and the patterning cloudy and not well defined. The body is dark green with black or

Right: *Polycentrus schomburgki* (to 4″)

Monocirrhus polyacanthus South American Leaf Fish (to 3¼″)

bottle-green blotches, and a strong dark stripe extends from the eye to the bottom of the gill plate. The dark colour tends to fade on the flanks and the belly is often pale pink. The fins are yellowish, carrying a few faint dark marks in continuation of the body pattern. The female is usually paler, with an even less clearly defined colour and pattern.

The male builds the bubble nest under any floating vegetation, Floating Fern for preference. He then attracts the female to the nest in the manner of the Gouramies. She turns on her back and extrudes a single egg into the nest and this is repeated until she has laid some 150 eggs. After this she must be removed in order to prevent damage from the male in his eagerness to protect the eggs. Breeding should not be attempted from any but fully mature specimens as young fishes tend to be highly irritable,

with the males acting savagely towards the females. Hatching time for the eggs, at 78°F., is approximately forty-eight hours. Remove the males as soon as the fry can swim properly. The young are good feeders and easy to rear.

Polycentrus schomburgki: Another Leaf Fish from South America, with a deep leaf-shaped body and a habit of swimming that gives it not only the colour but also the appearance of a dead leaf floating on the surface. The body colour is deep brown to black, with dark markings that emit a silver gleam. Three dark bands radiate outwards from the eye to the nose, covering the lower edge of the gill plate. The rigid parts of the anal and dorsal fins are blue or bottle-green, with light blue-green borders, and also some darker splashes where they join the body.

The ventral fins are yellowish, long and pointed.

The soft-rayed portion of the dorsal and the caudal fin are colourless and almost invisible, giving the fish a strange and characteristic truncated appearance.

During spawning and often during courtship, the males are richer in colour, the females brown and paler. Breeding in aquaria is rare.

This is a beautiful fish, which, like all Nandids, must be given live rather than dry foods. Slightly acid water is preferred, in common with other members of the family.

NOTOPTERIDAE

The Knife Fishes are large fishes with long, compressed bodies. The extended anal fin running the length of the body and joining the small caudal fin gives them a tailless appearance, and it is this long fin that propels them through the water. The fishes have considerable mobility and are able to swim backwards or forwards with equal facility. The very small scales give the skin an Eel-like texture.

Xenomystus nigri **African Knife Fish:** This is a typical member of the family, though distinguished by the complete absence of a dorsal fin. Dark grey or brown in colour, it is a nocturnal fish, disliking well-lit aquaria. Plenty of shade must therefore be provided at all times. Although it will coexist with fishes of its own size it cannot be trusted with smaller species, so is not a good community fish. It should be given clean, slightly acid water, with temperatures ranging from 70° to 80°F. Live foods are preferred. Not known to have bred in captivity.

OSTEOGLOSSIDAE

These large fishes are found in South America, Africa, Malaysia and Australia, and recommended only to the specialist. Given plenty of aquarium space, they will exceed 2 feet in length, and even as fry they need a large tank.

Osteoglossum bicirrhosum **Arowana:** This is the best known of the South American species, growing to about 16″. The body is compressed, the anal fin extending almost the entire length and tapering to a small tail. The large scales are deeply imprinted, giving a trellis-like effect to the body. The mouth is large, and two barbels protrude from the chin. The overall appearance of the Arowana is graceful and streamlined. Its colour is very changeable, with a general iridescent rainbow sheen. The water temperature should be kept at 75°–80°F. Diet should consist of fishes and large live foods.

POLYPTERIDAE

Representatives of the Bichirs and Reed Fishes may sometimes be seen in public aquaria, but all are too large for the average home aquarium, often growing to 2 feet in length.

Osteoglossum bicirrhosum Arowana (to 16″). This specimen is about 4″ long

Xenomystus nigri African Knife Fish (to 8″)

Polypterus ornatipinnis **Ornate Bichir:** This is a beautiful and fairly common species which, like other members of the family, comes from tropical Africa. It displays the typical physical features of the family, the dorsal being a series of finlets instead of a single fin, and the pectorals being used as props when the fish rests on the bottom. Like the Anabantidae, the Bichirs take air from the water surface, but having no special organ to absorb the oxygen, adapt the swim bladder for this purpose. Another unusual feature of this and related species concerns the fry. The young, when they hatch from

Polypterus ornatipinnis Ornate Bichir (to 15″)

the egg, are mere larvae, with external gills like the young of newts.

The Ornate Bichir has beautiful, irregular dark markings on a white or grey background colour, the belly being yellowish. The white dorsal finlets have black spots, the other fins being yellow with transverse black streaks.

SCATOPHAGIDAE

The Scats are brackish water fishes frequenting the river mouths, estuaries and coastal waters of India, the Malay Archipelago, Northern Australia and the Melanesian islands. Disc-shaped, with compressed bodies, they are scavengers, feeding on animals, plants and refuse. Only one of the family, *Scatophagus argus*, is readily available to the aquarist.

Scatophagus argus **Argus Fish, Leopard Scat, Tiger Scat:** Variously named because of its colour differentiations, this fish may be recommended to the discriminating aquarist with sufficient tank space. It is flat and deep bodied, very

beautiful and extremely sociable. Although it grows to about 10″ in captivity, it can be trusted even with tiny Guppies and becomes tame enough to take food from the fingers.

The most common form, the Leopard Scat, is a metallic bronze-green with dark round spots. The Tiger Scat, once thought to be a different species and wrongly described as *S. rubrifons*, has strong red embellishment on the head and first dorsal fin. Both are at their most colourful at 3″–4″, and although the hues remain fine at any stage, they tend to fade a little with growth. The fishes prefer slightly alkaline water of 72°–77°F.

TETRAODONTIDAE

Most of the Puffer Fishes are exclusively marine fishes, but the various members of the genus *Tetraodon* are unusually quaint and charming additions to the freshwater aquarium.

Tetraodon fluviatilis **Green Puffer Fish:** This is a beautiful species, from India and South-east Asia,

Scatophagus argus Leopard Scat (to 10″)

Tetraodon fluviatilis Green Puffer Fish (to 6½″)

Toxotes jaculator Archer Fish (to 4″)

with the usual squat, rounded shape. The head is very large and the body tapers away to a tiny tail. This tail is used solely for steering, propulsion being obtained through the rotating action of the small dorsal fin. The fish indeed appears to glide through the water, with sudden stops, starts and hovering movements, rather reminiscent of a hummingbird. It grows to about 6½″.

The unusual mouth and dentition of this and related species enable it to crush and devour shelled creatures such as water snails and other molluscs. They prefer water snails to daphnia and tubifex and are valuable in ridding a tank of these pests.

The common name is derived from the fish's habit of inflating itself with air to twice its normal size, when alarmed. It can be induced to do this by removing it from the water and gently stroking its belly, though as a regular practice this is not to be recommended. In fact, they are not easily alarmed and when properly settled they rarely inflate.

Both colour and patterning are variable, the back and sides being bright green or yellowish-green and the entire body and head irregularly covered with dark brown or black square patches, which sometimes form broad bands. The belly is white, sometimes showing the characteristic dark spots.

They are not particularly good community fishes, with unpredictable snapping habits, though they do mix well with certain species, for example *Monodactylus argenteus*. If properly cared for, preferably in salty water (though they can manage in completely pure water), they are hardy and long lived. Breeding is reported to be difficult and the young not easy to feed.

TOXOTIDAE

The Archer Fishes are found in the coastal waters of the Persian Gulf, India, the Malay Archipelago, Indonesia, Australia and the adjoining islands. They are brackish water fishes and the following species is easily the best known.

Toxotes jaculator **Archer Fish:** A beautiful fish which, like its relatives, earns its name from its habit of shooting down winged insects by means of a jet of water directed from its mouth. It can hit targets up to 5 feet distant with astonishing accuracy. A powerful contraction of the gill covers pushes the stream of water through a tube formed by the tongue and the roof of the mouth, the thin anterior end of the tongue giving the final thrust. The habit seems to be an acquired ability for the young fishes spit small jets more or less at random, only later becoming adept at the exercise. At that stage they will even allow for light refraction in water in gauging the position of their prey.

These fishes make interesting aquarium inmates. The silver and black bands and greenish-gold sheen show up well and the smart, compact shape is very pleasing. Naturally, they cannot be trusted with smaller fishes, but when settled they will readily take food from the hand. Old, brackish water suits them best, with a temperature between 77° and 82°F. They need plenty of swimming space, growing to around 4″.

No method of distinguishing the sexes externally has yet been discovered and they have not yet been bred in captivity.

DISEASES OF FISHES

Fishes suffer ill-health for a variety of reasons. Many disorders are caused by unfavourable environmental conditions, such as lack of oxygen or faulty nutrition, most of which can be rectified with little difficulty. Others are caused by infectious organisms such as protozoa, helminths, fungi, bacteria or viruses. For these, cure may also be a straightforward matter, although for some there is no known treatment. In the following pages, diseases commonly encountered by the aquarist are discussed together with recommended treatments where these are available. For more detailed coverage, the reader is referred to the books by Davis, Reichenbach-Klinke and Elkan, Sterba and van Duijn, listed on page 242.

The amateur aquarist can frequently diagnose the more common diseases, particularly those in which the skin is affected. A hand-lens is often adequate for identifying surface parasites such as helminths, but many of the smaller organisms like protozoa cannot be accurately identified without a microscope, and few aquarists wish to go to the trouble and expense of obtaining such equipment. It is therefore necessary to observe closely the behavioural pattern and deportment of the fishes, particularly new arrivals, so that early signs of disease or distress may be recognised and dealt with promptly.

For this reason an invaluable piece of equipment is an extra tank set aside for quarantine purposes; a sure way of maintaining disease-free tanks is to isolate all new stock for a few weeks.

SIGNS OF ILL HEALTH

Before specific diseases are described, it is worthwhile to consider some of the ways by which ill-health in fishes can be recognised. Symptoms depend mainly on the causative agent, but there are several guide-lines to indicate that fishes are unwell and in need of remedial treatment.

Healthy fishes are normally clean, erect-finned, bright-eyed and of crisp colour. The skin should be smooth and the fins untorn. They should also be alert, darting away when disturbed. In unhealthy fishes, any or all of these features may change. If, for example, the skin becomes ragged or excessively slimy, or if the fish continually rubs its body against objects in the tank, a skin infection is probably present. Discolouration can be due to skin parasites or even to an internal complaint, although it should be realised that temporary colour changes may occur, if, for example, the fish is frightened. Difficulty in breathing, often accompanied by pallid gills, is a sign of ill-health. Internal disorders are sometimes indicated by abdominal swellings or cysts. Perhaps the clearest indication of ill-health, however, is a persistent change in behaviour; to detect this, the owner must be familiar with his fishes' normal movements. When, for instance, an active fish becomes sluggish for prolonged periods, a disease must be suspected.

ILL HEALTH DUE TO ENVIRONMENTAL CONDITIONS

Let us look first at some examples of ill-health which may be caused by an unfavourable environment, and which are often mistaken for infections.

Lack of Oxygen. Fishes other than the Labyrinths (Anabantids), show characteristic signs of distress if the oxygen content of the water in the tank falls below the minimum required. Often they swim close to the surface and take in bubbles of air. Fast swimmers may swim more rapidly.

There are several ways in which lack of oxygen

can arise, such as over-crowding, lack of sufficient plants, inadequate sunlight, rise in temperature, or excessive decaying organic matter such as dead plants. Prevention, therefore, is achieved by ensuring that the tank is clean, well-lighted, not over-crowded and correctly planted. Artificial aeration may be necessary.

Faulty Nutrition. Incorrect food can give rise to various troubles, not all of which are immediately evident. Over-abundance of one type of food can cause inflammation of the intestine, which causes a loss of appetite; the excreta may be flecked with blood. If this should occur, feeding must be stopped for a few days, after which another type of food should be given. Too much fat and carbohydrate can lead to deposition of fatty tissue and degeneration of organs such as the liver. The disease may be difficult to recognise until after death, but can be avoided by maintaining a properly adjusted diet.

Temperature Change. Many fishes, particularly tropical species, can adapt to changing temperature, provided that the change is not too sudden. Care should be taken, therefore, when fishes are transferred to new tanks. A sudden lowering of temperature may cause shock, as a result of which the affected fish may develop a slow, weaving motion, a condition known as the 'shimmies'. A sudden rise in temperature may cause difficulties in respiration, when gasping and surface-hugging may occur.

Poisons. Fishes are highly susceptible to low concentrations of many metals and chemical compounds. Copper and zinc, for example, are extremely toxic. Their solubility in water depends on many factors such as aeration, salt concentration and pH, but they may be a cause of death when used in the frames of aquarium tanks. Insecticides are particularly harmful, low concentrations in the water often proving lethal. Refrain from using aerosol sprays in rooms where fishes are housed.

ILL HEALTH DUE TO INFECTIOUS ORGANISMS

All organs and tissues of fishes are possible sites of infection. In aquarium fishes the diseases most commonly encountered are those affecting the skin and gills, perhaps because these are more readily seen and diagnosed. In the first part of this section, common skin parasites are described, together with the symptoms they produce, and means of diagnosis. In the second part, infections of internal organs are discussed. Finally, a section on methods of treatment is given.

INFECTIONS OF THE SKIN AND GILLS

Of the wide variety of skin diseases, the two which probably cause most trouble in aquaria are 'white-spot' and 'velvet', both of which are caused by protozoa (single-celled organisms). Other diseases are caused by parasitic crustacea, helminths (parasitic worms), fungi, bacteria and viruses.

Protozoal diseases

'White-spot' disease: This disease is easy to recognise, as the skin of the infected animal becomes covered with small white spots, each approximately the size of a pinhead (Fig. 1). Each spot represents the site of one, or sometimes two, parasites. All parts of the body surface, including the fins and gills, may be attacked.

The causative agent is named *Ichthyophthirius multifiliis* (Figs. 2, 3). It is spherical and large by protozoan standards, measuring up to 1 mm. in diameter. Short, hair-like processes known as cilia are spread densely over the surface. A horseshoe-shaped nucleus is also present which is clearly visible under the microscope.

By means of its cilia the parasite rotates vigorously and burrows into the surface layer (epidermis) of its host. It feeds on skin cells and surface debris. The burrowing action causes a local irritation and the epidermis eventually grows across the parasite to enclose it, thus forming a white spot.

Reproduction occurs away from the host (Fig. 2). After maturing in the skin, which takes from a few days to three weeks, depending on the temperature, the parasite bores out, swims away and comes to rest on a submerged object such as a stone or plant. Here it forms a jelly-like cyst within which a series of rapid cell divisions takes place. In a few hours, several hundred daughter cells, or swarmers, are produced, which break out of the cyst to find a new host. Alighting on the skin, they burrow in to recommence the life-cycle. If they fail to find a host within three or four days, they perish.

SYMPTOMS: If the protozoan is introduced into a tank containing healthy fishes, little harm may occur, other than a fleeting infection with a few parasites. If, however, the fishes are already weakened for some other reason, e.g. lack of

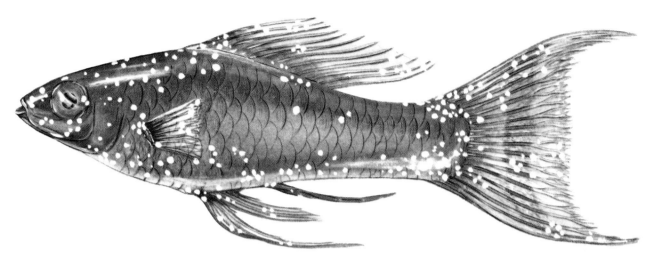

Fig. 1. White-spot, a protozoal skin disease, shown on Guppy

Fig. 2. Life cycle of White-spot parasite, *Ichthyophthirius multifiliis*

Fig. 3. *Ichthyophthirius multifiliis*, enlarged ×50

oxygen, the parasite will quickly cover the whole body surface, causing irritation and opening up wounds for secondary infections. The host's mobility may become affected. In severe cases, death may result.

DIAGNOSIS: The white spots are easily seen, being up to 1 mm. in diameter. If scrapings of mucus were taken from the surface for microscopical examination, the constantly rotating parasites would be seen.

PREVENTION: If White-spot appears in an otherwise healthy tank, the parasite must have been introduced either as the adult on a newly-acquired fish, or as the cyst form on, for example, new stones or plants. The only certain method of prevention, therefore, is to quarantine all new stock, including stones, plants, etc., preferably in water at a temperature of 77°F. Allow one week's quarantine.

TREATMENT: The adult parasite on the body surface and the multiplying forms in the cyst are protected, so curative treatment must be directed against the free-swimming adults and swarmers. The subject is covered in some detail by Ghadially (1956) and van Duijn (1967), who recommend the following treatments: methylene blue, quinine, mepacrine, mercurochrome, acriflavine or chloramine. Details of treatment are given at the end of this chapter.

'*Velvet*' *disease*: This disease is characterised by the skin taking on a dusty appearance of yellow or rust colour. 'Rust' or 'gold-dust' are alternative names. The protozoan responsible is *Oodinium*, there being two species of importance, *O. limneticum* giving the characteristic rust-powder appearance, and *O. pillularis* a greyer colouration.

Oodinium (Fig. 5) is smaller than *Ichthyophthirius*, the adult parasite being about 13 μ long (1 μ = 0.001 mm.). It is pear-shaped. At the narrow end are small outgrowths, or pseudopodia, with which the organism can penetrate its host's epithelium and feed off skin cells.

On the skin of its host, the parasite matures in a few days. Multiplication takes place within a cyst, as in *Ichthyophthirius*. In *Oodinium limneticum* the animal rounds itself off, and a series of divisions

233

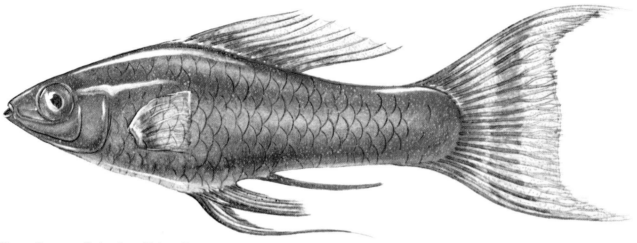

Fig. 4. Guppy suffering from Velvet disease

Fig. 5. *Oodinium* parasite, cause of Velvet disease, enlarged ×3,000

results in several hundred daughter cells, or dinospores. In *O. pillularis* the parasite leaves the fish and sinks to the bottom before encysting; in this species only 32 or 64 dinospores are produced. Dinospores possess two hair-like processes known as flagella which are used in locomotion. On finding a new host, they lose their flagella and grow into adults; they perish within twenty-four hours if they fail to find a new host.

SYMPTOMS: Skin damage is caused by the burrowing action of the parasites. Heavy infections may spread to the gills and mouth cavity. In tropical species, swelling of the gill cover may occur. Severe infections are often lethal.

DIAGNOSIS: The dusty appearance of the skin is sufficient for immediate recognition.

PREVENTION: As with White-spot, the best way of preventing an outbreak of Velvet is to quarantine new stock for at least ten days. If an outbreak has occurred, difficulty may arise in eradicating the organism as it can apparently survive for long periods in a non-parasitic form, making use of its chlorophyll for the process of photosynthesis. Treatment, therefore, is best carried out in a darkened tank.

TREATMENT: Available treatments are: methylene blue, acriflavine, quinine, sodium chloride.

Costia necatrix: This protozoan gives rise to a condition sometimes referred to as 'infectious turbidity of skin and gills', characterised by a slimy bluish-white appearance of the skin.

The parasite responsible (Fig. 6) has two long and two short flagella, used for locomotion in the free-swimming state. On attaching to the host's body, it feeds on mucus, surface debris and epithelial cells. The parasite divides rapidly on the skin, being able to cover a fish in a few days. It can survive only one hour when detached. In unfavourable conditions, it may encyst.

SYMPTOMS: Epithelial damage is caused, and respiration and mobility may become affected. Death may result if the fish remains untreated.

DIAGNOSIS: If a fish develops sliminess of the skin it may well be *Costia necatrix*, but identity of the parasite is not possible without microscopical examination, and the condition may be caused by more than one protozoan. *Costia* is the most serious of these parasites.

PREVENTION AND TREATMENT: Because of the short survival time of the organism away from its host, a tank can be disinfected by removing diseased fish to another tank and letting the water stand unoccupied for several hours. The treatments available include quinine, acriflavine, sodium chloride and formalin.

Chilodonella cyprini: This parasite causes a slimy skin appearance similar to that caused by *Costia*.

Chilodonella cyprini is ciliated, most of the cilia being arranged in rows along its underside. There are also a number of larger cilia at one end. It feeds on epithelial cells and debris. Like *Costia*, the parasite dies quickly if separated from its host for more than a few hours. The organism reproduces by division on the body surface.

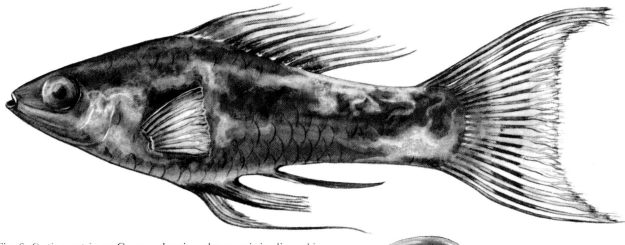

Fig. 6. *Costia necatrix* on Guppy, showing characteristic slimy skin

SYMPTOMS: Very similar to *Costia*. The parasite causes epithelial damage when present in large numbers, and may spread to the gills to interfere with respiration. Death may sometimes occur.

DIAGNOSIS: As for *Costia*. Microscopical examination of scrapings of skin is necessary for recognition.

PREVENTION AND TREATMENT: As for *Costia*. Quinine, acriflavine and sodium chloride are recommended for treatment.

Trichodina (Fig. 7) is another ciliate protozoan, generally round or disc-shaped, with a flattened underside. Other notable features, visible under the microscope, include an adhesive attachment organ underneath, and a circular ring of hooks inside. Like *Costia* and *Chilodonella*, the parasite may cause the skin to produce slimy secretions. Several species are known, of which *T. domerguei* is possibly the most common.

The parasites rotate continuously, feeding on dead cells and particles caught up in the mucus. Unlike the protozoa described above, they seem to survive for long periods away from their host.

SYMPTOMS: As for *Costia* and *Chilodonella*. The parasite is probably the least harmful of the three, but can cause irritation and skin damage. It may spread over the whole surface of fishes weakened by other infections.

DIAGNOSIS: As for *Costia*.

PREVENTION AND TREATMENT: As for *Costia*. Quinine and sodium chloride are recommended cures.

Helminth diseases

Helminths are extremely common fish parasites. Many have complicated life-cycles requiring secondary hosts such as snails, crustacea or even birds and mammals to complete their development, and

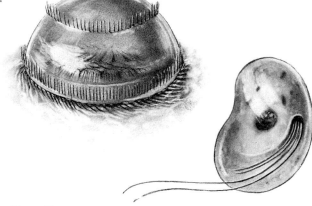

Fig. 7. Two parasites causing slimy skin condition. Left: *Trichodina* ×750. Right: *Costia* ×3,000

so are rarely found in aquaria. The skin flukes *Gyrodactylus* and *Dactylogyrus*, however, with no need of an intermediate host, may cause trouble.

Skin flukes: *Gyrodactylus* (Fig. 8) is found on the body surface and gills. It can be seen with the naked eye, some species measuring up to 1 mm. long. It attaches itself by a cluster of hooks at its posterior end and by a sticky secretion produced by glands in its head. A remarkable feature is that the fluke bears its young alive, the unborn worm being visible near the centre of its parent's body. After birth, the young worm may remain on the same host or search for another.

Dactylogyrus (Fig. 9) is found only on the gills. Certain features distinguish it from *Gyrodactylus*, for example, the number of hooks. In this genus, eggs are produced which hatch after leaving the parent worm. Several species are known.

SYMPTOMS: *Gyrodactylus* causes the skin colours to fade, and stimulates secretion of excessive mucus. Small spots of blood may be seen, produced by the action of the parasite's hooks. In heavy infections, mobility may be affected. If present on the gills,

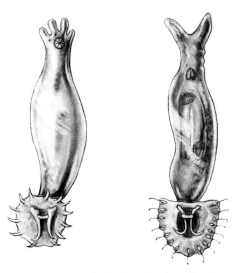

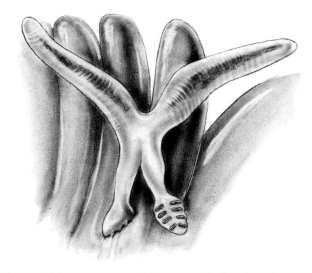

Figs. 8, 9. Skin flukes. Left: *Gyrodactylus*, showing unborn young worm, approximately 1 mm long. Right: *Dactylogyrus*

Fig. 10. *Diplozoon*, seen on gill filaments. Much enlarged

gill filaments may become pallid, and the gill cover may open wider than usual.

Dactylogyrus causes difficulty in respiration. Gill filaments become covered in slime.

DIAGNOSIS: The worms may be seen with the naked eye, and can be distinguished by their sites of infection.

PREVENTION: The larvae of each parasite die within a few days if they fail to find a new host. Infected fishes, therefore, should be removed from the tank for treatment. The tank can be used again after a week.

TREATMENT: Several treatments are effective, including methylene blue, formalin and chloramine.

Other helminths: Another worm which completes its life-cycle without the need of an intermediate host is *Diplozoon* (Fig. 10), which is found on the gills. The parasite rarely causes trouble in aquaria, but may be seen on fishes newly imported from open waters. Two other important skin parasites are *Diplostomum* and *Clinostomum*, both of which require snails and water-birds for transmission. They have been found occasionally in aquarium fishes after infected snails have been accidentally introduced into the tank. It is advisable, therefore, to quarantine all new snails for a few weeks to make sure they are parasite-free.

Crustacean diseases

There are two crustacean parasites of the skin which occasionally occur in aquaria, *Argulus*, sometimes called the 'fish-louse', and *Lernaea*, the

anchor worm. Several species of each are known.

Argulus (Fig. 11): The parasite is much larger than any described so far, measuring up to 7 mm. in length, and can thus be seen easily with the naked eye. Under the microscope, its four pairs of legs, two suckers, and proboscis with poison spine can be seen. The organism penetrates the upper layers of its host's skin with its proboscis and feeds on blood. It does not remain permanently attached, and is capable of swimming freely.

The adults leave their host for spawning. Eggs hatch into first stage larvae after about one month. After a moult, the larva is then ready to find a suitable host. The adult is formed after several further moults.

SYMPTOMS: The parasite by itself causes little serious damage, although it is said to be capable of transmitting bacterial and viral infections.

DIAGNOSIS: *Argulus* is readily seen without the need for microscopical examination. It varies in colour, from light green to brown.

PREVENTION AND TREATMENT: The parasites are not often seen in aquaria, but may be introduced with food such as *Daphnia*, particularly during the late summer when larvae are hatching out. They can be removed from fishes with the aid of forceps, or by dropping a few drops of strong salt solution on them and rubbing them off.

Lernaea: Although this parasite is a crustacean, it looks more like a helminth (Figs. 12, 13). The adult female is relatively long, measuring up to 20 mm., and is characterised by anchor-like appendages at

Fig. 11. Left: Underside of 'fish-louse' *Argulus*. Size about 7 mm

Fig. 12. Top: *Lernaea*, the anchor worm, embedded in fish

Fig. 13. Above: Isolated *Lernaea*, much enlarged. Actual size about 15 mm

its anterior end, and egg-sacs at the posterior.

The life-cycle is a seasonal one. Infections begin in the early summer when female larvae alight on the skin of their host and burrow in. The following spring, the parasites are mature, and produce egg-sacs, from which typical crustacean larvae hatch. After several moults throughout the summer, larvae settle on the skin to restart the cycle.

SYMPTOMS: Damage to the skin and sub-epidermal layers is caused by the parasite's burrowing action. Secondary bacterial and fungal infections may occur. In the spring, when the larvae are released, the adults die, leaving holes in the skin with openings to deeper tissues in which further secondary infections may take hold.

DIAGNOSIS: The crustacean is large and easily visible.

PREVENTION: As with many other surface parasites, the organism dies if it fails to find a new host. Infected fishes, therefore, should be placed in tanks free of other fishes, especially in spring and early summer when larvae are hatching.

TREATMENT: Potassium permanganate and mercurochrome are effective.

Fungal diseases

Fungi are commonly seen on the skin of freshwater fishes as white or grey outgrowths, resembling tufts of cotton wool. They occur only in fishes suffering from other diseases in which skin damage has occurred, and so are unlikely to cause trouble in a healthy tank.

Many types of fungus can affect fishes and expert advice would be necessary to identify them. Most skin infections are caused by *Saprolegnia* species (Fig. 14). If established, a fungus is difficult to eradicate as it spreads under the skin as thread-like filaments or hyphae, forming a so-called mycelium. These filaments, or hyphae, project from the mycelium to form the characteristic tufts. Reproduction is by means of spores.

SYMPTOMS: Fungal infections may aggravate disorders caused by other organisms.

DIAGNOSIS: Infections are usually apparent only some time after they have taken hold. Tufts of hyphae, particularly near the fins and tail, are easily seen.

PREVENTION: The fungi which affect fishes do not

Fig. 14. *Saprolegnia* fungus affecting tail region

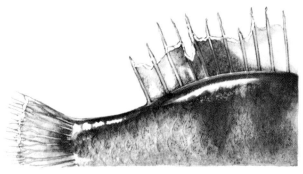

Fig. 15. Fin-rot and Tail-rot are common bacterial diseases

depend on their host for survival. They commonly live in dead or decaying organic matter, particularly in poorly aerated tanks. Prevention is best achieved, therefore, by maintaining clean and healthy tanks.

TREATMENT: By using baths of potassium permanganate or phenoxethol, or by swabbing affected regions with mercurochrome or merthiolate.

Bacterial diseases

Many fish diseases are caused by bacteria, but relatively little is known about them. Bacteria are smaller than any of the organisms described so far, a typical length being only 5μ. They are barely visible under the light microscope. Special methods of staining and culture are necessary for species diagnosis, which is thus a matter for the expert only. Certain diseases, however, have fairly distinctive symptoms, and so the amateur can often take precautionary measures.

Fin-rot and Tail-rot: These are common complaints (Fig. 15), which particularly affect fishes kept for long periods. Highly pigmented fishes, such as Black Mollies, seem especially susceptible. It is not clear which bacteria are responsible. Several species have been isolated from infected animals, e.g. *Haemophilus piscium, Aeromonas punctata,* but it appears that others may also cause the disease.
SYMPTOMS AND DIAGNOSIS: A gradual shortening of the fins and tail, usually starting at the extremities.
PREVENTION: The disease usually affects only injured fishes living in poorly maintained tanks. The bacteria appear to enter through wounds. Trouble is avoided by ensuring healthy tanks.
TREATMENT: Several drugs are available, e.g. acriflavine or phenoxethol. Should these fail, it is necessary to carry out surgery and cut away the affected portions of the fins and tail.

Columnaris: In the past, this term has been used to cover a variety of diseases caused by bacteria, fungi and even viruses. Strictly, however, it should be reserved for the bacterium *Chondrococcus columnaris,* which affects the mouth and causes difficulty in breathing. In later stages, a white fungus-like growth appears around the mouth and anterior regions of the head, the condition being sometimes wrongly called 'mouth-fungus', or 'cotton-wool disease'. In acute cases the whole frontal region is attacked and eroded away.
SYMPTOMS AND DIAGNOSIS: As described above; expert advice is needed for precise identification.
PREVENTION: By quarantine of newly acquired fish, particularly those from the wild where *Columnaris* sometimes causes great mortality.
TREATMENT: By swabbing affected regions with merthiolate, or using chloromycetin as a bath.

Scale protrusion: Several bacteria appear to cause this disease, although the most common is probably *Bacterium lepidorthosae.* The infective organisms enter through open wounds, so healthy fishes rarely develop the disease. Van Duijn (1967) describes two ways in which infections may proceed: either slowly, taking three or four weeks before the scales protrude, or fast, when the characteristic symptom of scale-raising does not occur, but red patches (ecchymoses) appear over the skin. In both cases, death may result if the fishes remain untreated.
SYMPTOMS AND DIAGNOSIS: As described.
PREVENTION: By maintaining a close watch for injury (e.g. due to fighting).
TREATMENT: Chloromycetin is generally effective against this disease.

Viral diseases

Even less is known of viral fish diseases than those caused by bacteria. Viruses are considerably smaller than bacteria, being visible only in the electron microscope. Diseases of the skin known to be caused by viruses include the following:

Lymphocystis is readily recognised by cauliflower-like growths on the skin and fins (Fig. 16).

Fig. 16. *Lymphocystis,* a viral skin disease

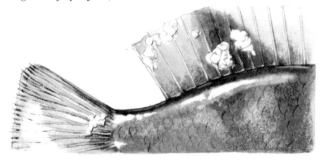

Fig. 18. *Myxosporidia* protozoa. Right: *Myxobolus* cysts on gills. The gill cover has been removed. Far right: *Myxobolus* spore enlarged × 3,000

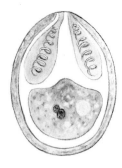

Fig. 17. Skin spotting caused by Pox

Fig. 19. Characteristic orange cysts on Stickleback, caused by Microsporidian *Glugea anomala*

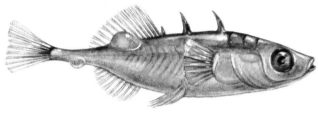

Pox, giving rise to hard, milky-white spots all over the surface, which eventually merge to cover large areas of skin (Fig. 17).

Kryo-ichthyozoosis, causing swellings at the fin bases, affecting swimming movements.

No treatments are available for lymphocystis or pox, although pox often cures itself spontaneously. For kryo-ichthyozoosis, raising the water temperature about 61°F. is said to effect a cure.

INFECTIONS OF THE INTERNAL ORGANS

As is the case for skin diseases, a wide variety of organisms can cause internal disorders. Most of these are dealt with only briefly here as they rarely occur or are diagnosed in aquaria. No treatments are available unless otherwise stated.

Myxosporidia: These are perhaps the most common of all fish protozoa, although not many are pathogenic. All organs and tissues are possible sites of infection. The infective stage is the spore (Fig. 18), the features of which are used in species identification. The spore valves, or shell, enclose polar capsules and a sporoplasm. On entering a new host the sporoplasm is released from the spore and makes its way to its specific site of infection, where it develops into a trophozoite. Spores develop inside the trophozoite.

One of the most serious myxosporidians is *Myxosoma cerebralis,* which affects the brain of young Trout, causing 'twist' disease. Some species form boils or cysts on the body surface, e.g. *Myxobolus*

pfeifferi of the barbel, or on the gills, e.g. *Myxobolus piriformis.*

Microsporidia: These parasites have a similar life-cycle to the Myxosporidia, the infective stage being a spore. One of the most easily recognised species is *Glugea anomala* which produces large spherical orange cysts on the surface of Stickleback (Fig. 19). A species of importance in tropical fish is *Plistophora hyphessobryconis* which causes 'Neon Tetra disease'. The parasites attack muscle tissue, and produce regions of whitish discolouration on the body surface. Death frequently results. Several other tropical fishes besides Neon Tetras may be infected, including Glowlight and Rosy Tetras, Swordtails and Zebra Fishes.

Coccidia: Coccidia are common in domestic animals as parasites of the gut. In fishes, other organs may be attacked.

Trypanosomes and Trypanoplasms: These organisms are flagellated and live in the blood, being transmitted from one fish to another by leeches (Figs. 20, 21). *Cryptobia cyprini* infects many Cyprinids and is said to cause a type of sleeping sickness in Goldfish, producing anaemia and loss in weight.

Helminth diseases

An enormous number of helminths parasitise fishes, but they are rarely seen in aquaria because of their need of secondary hosts. Fish themselves may act as secondary hosts of worms found in mammals and birds; examples are the following:

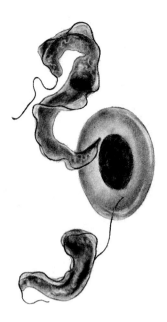

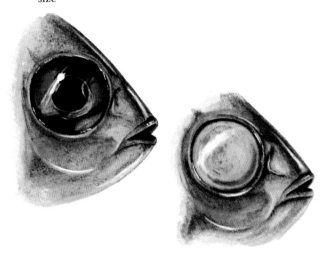

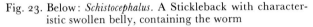

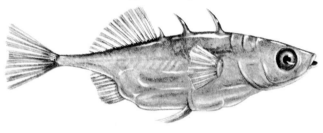

Fig. 22. The *Diplostomum* parasite attacks the eyes of many species. Above left: a healthy eye. Above right: a 'clouded' eye

Fig. 23. Below: *Schistocephalus*. A Stickleback with characteristic swollen belly, containing the worm

Diplostomum: The parasite invades the eye of many fish species, causing 'worm cataract' which can lead to blindness. The adult worm is found in birds, while water snails provide a second intermediate host (Fig. 22).

Ligula and *Schistocephalus* (Figs. 24, 23): These parasites occur in the abdomen of their hosts as the larval plerocercoid. The adults occur in birds, and the crustacean *Cyclops* is a second intermediate host. *Ligula* is common in Carp, while *Schistocephalus* is found only in Stickleback.

Diphyllobothrium: This genus includes several species of tape-worm which infect a variety of land-living animals including birds, mammals and man (*Diphyllobothrium latum*). In fishes, the stage found is the larval plerocercoid, which infects musculature and other organs. Man acquires the infection on eating uncooked fish.

Fig. 24. Below: *Ligula*. Dissection of an affected fish

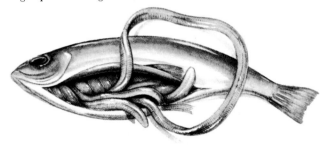

Fungal diseases

The most important internal infection due to a fungus in aquarium fishes is caused by *Ichthyophonus* (*Ichthyosporidium*) *hoferi*.

Fishes become infected by eating cysts floating free in the water, or by eating infected fishes. In the intestine the cysts open to free the parasite. Hyphae penetrate the gut wall to enter blood-vessels, by which the parasite is carried to various organs of the body.

Symptoms depend largely on the site of infection. When the skin is invaded, small pea-sized ulcers may be formed. In the brain the sense of balance is frequently affected. Eye protrusion can also occur. If the liver is attacked, abdominal swellings may appear, together with loss of muscle substance, skin pallor and even loss of fins. If the ovaries are attacked, sterility may result; in Guppies, sex reversal has been reported.

DIAGNOSIS: This may be difficult, owing to the variety of symptoms. The fungus can be isolated from live fishes only when the skin is infected. Otherwise, post-mortem examination is necessary.

PREVENTION AND TREATMENT: Infected fishes must be isolated, as diseased skin may be eaten by other fishes. Phenoxethol is an effective drug.

Fig. 25. A fish suffering from Dropsy, viewed from above

Bacterial diseases

Dropsy: The chief symptom of this disease is a large abdominal swelling (Fig. 25) caused by accumulation of fluid. Post-mortem examination shows deterioration of the liver and spleen enlargement. Other symptoms which may occur include scale protrusion, ulcers, and, in severe cases, deformity of the head and spine caused by internal fluid pressure.

The bacterium *Pseudomonas (Aeromonas) punctata* has often been incriminated as the causative organism, although more recent work suggests that viruses may be the cause, the bacteria being secondary invaders.

PREVENTION AND TREATMENT: The disease is very contagious, and so affected fishes must be isolated.

The body fluid can be extracted with a hypodermic syringe, after which treatment with chloromycetin or streptomycin is normally effective.

Tuberculosis: There are a number of species of the tubercle bacillus *Myxobacterium* which are known to infect fishes. Almost any organ may be attacked, the infection being recognised by the presence there of small grey cysts, or tubercles, visible under the microscope. The symptoms are various, ranging from deformity of the spine to skin ulcers. Diagnosis is a matter for the expert, a post-mortem examination usually being necessary.

TREATMENT: Streptomycin and terramycin are effective drugs.

METHODS OF TREATMENT

Several drugs are effective in combating the common infectious organisms of aquaria, some of which can be used against many diseases. The following list includes some of the drugs in common use which are readily available to the aquarist. For more details, the reader is referred to van Duijn (1967).

Acriflavine: *Effective against:* White-spot, Velvet, *Costia, Chilodonella, Trichodina,* Fin-rot, Tail-rot, fungal diseases.

Stock Solution: 0.001% using neutral acriflavine. To be kept in darkness.

TREATMENT: 10 ml. of stock solution added to each

Imperial gallon. Treatment may need to be extended for several days.

PRECAUTION: Toxic to fishes and to some aquatic plants if treatment is too prolonged.

Chloramine: *Effective against:* White-spot, *Costia, Chilodonella, Trichodina, Gyrodactylus.*

Stock Solution: 1%. Use freshly made.

TREATMENT: 4.5 ml. of stock solution added to each Imperial gallon. Fishes treated for twenty-four hours.

PRECAUTION: Must not be allowed to contact bare metal, as poisoning may result.

Chloromycetin: *Effective against:* Many bacterial and viral infections. Also against White-spot and Velvet.

TREATMENT: 25–50 mg. added to each Imperial gallon. Alternatively, added to food, 1 g. per kg.

Formalin: *Effective against:* Costia, *Gyrodactylus*, *Dactylogyrus*.

TREATMENT OF COSTIA: A 10% solution of 32% formaldehyde is made up as stock. A bath is prepared using 10–25 ml. of stock solution per Imperial gallon. Infected fishes are placed in the bath for 15–30 minutes. The treatment is repeated several times every two days.

TREATMENT OF GYRODACTYLUS AND DACTYLOGYRUS: A 1% stock solution of 32% formaldehyde is made up. 165 ml. of stock solution are added to each cubic foot of tank water. Infected fishes are kept in the bath until the flukes disappear.

Mepacrine: *Effective against:* White-spot.
 Stock solution: 0.1%, using mepacrine hydrochloride.

TREATMENT: 15 ml. of stock solution added to each Imperial gallon, given as three doses of 5 ml. every forty-eight hours.

PRECAUTION: Relatively toxic. Lethal to Guppies.

Mercurochrome: *Effective against:* Many skin diseases, especially White-spot, *Lernaea* and fungi.
 Stock solution: 0.2%.

TREATMENT: By swabbing affected regions with cotton-wool. For White-spot, 2 ml. of stock solution added to each Imperial gallon.

PRECAUTION: May be toxic, causing kidney and liver damage.

Merthiolate (Thiomersal): *Effective against:* Fungal diseases. Also *Columnaris*.
 Stock solution: 0.1%.

TREATMENT: By swabbing wounds. Not to be used as a bath.

Methylene blue: *Effective against:* White-spot, Velvet, *Gyrodactylus*, *Dactylogyrus*.
 Stock solution: 1%, using pure grade solid.

TREATMENT: 1 ml. of stock solution added to each Imperial gallon. Repeated every two days. A stronger solution, up to 4 ml., may be necessary for Velvet.

PRECAUTION: May be toxic to aquatic plants.

Potassium permanganate: *Effective against:* Many skin diseases, especially Velvet and *Lernaea*.
 Stock solution: 1%.

TREATMENT: 4.5 ml. of stock solution added to each Imperial gallon. Used as a bath, 30 minutes only.

PRECAUTION: Toxic to fishes if used in excess.

Phenoxethol: *Effective against:* Fin-rot, Tail-rot, some helminth infections, *Ichthyophonus*.
 Stock Solution: 1%.

TREATMENT: 45–90 ml. of stock solution added to each Imperial gallon.

For internal worm infections and *Ichthyophonus*, food is soaked in the stock solution.

Quinine: *Effective against:* White-spot, Velvet, *Costia*, *Chilodonella*, *Trichodina*.
Stock solution: 1%, using quinine hydrochloride.

TREATMENT: For White-spot: 15 ml. of stock solution per Imperial gallon, given as three doses of 5 ml. every twelve hours. For other diseases: 9 ml. of stock stolution added to each Imperial gallon, given as two doses of 4.5 ml. at twelve-hour intervals.

PRECAUTION: Very toxic to Prussian Carp. May affect plant growth.

Sodium Chloride: *Effective against:* Costia, Chilodonella, Trichodina, Gyrodactylus, Lernaea, some bacterial diseases.

TREATMENT: 2.5–5 oz. per Imperial gallon for 15–30 minutes, or 1 oz. per Imperial gallon for indefinite periods. Change to fresh water should be made gradually.

Streptomycin: *Effective against:* Tuberculosis and dropsy.

TREATMENT: 0.7 g. per Imperial gallon, or by injection of 0.1 mg. in 0.1 ml. of water per 10 g. body weight.

Terramycin: *Effective against:* Internal bacterial diseases.

TREATMENT: In the food. 1.8 mg. per gram of food per 3% of body weight.

Suggested further reading

DAVIS, H. S. (1961). Culture and Diseases of Game Fishes. Cambridge University Press.

GHADIALLY, F. N. (1956). White-spot Disease. *The Aquarist*, 20, 216–218, 239–242. *21*, 12–13.

REICHENBACH–KLINKE, H. and ELKAN, E. (1965). The Principal Diseases of Lower Vertebrates. Academic Press.

STERBA, G. (1967). Aquarium Care. A comprehensive guide. London, Studio Vista Ltd.

VAN DUIJN, C. (1967). Diseases of Fishes. 2nd edition. London, Iliffe Books Ltd.

Acknowledgments

Thanks are due to Peter Bird of the British Aquarists
Study Society for his generous assistance throughout
the preparation of this book; to James Chambers of the
Fish Section, British Museum (Natural History),
London; The North of England Zoological Society,
Chester; Keith Barraclough Tropicals, Bradford, and
to the photographers for all their help.

Illustrations of diseases of fishes by Margot Cooper.
Line illustrations by Carole Tyler with the following
exceptions:
page 12 by Annabelle Milne
pages 22, 23 (top) by Sharon Chambers
page 23 (bottom) by Penelope Wood
Colour illustration of *Barbus Schwanenfeldi* on page 12 by Norman Weaver.

Design and layout by Victor Giolitto.

INDEX

INDEX OF FISHES

INDEX OF DISEASES

INDEX OF PLANTS